Foundations of Programming

This is volume 23 in A.P.I.C. Studies in Data Processing
General Editors: Fraser Duncan *and* M. J. R. Shave
A complete list of titles in this series appears at the end of this volume

Foundations of Programming

Jacques Arsac

Ecole Normale Supérieure
Paris, France

Translated by Fraser Duncan

1985

ACADEMIC PRESS

(Harcourt Brace Jovanovich, Publishers)
London   Orlando   San Diego   New York
Toronto   Montreal   Sydney   Tokyo

ACADEMIC PRESS INC. (LONDON) LTD.
24–28 Oval Road
LONDON NW1 7DX

United States Edition published by
ACADEMIC PRESS, INC.
Orlando, Florida 32887

British Library Cataloguing in Publication Data

Arsac, Jacques
    Foundations of programming. – (APIC studies
    in data processing)
    1. Electronic digital computers – Programming
    I. Title   II. Les bases de la programmation.
    English   III. Series
    000.64'2   QA76.6

Library of Congress Cataloging in Publication Data

Arsac, Jacques.
    Foundations of programming.

    (A.P.I.C. studies in data processing)
    Translation of: Les bases de la programmation.
    Includes index.
    1. Electronic digital computers--Programming.
I. Title. II. Series.
QA76.6.A75813   1985   001.64'2   84-14436
ISBN 0–12–064460–6 (alk. paper)

PRINTED IN THE UNITED STATES OF AMERICA

85 86 87 88   9 8 7 6 5 4 3 2 1

FOUNDATIONS OF PROGRAMMING. Translated from the original French edition
entitled LES BASES DE LA PROGRAMMATION, published by Dunod, Paris,
© BORDAS 1983.

Vingt fois sur le métier remettez votre ouvrage;
Polissez-le sans cesse et le repolissez.

Nicolas Boileau

Contents

Preface   xiii

List of Programs Discussed in the Book   xxiii

Notations   xxvii

Translator's Introduction   xxxi

Chapter 1   Iterative Programming

1.1   An Incorrect Program   1
1.2   The Assignment Instruction   2
1.3   Assertions and Instructions   4
      1.3.1   Assignment   4
      1.3.2   Selection   6
      1.3.3   Branching Instruction   6
      1.3.4   The WHILE Instruction   7
      1.3.5   The Loop   8
1.4   The Interpretation of a Program   9
1.5   Recurrent Construction of Iterative Programs   11
1.6   Partial Correctness   13
1.7   Strengthening the Recurrence Hypothesis   16
1.8   The Effect of the Choice of the Recurrence Hypothesis   17
1.9   "Heap Sort"   22
      Exercises   24

Chapter 2   Recursive Programming

2.1   Recursivity Recalled   27
2.2   The Construction of Recursive Definitions   28
      2.2.1   The Factorial Function   28
      2.2.2   The Exponential Function   29
      2.2.3   Reverse of a String   30
      2.2.4   Expression of an Integer in Base b 31

	2.2.5 Fibonacci Numbers	31
	2.2.6 The Product of Two Integers	32
2.3	Computation of a Recursively Defined Function	32
	2.3.1 Monadic Definition	32
	2.3.2 Dyadic Definition	33
2.4	The Nature of a Recursive Definition	34
2.5	Properties of a Recursively Defined Function	35
	2.5.1 A Simple Example	35
	2.5.2 Computational Precision	36
	2.5.3 Complexity	38
2.6	The Choice of a Recursive Form	39
	2.6.1 The Problem of the Termination	39
	2.6.2 Complexity	40
2.7	Transformation of Recursive Definitions	41
2.8	The Proper Use of Recursion	43
	2.8.1 Function 91	44
	2.8.2 Call by Need	46
2.9	Functional Programming	46
	Exercises	49

Chapter 3   Recurrent Programming

3.1	Direct Algorithms	51
3.2	Construction of Algorithms	53
3.3	The Precedence Relation	55
3.4	Transformation into a Program	56
3.5	"Lazy" Evaluation	58
3.6	Recurrent Algorithm	60
	3.6.1 An Example	60
	3.6.2 The General Form	63
	3.6.3 Deep Recurrences	64
3.7	Execution of a Recurrent Algorithm	65
3.8	Transformation into an Iterative Program	67
	3.8.1 The General Case	67
	3.8.2 An Example	68
	3.8.3 The Reduction of the Number of Variables	69
3.9	The Use of Recurrence in the Writing of a Program	70
3.10	Giving a Meaning to a Program	76
	Exercises	78

Chapter 4   From Recursion to Recurrence

4.1	The Recurrent Form Associated with a Recursive Scheme	81
	4.1.1 The Scheme to Be Considered	81
	4.1.2 The Associated Recurrent Form	82
	4.1.3 The Iterative Program	83
	4.1.4 Example	84
4.2	The Stack	85
4.3	Programs without Stacks	90
4.4	A Program with Only One Loop	92
4.5	Interpretation of the Recursive Scheme	93

Contents

4.6	Other Simplifications	93
	4.6.1 Associativity	93
	4.6.2 Permutability	95
4.7	A Degenerate Form of the Recursive Scheme	96
	4.7.1 The Degenerate Form	96
	4.7.2 When a Is Constant	97
	4.7.3 When b Is the Identity Operation	98
4.8	Special Cases	99
	4.8.1 A Dyadic Scheme	100
	4.8.2 Non-Associativity	101
	Exercises	104

Chapter 5   From Recursion to Iteration

5.1	An Example of Direct Transformation	105
	5.1.1 Invariance in a Loop	105
	5.1.2 Construction of the Iterative Program	106
5.2	Extension	107
	5.2.1 Generalisation	107
	5.2.2 The Test for Exit	107
	5.2.3 Progression	108
	5.2.4 Initialisation	108
5.3	Examples	108
	5.3.1 The Reverse of a String	108
	5.3.2 Expression in Base b	110
5.4	Program Synthesis	113
5.5	A Complex Recursion	116
5.6	Happy Numbers	118
5.7	The Hamming Sequence	125
	Exercises	127

Chapter 6   Regular Actions

6.1	Intuitive Presentation of the Idea of an Action	129
6.2	Systems of Regular Actions	131
6.3	Interpretation of a System of Regular Actions	133
	6.3.1 Interpretation as Label	133
	6.3.2 Decomposition of a Program into Actions	135
	6.3.3 Actions as Procedures without Parameters	136
6.4	The Graph of a System of Actions	137
6.5	Substitution	138
	6.5.1 The Copy Rule	138
	6.5.2 The Inverse Transformation	139
6.6	Transformation from Terminal Recursion to Iteration	140
	6.6.1 A Particular Case	140
	6.6.2 The General Case	142
6.7	The Structure of a System of Regular Actions	144
	6.7.1 The General Case	144
	6.7.2 Example: Finding a Substring of a String	145
6.8	Identification	150
	Exercises	156

Chapter 7   Program Transformations

7.1   Definitions and Notations   159
7.2   Simple Absorption and Simple Expansion   161
7.3   Double Iteration and Loop Absorption   163
7.4   Proper Inversion   167
7.5   Repetition   170
7.6   Local Semantic Transformations   170
       7.6.1   Assignments   170
       7.6.2   Selection Instructions   173
7.7   The Development of More Complex Transformations   175
       7.7.1   WHILE Loops   175
       7.7.2   A Transformation due to Suzan Gerhardt   177
       7.7.3   Remark on the AND Operator   181
7.8   Application to a Problem of Termination   182
7.9   Change of Strategy   184
       Exercises   193

Chapter 8   The Transformation of Sub-Programs from Recursive to Iterative

8.1   Generalised Actions   195
       8.1.1   Intuitive Presentation   195
       8.1.2   Definition   196
       8.1.3   Interpretation   197
8.2   Regularisation   200
       8.2.1   The General Case   200
       8.2.2   The Use of Predicates   200
       8.2.3   The Property of Invariance   200
       8.2.4   The Activation Counter   201
       8.2.5   The n-ary Counter   202
8.3   Example   203
8.4   The Schemes of Irlik   205
8.5   Formal Parameters and Global Variables   210
       8.5.1   Local Variables   210
       8.5.2   Formal Parameters   210
8.6   A Known Recursive Scheme   211
       Exercises   217

Chapter 9   Analytical Programming

9.1   Analytical Programming   221
9.2   An Old Friend   223
       9.2.1   Creation of the Recursive Sub-Program   223
       9.2.2   Regularisation   225
       9.2.3   First Realisation of the Stack   226
       9.2.4   Second Implementation of the Stack   226
       9.2.5   Variations   229
9.3   A Problem of Permutations   230
       9.3.1   The Recursive Procedure   230
       9.3.2   First Iterative Form   232
       9.3.3   Second Iterative Form   235

Contents

9.4   The Towers of Hanoi   242
      9.4.1   Recursive Procedure   242
      9.4.2   The First Form   243
9.5   A General Result   250
      9.5.1   The Stack   251
      9.5.2   Recomputing the Arguments   251
9.6   The Towers of Hanoi — Second Form   252
9.7   Remarks on the Two Solutions of the Towers of Hanoi   255
      Exercises   258

Bibliography   261

Index   263

Preface

Informatics (or computer science or information processing) is too young a science to have become the subject of many historical studies or philosophical analyses. To me, however, its history seems quite exceptional. It is normal for a science to be born out of the observation of nature. When a sufficient number of duly observed facts have been recorded, the outline of a model can be sketched, and this in its turn allows the prediction of new patterns of behaviour which are then subject to experimental verification.

Technology comes later; the model being confirmed, to a certain degree of precision, by experiment, possible applications are conceived and come to birth. The discovery of electricity is typical of such an evolution. The electric motor and incandescent lamp did not appear until well after the development of the first theoretical models of electrostatics and of electromagnetism.

Much more rarely, technology has come before science. The steam engine was built long before the science of thermodynamics enabled its output to be calculated. In informatics we have an extreme example of this class.

The computer was engendered by the necessity for computation experienced during the Second World War. It was not the brainchild of some brilliant dabbler, but the product of a technology founded on a well-established science, electronics, and supported by a no less well-founded mathematical model, Boolean algebra. There is nothing unusual about this. But it was followed by wild speculation on the part of industrialists who believed that such monsters might have applications in everyday life and who engineered these machines for the market. This theme is to be found developed in a book by Rene Moreau [MOR].

From then on we have witnessed an incredible development of the means of computation, requiring the support of numerous technicians—operators, programmers, ... This in turn led to the need to establish numerous new educational programmes, which began to be satisfied in about 1960. But the universities which took responsibility for this realised very quickly that they were not dealing simply with an application of the science of electronics aided by a very old branch of mathematics, numerical analysis. We were face to face with something fundamental, with a very old activity of the human mind, but one whose significance we were not able to grasp because there was no technical means of allowing it to take full flight.

In the same way as astronomy began with the telescopes of Galileo, but was unable fully to develop until better means of observation became technically possible, so informatics, the science of information processing, will not be able to show itself clearly until the proper means are found to exercise it [AR]. It would not be right to allow the reader to believe that what is said here is an absolute and proven truth, recognised by universal consensus. There are very many who believe in the existence of a science of informatics, as is shown, for example, by academic instances in every country: in all the great universities there are departments of "computer science"; the French Academy defines "l'informatique" as a science, and the French Academy of Sciences has two headings "informatique" in its proceedings. But there are just as many again who would restrict its scope, and deny it all claim to a character of its own. In this sense, the position of the Academy of Sciences is ambiguous: there is not one unique classification for informatics, as would be the case for a well-established discipline, but rather two, one for theoretical information science, a branch of mathematics concerned with the problems posed by information processing, and the other at the level of "science for the engineer." Many professionals see in informatics nothing more than a technique, sufficiently complicated to require a specific training, but of narrow breadth. Bruno Lussato has become a champion of this idea, asserting that informatics can be learnt in three weeks [LUS].

I believe this to be a consequence of the very peculiar development of the discipline. As had been said, the technology came first, founded as always on a science, solid-state physics, but remote from its proper concern, the treatment of information. Since then we have spent much energy trying to master techniques for which, the need not having been foreseen, we were never adequately prepared. There has hardly been time to think. The history of programming, within the history of informatics, is in this respect very revealing.

In the beginning there were the first computers, for which we had to write programs in the only language which they could interpret, their own, the machine language. This was extremely tedious, with a very high risk of error; and so machine languages were very soon replaced by assembly languages, maintaining in their forms the structures of the machine languages, and offering no more distinct operations than the machines could cope with by hardware. It very soon became clear that the fragmentation of thought imposed by the very restricted set of these primitive operations was a handicap, and the first developed language, Fortran, appeared about 1955. This was a decisive step. The choice of structures for this language and the manner of writing of its compiler were to leave a deep mark on the history of programming.

In fact, the language was conceived fundamentally as an abbreviation of assembly languages, and maintained two of their principal characteristics:

— the assignment instruction, or modification of the contents of a unit storage in the computer,

— the idea of the instruction sequence, broken by the GO TO instruction, conditional or unconditional.

Very many languages developed rapidly from this common origin. The principal languages still in use today, Algol 60, Cobol, Basic, . . . , appeared over a period of at most five years. Lisp is of the same period, but it deserves special mention; it was not constructed on the same universal primitives, having no concept of assignment, no loop, no instruction sequence, but it was based on the recursive definition of functions.

This language explosion, this modern Babel, has caused much dissipation of energy in the writing of compilers, and in heated argument over a false problem—that of the comparative merits of the different languages. Unhappily, this game has not yet stopped. Take any assembly, anywhere, of sleepy computer scientists, and turn the discussion on to a programming language. They will all wake up and throw themselves into the debate. If you think about this, it is worrying, indeed deeply disturbing. All these languages in fact have been built upon the same universal primitives, as has already been pointed out; and the principal problems flow from this fact. Two of the chief difficulties in programming practice arise from the assignment instruction and the branch instruction. Why such rivalry between such close cousins?

As long as we work ourselves into such excitement over these languages, we are apt to forget that they are only a means of expression and that the essential thing is to have something to say, not how to say it.

Ce que l'on concoit bien s'énonce clairement et les mots pour le dire arrivent aisement [BOI].

["That which is well conceived can be expressed clearly, and the words for saying it will come easily"—Nicolas Boileau, 1636–1711.]

The means for the construction of programs were rudimentary, indeed non-existent. The literature of the period abounds in works of the type "Programming in Basic" or "Programming in Fortran IV." Teaching was no more than the presentation of a language, a trivial matter for these languages are remarkably poor. After that, the programming apprentice was left to his own devices. Consequently, each one became self-taught, and no transmission of competence was possible. The programmer of the eighties is no better off than the programmer of the sixties, and the accumulated mistakes of twenty years are there to prevent him avoiding the many programming traps into which he will fall.

All this was done in an entirely empirical fashion. (I hardly know why I use the past tense. If it is true that a few universities now operate differently and that a small number of industrial centres have at least understood the significance of new methods and adopted them, how many more practitioners go on in the same old way! More seriously, how many teachers, not to say recent authors, remain faithful to what cannot in any way be described by the name of "method.") The programmer sketches out the work to be done and makes a schematic representation of his program, setting out all the branch instructions, in the form of a flow-chart. Then he writes out the instructions, and begins the long grind of program testing. The program is put into the computer, and a compiler detects the syntactic errors. Some sophisticated compilers now even detect semantic errors (chiefly errors concerned with data types). The program is corrected and eventually accepted by the compiler, but that does not yet mean that it is correct. It still has to be made to run with test data. If the results appear correct, the program is declared to be correct. Otherwise, the program is examined for any apparent abnormalities, and modified to prevent their unfortunate consequences. It is the method called "trial and error" or, in the professional jargon, "suck it and see." I have seen it as practiced by a research worker in biology. His Fortran program was causing problems, and he had, by program-tracing (printing instructions as executed, with intermediate values), finally isolated his error. He then told me with great satisfaction how he had put it right. His program began with the declaration of two arrays:

DIMENSION A(1000), B(1000)

One loop involving the array A was running beyond the array bounds and was destroying the values of B. I asked him how he had found the error which caused the bounds to to exceeded, and how he had gone on to correct the loop. But his reply showed he had done neither. He had simply doubled the size of A:

DIMENSION A(2000), B(1000)

How can anyone expect correct results from a program which is manifestly false? How can he go on to publish a paper, saying "It has been found by computation that. . ."?

It has been all too easy to denounce this lamentable state of the art [BOE]. Statistics for 1972, dealing with sums of millions of dollars, give the cost of writing as $75 per instruction, but after program testing $4000 per instruction. In its estimates at the beginning of its bid for support for ADA, the United States Department of Defense declared that if the cost of programming errors were to be reduced by only 1%, the total saving would be $25 million per annum. . . .

The answer has been sought in languages with tighter constraints. Increase control by having more data types. I must be permitted to say that I do not appreciate this line of reasoning. Let us take a comparison. Because certain reckless drivers take needless risks and so endanger the community of drivers and passengers, we need to multiply the methods of control and surveillance — traffic lights, automatic barriers at stop signs, weighing devices at the approaches to bridges, radar for speed control, ... All this translates into inconvenience for the reasonable driver, penalised for the brutishness of a few clods. Programming is going the same way. Just because my biologist does not know how to look after his subscripts and lets them exceed their declared bounds, at every call of a subscripted variable the run-time system will make tests to ensure that there is no error, and too bad for me if I have not made an error. These tests cost computing time, which costs money. I am paying for fools.

The other cure, the one in which I believe, lies in teaching. The programmer can be taught to work properly, to write correct programs, which he knows are right, and why.

It is difficult to say who first launched this idea. "Notes on Structured Programming" of Edsger Dijkstra is, in the view of many, the first important text in this domain [DI1]. "Testing a program can show only that it contains errors, never that it is correct. . . ."

Many research workers have addressed themselves to the problem of the creation of programs, and we shall not attempt here to give an exhaustive bibliography, being unable to do so and unwilling to risk being unfair. But two works stand out along the way. In 1968, Donald Knuth began the publication of a series of books entitled "The Art of Computer Programming" [KNU]. In 1981, David Gries published "The Science of Programming" [GRI]. From art to science in ten years! As far as we are concerned, the most important step has been the introduction of inductive assertions by R. Floyd [FLO] in 1967, the system axiomatised by Tony Hoare [HOA] in 1969. At first this was regarded as a tool for proving the correctness of programs. But experience has shown that it can be very difficult to prove a program written by someone else.

Assertions have been used, therefore, as the basis of a method of program construction [AR1] [AR2] [GRI]. This method will be recalled in the first chapter, below. We presented it first in 1977, and again in a book in 1980, trying to avoid as far as possible all mathematical formulation; that book was intended primarily for school teachers, some of them certainly literate in the humanities, and it was essential that its language should discourage none of them. David Gries, on the other hand, regards it as essential to formulate the assertions in terms of first-order logic, and discusses the relationship between this and the logic expressible in natural language with AND and OR. We shall say a few words here about this point. Because we have no wish to write a book of mathematics, we shall as far as possible keep to assertions expressed in natural language.

The program construction method is founded on recurrence. "Suppose that I have been able to solve the problem up to a certain point. . . ." If that is the end, we stop. Otherwise, we move a step nearer the solution by going back to the recurrence hypothesis. Then we look for a way to begin. In other words, and in simplified, schematic fashion, suppose I have been able to compute $f(i)$. If $i = n$, and $f(n)$ is required, the work is finished. Otherwise, I compute $f(i + 1)$ in terms of $f(i)$, then I change $i + 1$ into i and start again. Finally I compute $f(0)$.

It is remarkable that the same reasoning, with little or no modification, will produce a recursive procedure. We shall give in the second chapter a certain number of examples of procedure construction for recursive functions. They do not use the assignment instruction, and so their programming style is very different. It is nearer to axiomatic definition than to computing strategy. It is computed through a very complex execution mechanism, but also gives the possibility of deduction from the properties of the recursive definition. We shall give several examples of this, particularly in connection with the complexity or precision of computations.

If recurrence is the common base of iteration and recursion, we can build it into a true programming language. It uses recurrent sequences of depth 1, and the minimisation operator. In this sense, we can say that it is constructed on the same universal primitives as its contemporary Lucid [ASH], proposed by Ashcroft and Wadge. But we would not seek to develop a formal system, and we use numerical indices for the sequences, although in fact we would call only on the successor function of natural integers. The important thing is to have a simple means of expressing recurrence, which is at the centre of the whole of this study. We shall show how a recurrent algorithm can be interpreted and transformed into an iterative program. Our aim is much less to make of this a true programming language, endowed with good data structures, and compilable by a computer, than to be able to write recurrent algorithms in a recurrent language, and to have a simple method of extracting iterative programs from them. But why this diversion, when in the first chapter we have shown how to create the iterative program directly? One of the reasons is that this recurrent language has no assignment instruction, and so makes possible substitution, and hence the whole of algebraic manipulation. This allows a recurrent algorithm to be transformed easily into the form best adapted for translation into a good iterative program. We shall give several examples of this.

This language proceeds at the same time from recursion, for like that it is not founded upon assignment, and from iteration, for like that it shows sequences of values to be computed to reach a result. It is thus not surprising that it can serve as an intermediary between recursion and iteration. We shall show how a recurrent program can be created from a recursive function definition. This will allow us to expose for examination the execution mechanism of a recursive procedure, to study in depth the concept of the stack, not laid down *a priori,* but deduced from the recurrent scheme, and to discuss the further significance of this. We shall show afterwards how stronger hypotheses allow simplication of the iterative form, making the stack redundant in some cases, and often leading finally to the reduction of a program to a single loop.

Because recursion and iteration are two expressions of the same recurrence, there must exist a simple transition from one form to the other. We shall show in Chapter 5 how we can pass directly form the recursive definition to an iterative program. A generalisation of the recursive definition gives the recurrence hypothesis on which the iterative program can be constructed. A substitution, a little algebraic manipulation, and then a unification lead to the body of the loop. This method is extremely powerful when it can be used. Thus it provides a true mechanism for program synthesis. Beginning with a recursive definition which describes the function, but says nothing as to how it can be computed, we obtain an iterative program which exhibits a computing strategy.

This method is valid only for recursively defined functions. For sub-programs, other tools are needed. Just as recurrent sequences have played their part as the hinge between recursion and iteration, so regular actions, presented in Chapter 6, take on this double aspect, both iterative and recursive. They can be interpreted as segments of a program which has branch instructions, but also as recursive procedures without formal parameters or local variables. In particular they are amenable to substitution (the replacement of a procedure name by the procedure body), to identification (an expanded form of identity between two actions), and to the transformation of their terminal recursion into iteration. We show how this can be used to formulate the program representing an automaton.

It can also be used for program transformations. We give in Chapter 7 three frequently used syntactic transformations, which do not depend on the program's semantics and which do not modify the sequence of computations defined by the program. But we may well need transformations acting on this sequence if we are to modify, principally to shorten, it. We give some transformations which depend only on local properties. With these tools, we can build up more complex transformations or operate upon programs, for example to make their termination become clear or to pass from one strategy to another.

Regular actions and syntactic or local semantic transformations allow operations on iterative programs. To operate on recursive sub-programs, we need a more powerful tool. Thus we introduce generalised actions, and show how they can be regularised. This allows us to pass from parameterless recursive procedures to iterative procedures, if necessary through the introduction of an integer variable. To operate upon procedures with formal parameters and local variables, we must first make semantic transformations replacing the formal parameters and local variables by global variables. We give a first example in Chapter 8.

But that is concerned with the most powerful tool we have for operating on programs, and its presentation leads us to develop some examples which are both longer and apparently more sophisticated. We delve more deeply into the study of the replacement of formal parameters and local variables by global variables. We try to spell out the choices which are made during the transformation process and to demonstrate their importance.

For we end up, in fact, with a new method of programming. We create a recursive procedure; by semantic transformations we pass to global variables; by transformations into regular actions, and their subsequent manipulation, we obtain an iterative program which often seems to have very little left in common with the initial procedure. During a meeting of an international working group at the University of Warwick in 1978, where I presented this mode of operation, Edsger Dijkstra strongly criticised it, comparing it with the analytical geometry of Descartes. For him, it is worse than useless to spend hours in covering pieces of paper with tedious computations, just to get in the end a simple program which a little reflective thought would have revealed directly. He thinks that it is a waste of time for me to teach methods of computation which apply to programs and that I would do better to teach people how to think and how to ponder.

I am sensitive to this criticism. It has truly become an obsession with me — how does one invent a new program? How do you get a simple idea which turns into a simple program? I have not for the moment any answer, and I am afraid there may not be one. Human beings have been confronted with the problem of creativity for thousands of years, and we still have not a chance of being able deliberately to create anything new. Nonetheless, the constraints of computer technology have thrust the assignment instruction on us, and obliged us to invent new forms of reasoning. Recurrence is an old form of reasoning; iteration and recursion are creations of informatics. This book tries to shed some light on their relationships. Will this result in new ways in matters of program creation, and thence, in problem solving?

For me, analytical programming is a new path of discovery. From simple premises, and by computational methods which hardly change from one example to another, I can obtain a simple program in which what I am looking for — a simple strategy — is to be found. In his book, David Gries says that when we have obtained a simple program in this way, we should forget the twisted path by which we have come, and look for the straight road which leads directly to it [GRI]. It would indeed be a good thing to have only a simple way of producing a simple result. But I do not think that this would necessarily benefit the student or programming apprentice. He may well be filled with admiration for the master, but is it not a deceit to be made to believe that the master has an excess of inventive genius when, on the contrary, it is computation which has been the principal instrument of his success?

In this book, we should like to illustrate the mechanism for the creation of programs by computation, that is, "analytical programming." We have not hesitated, in developing the working, freely to jump over several clear but tedious steps from time to time. We immediately ask the reader on each of these occasions to do the computations himself, if he wishes to make the most of what is in front of him.

Henri Ledgard [LE1] has recognised good style with his programming proverbs. He might have included, from Boileau: "Qui ne sut se borner ne sut jamais écrire" ["No one who cannot limit himself has ever been able to write"]. A cruel proverb, and I have suffered a lot here. There are so many extraordinary examples of program transformations, revealing altogether unexpected strategies. . . . How to choose the best of them? Where to publish the others? I have tried to be content with examples not requiring too much computation and yet producing spectacular results. I have tried hard not to reproduce the examples of my previous book, still valid even if I have abandoned its notation as too unreadable and my methods of computation rather too sketchy [AR2]. The reader may wish to refer to it if he needs further examples.

If he learns from this book that recurrence is the foundation of methodical informatics, that recursion is an excellent method of programming, and that there are in general simple transitions from recursion to iteration, I shall already have achieved an important result. But I have been a little more ambitious: has the reader been convinced that computation is a reliable tool for the creation of programs?

I am anxious to warn the reader that this book revives my previous work [AR2], continuing much of its argument in terms which are, it is hoped, more simple. Since it was written I have had much new experience, both in transforming programs and in teaching students. This new book brings all these things together. I hope the result is rather more readable. . . .

Finally, exercises have been given, because it is not the result which is significant, but the way in which it is obtained. This aspect needs to be developed completely—but to do that I shall have to write another book.

List of Programs Discussed in the Book

(Numbers in parentheses are chapter and section numbers.)

Exponentiation

Computation of x^n, x real, n natural integer: An incorrect program (1.1), discussed (1.4), corrected (1.4). Recursive forms (2.2.2), precision (2.5.2), complexity (2.5.3). Computation (2.3), transformation to iterative (4.2).

Factorial

Computation of $n!$: recursive form (2.2.1), aberrant form (2.6.1). Variously derived iterative forms (4.6.1, 4.6.2).

String reversal

Mirror image of a character string, NOEL giving LEON: Recursive definition (2.2.3), its nature (2.4), complexity (2.6.2). Transformation to iteration (5.3.1), added strategy (5.3.1). Application to the representation of an integer in binary; conversion of an odd binary integer into the integer whose binary representation is the image of that of the given number; recursive and iterative forms (5.5).

Conversion of an integer to base b

Regarded as a character string: recursive definition (2.2.4), property (2.5.1). Regarded as a decimal number: beginning with $n = 5$ and $b = 2$, write 101 (the number one hundred and one, not the string one, zero, one). Recursive definition (4.8.2), transformation to recurrent (4.8.2), to iterative (5.3.2).

Fibonacci sequence

Dyadic recursive definition (2.2.5): computation (2.3.2), complexity (2.7), transformation to monadic recursive procedure (2.7), complexity (2.7), recurrent form (3.6.3).

Product of two integers

Dyadic recursive form (2.2.6): transformation to monadic (4.8.1), then to iterative (4.8.1). Other iterative forms (9.2). Recurrent form from another algorithm (3.6.1), associated iterative form (3.8.2).

Hamming sequence
Sequence, in increasing order of integers with no other prime factors than 2, 3, or 5:

2   3   4   5   6   8   9   10   13   15   16   18   20   24   25
27   · · ·

Recursive definition (2.7), iterative form (5.7).

"Function 91"
A dyadic recursive definition which computes a constant: Definition, value, complexity (2.8.1).

Christmas Day
Recurrent algorithm giving the day of the week on which Christmas Day falls in a given year (3.1).

Perpetual calendar
Gives the day of the week corresponding to a specified date (3.2).

Integral square root
Recurrent algorithm and improved forms, associated iterative forms (3.9). Iterative form operating in base b by subtraction of successive odd numbers (3.10).

Euclidean division of integers
Recursive form (4.1.1), associated iterative form (4.3).

Addition of integers by successor and predecessor functions only
Recursive and associated iterative forms (4.7.2, 4.7.3).

Longest common left-prefix of two integers in base b
In base b, the two integers are represented by character strings; the longest common prefix (leftmost part) of the two strings is taken as representing an integer in base b, the required result (5.4).

Greatest common divisor of two integers
Recursive form based on Euclid's algorithm and associated iterative form (5.4), automatic change of strategy (7.9).

Happy numbers
Sequence of integers obtained from a variant of the sieve of Eratosthenes, by crossing out at each stage only numbers which have not yet been crossed out. Complete elaboration of an iterative form, improvement, and comparison with another form (5.6).

Equality of two character strings apart from blanks
Automaton (6.1), change to an iterative program and improvement (6.8).

Search for a sub-string in a given string
Automaton (6.7.2), iterative form (6.7.2), change of form (6.3).

A problem of termination, due to Dijkstra (7.8)

Closing parenthesis associated with an opening parenthesis
Recursive form (8.1.1), assembly language form (8.1.3), iterative form with counter (8.3).

Permutations of a vector (9.3)

Towers of Hanoi (9.4, 9.6, 9.7)

Notations

These are not intended to be learnt by heart, but only, should the need arise, to be consulted in cases of doubt.

$*$	Multiplication sign
$:$	Integer quotient (only for natural integers)
$/$	Real division
$!$	Sign for concatenation of character strings giving the string resulting from placing the operand strings end to end
$\uparrow$	Exponentiation, $x \uparrow n = x^n$
$a[i \ldots j]$	Sequence $a[i]$, $a[i+1]$, . . . $a[j]$, empty if $j < i$
$a[i \ldots j] < c$	Equivalent to $a[i] < c$ AND $a[i+1] < c$ AND . . . $a[j] < c$
AND, and	Forms of the boolean operator giving the value TRUE if and only if the two operands both have the value TRUE
OR, or	Forms of the boolean operator giving the value FALSE if and only if the two operands both have the value FALSE
sbs(c, i, " ")	Sub-string taken from the string c beginning at the character in position i and finishing at the end of c
sbs(c, i, j)	Sub-string taken from the string c beginning at the character in position i and comprising j characters
sbs(c, i, i)	Special case of the foregoing: the character of c in position i
" < Sequence of characters not including a quotation mark > "	A constant string whose value is the string enclosed between the quotation marks
" "	Empty constant string
pos(c, i, d)	c and d are character strings; the value of this function is 0 if d does not occur within c with its

	leftmost character at a position $> i$; otherwise it is the position (rank) of the beginning of the first occurrence of d in c beginning at position i
$\Rightarrow$	Implication sign; $P \rightarrow Q$ is false if and only if P is false and Q is true
$\simeq$	Definition sign for recursive functions, or, depending on the context, syntactic equivalence of sequences of instructions (equivalence maintaining the history of the computation)
$f[a \rightarrow b]$	Its value is the string of characters representing f in which every occurrence of a has been replaced by an occurrence of b (substitution of b for a, or change of a to b)
FI	Closing parenthesis associated with the opening parenthesis IF; the selection instruction can take one or other of the two forms

$$\text{IF } t \text{ THEN } a \text{ ELSE } b \text{ FI}$$
$$\text{IF } t \text{ THEN } a \text{ FI}$$

If t is true, the sequence of instructions a is executed; otherwise b is executed if it exists, or nothing is done if it does not. The closing parenthesis FI makes it unnecessary to enclose the sequences a and b between BEGIN and END

WHILE t DO a OD   Is the loop, which can also be represented by

$$\text{L: IF NOT } t \text{ THEN GOTO L}' \text{ FI;}$$
$$a;$$
$$\text{GOTO L}$$
$$\text{L}': \text{continue}$$

REPEAT a UNTIL t Is the loop, which can also be represented by

$$\text{L : a;}$$
$$\text{IF NOT } t \text{ THEN GOTO L FI;}$$
$$\text{continue}$$

EXIT   Instruction causing the immediately enclosing loop to be left and execution to continue in sequence with the instruction written immediately after the loop

EXIT(p)   Leave p immediately enclosing nested loops and continue in sequence. EXIT(1) is the same as (is abbreviated to) EXIT

EXIT(0) Empty instruction

DO . . . OD Parentheses enclosing a loop; OD may be considered as an instruction to repeat the execution of the instructions of the loop, conditionally if the loop is prefixed by a WHILE clause

[[< Predicate >]] Assertion; relation between the variables of the program, true at the point at which it is written

INTEGER The set of natural integers

Translator's Introduction

No computer programmer of any experience can feel complacent about the state of his craft. It is, as it has always been, in a mess, and nowhere more so than in that part of programming practice to which the beginner is nowadays most likely to be first exposed — the software of the more popular microcomputers, including those provided by beneficent authorities in more and more of our schools. It seems as if nothing has been learned from the last thirty or forty years. Future professional programmers are helped neither by those of their teachers who become obsessed with the messier details of some assembly language or variation of "Basic" nor, at a "higher" level, by those who distance themselves as far as possible from actual computers and whose theories are developed upon pseudo-mathematical wishful thinking.

Professor Arsac's method is based on the definition and unification of many techniques known to, and practised by, good programmers over the years. In the hands of the new programmer who is prepared to work thoroughly and carefully, this book cannot fail to lead to the production of programs of which he can justly be proud. The teacher who may have despaired of finding a way of communicating a plain and straightforward approach to the programmer's task will find new hope and no little comfort in these pages. Only the "computer junky" with chronic "terminal disease" and the self-appointed high priest of fashionable programming theory will fail to appreciate the value of Arsac's work.

Good programming is not a mysterious art dependent on inspiration granted only to the genius, nor is it an automatic product of the use of the latest commercial system. Arsac shows, with numerous and remarkably appropriate examples, that it is the result of painstaking thoroughness helped sometimes by luck.

Arsac's book deserves a place on the desk of every programmer and would-be programmer whose concern for the quality of his work is more than superficial.

Clevedon   F. G. DUNCAN
1984

Chapter 1

Iterative Programming

1.1 An Incorrect Program

We have remarked already on the poor state of the art of programming—here is a piece of evidence of this. In the January–February 1979 issue of *Ordinateur Individuel* [in English, *Personal Computer*], Didier Caille [CAI] published the following program (the language used is LSE, which means very little here; the semantic intention of the instructions of this little program is self-evident):

```
1    * Personal computer
2    * example of arithmetical calculation
3      PRINT "this program calculates x to the power n"
4      PRINT "give me x please:"; READ x
5      PRINT "give me n please:"; READ n
6      IF n < 0 THEN BEGIN PRINT "n positive, please"; GOTO 5 END
7      a ← x
8      i ← 0
9      a ← a * x
10     i ← i + 1; t ← n − 1
11     IF i < t THEN GOTO 9
12     PRINT a
13     FINISH
```

From the text printed by line 3, we know the object of this program. From line 9 we can see that it is meant to work through repeated multiplication by x, but it is very easy to see that it is incorrect. Let us execute it "by hand" for a simple pair of input values, $x = 2$ and $n = 1$.

From line 6, $n = 2$ being greater than 0, the program continues at line 7, where a takes the value of x; that is, $a = 2$. In line 8, $i = 0$. In line 9, a is multiplied by x: $a = 2 * 2 = 4$. In line 10, i is increased by 1: $i = 1$; t takes the value of $n - 1$; $t = 0$. In line 11, $i = 1$ is not less than t ($=0$), and so the program passes to line 12, and the result 4 is printed for the value of $x = 2$ to the power $n = 1$—evidently false.

We should be astonished by this. In any other discipline, the publication of a false result would be considered abnormal, even scandalous. It is admitted in informatics that the writing of a correct program is exceptional, and thus that error is normal. As long as this point of view is sustained, no progress will be possible, but we should not throw stones at the author of this little program. We can find equally elementary mistakes in many other books.

Many programmers will react by carrying out tests on this program in order to localise the error, but this is no way out. For even if we arrive at a version of the program which will pass the tests, what can we infer if we still do not understand how it works and why it gives the expected results? "Testing a program allows us to show that it contains errors, never that it is correct" (Edsger W. Dijkstra [DI1]). We need tools and methods for describing the functioning of a program.

1.2   The Assignment Instruction

This instruction, which can change the value of a variable, is often a cause of obscurity in programs which use it. It is denoted by the sign $\leftarrow$ in APL and LSE. More frequently, we use the sign $:=$, as in ALGOL and PASCAL.

Consider the sequence

$$x := x + y; \qquad y := x - y; \qquad x := x - y$$

It is very difficult to see the effect of this by inspection alone. By its nature, an assignment instruction realises a transformation; it changes the state of a variable. To set out the effect of this sequence, we need to describe the set of states generated by the three instructions. We place the description of a state—represented by a relation involving the constants and variables of the program—between the signs [[and]]. Thus, if a and b are the initial values of the variables x and y, we may write

$$[[x = a \quad y = b]] \qquad x := x + y$$

We execute the instruction $x := x + y$ with the values a and b of the variables x and y; y remains unchanged.

$$[[x = a \quad y = b]] \qquad x := x + y \quad [[x = a + b \quad y = b]]$$

The next instruction changes only y:

$$y := x - y \quad [[x = a + b \quad y = (a + b) - b = a]]$$

The final instruction changes x:

$$x := x - y \quad [[x = (a + b) - a = b \quad y = a]]$$

Thus the final values of x and y are their initial values interchanged. Let us be quite clear as to what we have done. We have placed between the instructions comments in the form of predicates describing the state of the variables. The passage from one state to another is achieved by the execution of the instruction upon the values of the variables given by the predicates.

The affirmation of a relation holding among the variables of a program at a given point is called an "assertion". An instruction effects a transformation upon a predicate. To say how an instruction modifies the assertion which precedes it (its "preassertion") to give that which follows or succeeds it (its "postassertion") is to define the *semantics* of that instruction. We shall examine more closely the effect of the principal instructions on the assertions. First, however, we shall look again at the part played by the three instructions of our example. They are, with their assertions,

$$[[x = a \qquad y = b]] \qquad x := x + y$$
$$[[x = a + b \qquad y = b]] \qquad y := x - y$$
$$[[x = a + b \qquad y = a]] \qquad x := x - y$$
$$[[x = b \qquad y = a]]$$

Let us suppose that the numbers a and b are "real", and that b is very small in comparison with a. The calculations are carried out with a constant number of significant figures. To the precision of the arithmetic, b is *negligible* compared to a, and the addition of b does not change x. So,

$$[[x = a \quad y = b]] \qquad x := x + y$$
$$[[x = a \quad y = b]] \qquad y := x - y$$

Again, subtracting b from a has no effect:

$$[[x = a \quad y = a]] \qquad x := x - y$$
$$[[x = 0 \quad y = a]]$$

The exchange of values does not take place. There is 0 in x and a in y. This shows how the mechanism of assertions can be a very fine instrument describing even the way in which calculations are executed in the computer. It allows a very precise interpretation of the effect of a sequence of instructions. It is this which enables us to give a meaning to a program.

1.3   Assertions and Instructions

1.3.1   Assignment

Consider an assignment instruction modifying the variable x. Two cases are possible:

x is given a new value independent of its old value. We write for this case $x := a$ (constant relative to x).
x is given a value calculated from its old value. We write this as $x := f(x)$.

These notations say nothing about the possible dependence of a and $f(x)$ on other variables in the program. The preassertion will be denoted in the form of a predicate linking x to the other variables of the program; thus $P(x, y)$. This does not require x to depend on these other variables, symbolised by y, but implies only that in the most general case, x bears a certain relation to them.

If initially

$$[[P(x, y)]] \qquad x := a$$

the old value of x being destroyed, the relation with the other variables represented by P is also destroyed:

$$[[P(x, y)]] \qquad x := a \qquad [[x = a]]$$

If a is a function of y, we have created a new relation between x and y.

Suppose now $x := f(x)$. We shall introduce for the sake of clarity a new intermediate variable x' such that the sequence

$$x' := f(x); \quad x := x'$$

is equivalent overall to $x := f(x)$.

We now have two assignments of the preceding type:

$$[[P(x, y)]] \quad x' := f(x) \quad [[P(x, y) \qquad and \qquad x' = f(x)]]$$

Giving x the value of x' through $x := x'$ is the same as replacing x by x'. Suppose first that $f(x)$ has an inverse f^{-1} such that $x' = f(x)$ is equivalent to $x = f^{-1}(x')$. Then,

$$P(x, y) \qquad and \qquad x' = f(x)$$

is equivalent to

$$P(f^{-1}(x'), y) \qquad and \qquad x = f^{-1}(x')$$

If we now give x a new value, its previous value is destroyed, and x appears in the place of x'. Finally,

$$[[P(f^{-1}(x'), y) \qquad and \qquad x = f^{-1}(x')]] \quad x := x' \quad [[P(f^{-1}(x), y)]]$$

If we eliminate the intermediate variable by simplifying the assertions, we are left with

$$[[P(x, y)]] \; x := f(x) \; [[P(f^{-1}(x), y)]]$$

The algebra also comes out neatly if the predicate $P(x, y)$ is itself of the form $Q(f(x), y)$:

$$[[Q(f(x), y)]] \; x' := f(x)$$

We replace $f(x)$ by x'

$$[[Q(f(x), y)]] \quad x' := f(x) \quad [[Q(x', y)]]$$
$$x := x' \quad [[Q(x, y)]]$$

or, finally,

$$[[Q(f(x), y)]] \; x := f(x) \; [[Q(x, y)]]$$

Where f has an inverse, the two methods give the same result. If in fact $P(x, y) = Q(f(x), y)$, then the substitution for x of $f^{-1}(x)$ in P gives $P(f^{-1}(x), y) = Q(f(f^{-1}(x)), y) = Q(x, y)$.

These results are at first sight surprising. Let us therefore look at their application to some simple cases.

Suppose we have

$$[[x \geq 0]] \; x := x + 1$$

It is clear that increasing x still leaves it positive but does not allow it to be zero. We must therefore have as postassertion $x > 0$. With $f(x) = x + 1$, $f^{-1}(x) = x - 1$,

$$[[x \geq 0]] \; x := x + 1 \; [[x - 1 \geq 0]]$$

The postassertion is equivalent to $x \geq 1$ or $x > 0$. In the same way, for any preassertion involving x,

$$[[P(x)]] \; x := x + 1 \; [[P(x - 1)]]$$

This is one of the most serious difficulties in the explanation of information processing to those who are not scientifically trained. We can get across the idea of the situation (state of variables characterised by predicates) being modified by instructions which act as transformations. But it is not easy to explain why a situation involving x is transformed into the same situation but involves $x - 1$ by the execution of $x := x + 1$. Of course, we might say that if an observer has arrived at x, and if x is advanced, then everything happens as if the observer had stepped back relative to x, and so sees no more than $x - 1$. It is not entirely convincing.

We should also note that it is not at all certain in general that f has an inverse. If we suppose n to be an integer variable

$$[[P(n)]]\quad n:=n:2$$

we can affirm nothing more, at least not without introducing a new variable r having the values 0 and 1 for the *remainder* of the division by 2. Then,

$$[[P(n)]]\ n:=n:2\ [[P(2*n+r)]]$$

More precautions are now needed in the development of the assertions.

All this shows the extent to which the assignment instruction is difficult to manipulate and to interpret. We shall have many occasions to return to these problems.

1.3.2   Selection

The instruction of *selection*,

IF condition THEN ...... ELSE ...... FI

(where FI is the closing parenthesis associated with the opening parenthesis IF) distinguishes in a given situation between two sub-situations, depending on whether the condition is satisfied or not:

$$[[P]]\ \text{IF}\ t\ \text{THEN}\ [[P\ and\ t]]\ \text{ELSE}\ [[P\ and\ not\ t]]\ \text{FI}$$

The "test" part of the instruction is not transformational in nature and has no effect on situations; it serves only to distinguish the two possible cases.

This is why it would be indeed abnormal for the evaluation of the condition t to modify any variable whatever; for example, as a side effect of a function procedure. In the general case, it is difficult to say what this means for the postassertion of a selection. Let f be the set of instructions of the alternative "true" and g that of the alternative "false"!

$$[[P]]\ \text{IF}\ t\ \text{THEN}\ [[P\ and\ t]]\ \text{f}\ [[P']]$$
$$\text{ELSE}\quad [[P\ and\ not\ t]]\ \text{g}\ [[P'']]$$
$$\text{FI}\ [[P'\ or\ P'']]$$

However, in many cases the object of this instruction is to attain the same final situation whatever the initial condition t. We will then have $P' = P''$.

1.3.3   Branching Instruction

The GOTO instruction does not modify any variable of the program and thus does not operate upon states. If a is a label referring to an instruction and

P the preassertion of the GOTO instruction, then
$$[[P]] \text{ GOTO } a \, [[P]]$$
that is, $[[P]]$ is also the preassertion of the instruction labelled by a. In other words, the GOTO instruction links two points in the program characterised by *the same situation.*

This remark is of very great importance. It has been said that branching instructions are dangerous and to be avoided [DI2], [LE1]. They are inimical to the legibility of the program, the reader having to jump frequently from one place to another. This has happened as a result of the abuse of these instructions. Nevertheless, when we are confronted by a situation which has to be decomposed into two, we are obliged to consider these two one at a time. The human mind is constrained to consider first one and then the other. The branching instruction may involve the anticipation of a situation which will be considered later (GOTO "further down", "forward jump") or the reconciliation with a situation already encountered and dealt with (GOTO "back up", "backward jump").

The greatest danger arises out of the way in which the programmer considers this instruction. Most often, it is seen as the answer to the question, "What to do next?", being read as "go to such a point in the program to do such an action". Rather, it must be seen as a reply to the question, "Where are we now?". It is absolutely necessary first to think in terms of situations and then to deduce from these situations what to do. My experience of teaching extremely diverse groups has convinced me that the backward jump is in general less dangerous than the forward jump. In the former case, a situation already encountered is found again. The programmer knows enough about what he has written to find the right point in the program. The forward jump is in contrast an anticipation of a situation which is to be dealt with later and whose details are as yet unknown. The programmer rarely bothers to work them out there and then, promising himself to deal with them later. When he does so, he has forgotten some details, and the result is in error. For the sake of prudence, at every forward jump we should write, as commentary, a description of the corresponding situation which will have to be matched later on.

1.3.4   The WHILE Instruction

This instruction is written
$$\text{WHILE } t \text{ DO } a \text{ OD}$$
where t is a test, and a is a set of instructions. It is equivalent to
$$L: \text{IF } t \text{ THEN } a; \text{ GOTO } L \text{ FI}$$

Let P_0 be the situation at the beginning of the execution of this instruction. The preassertion of a is P_0 *and* t. The execution of a produces a postassertion P_1. The instruction GOTO L links two points of an identical situation so that either $P_1 = P_0$ or at least P_1 is a particular case of P_0 (P_1 implies P_0). Usually, P_0 and P_1 will be particular cases of the same general situation P encompassing all these particular cases, so we will have

$$[[P]] \text{ WHILE } t \text{ DO } [[P \text{ and } t]] \ a \ [[P]] \text{ OD}; [[P \text{ and not } t]]$$

The assertion P *and* t is true at each repetition of a and thus invariant over the execution of the loop. When t becomes false, P is still true so that at the exit from the WHILE instruction, we have P *and not* t. As at the entry we already have P, we can say that the effect of the loop is to obtain the realisation of *not* t while conserving P.

1.3.5   The Loop

The loop which we consider most often in this book comprises a list of instructions forming the body of the loop and including one or several EXIT instructions, denoted here by f(EXIT), including a sequence of instructions containing at least one occurrence of an EXIT instruction. The loop is enclosed in the loop parentheses DO ...... OD:

DO f(EXIT) OD

OD, the closing parenthesis of the loop, can be considered as an instruction sending one back to the head of the loop. EXIT means "leave the loop and continue in sequence". This loop is thus equivalent to

$L: f(\text{GOTO } L'); \text{GOTO } L;$
$L':$

As in the case of the WHILE loop, the postassertion of f is the preassertion of GOTO L and so must imply the preassertion of L. This assertion is thus invariant through the loop.

If P is the preassertion of the loop and Q that of the EXIT instruction (or the union of those of the EXIT instructions if there are several such), then

$[[P]]$ DO
        $[[P]]$ f($[[Q]]$ EXIT)
    OD;
$[[Q]]$

This loop being rather more general than the WHILE loop, there is not necessarily a simple relationship between P and Q. This depends on the structure of the sequence of instructions f. Experience shows, however, that it is amenable to a systematic analysis. We return to this point later in the chapter [AR1].

1.4 The Interpretation of a Program

The idea of assertion was proposed by R. Floyd [FLO], as a means of giving a meaning to a program, and then formalised by C. A. R. Hoare [HOA]. We shall use it to study the program by Didier Caille (Section 1.1).

There is a loop from line 9 to line 11, and so we must have at the entry to line 9 an assertion which will be invariant through the loop. It will involve the variables of the loop, which are a and i. As this program is intended to compute x^n, let us suppose, as hypothesis, that a is of the form x^i. We arrive for the first time at line 9 from line 7.

7. $\quad a \leftarrow x \; [[a = x]]$
8. $\quad i \leftarrow 0 \quad [[a = x \; and \; i = 0]]$

A possible assertion here is $a = x^{i+1}$. Let us see what will lead to this assertion:

9. $\quad [[a = x^{i=1}]] \; a \leftarrow a * x \; [[a/x = x^{i+1}, that \; is \; a = x^{i+2}]]$
10. $\quad [[a = x^{i+2}]] \; i \leftarrow i + 1 \; [[a = x^{i+1}]]$

We note that the assertion $a = x^{i+1}$ has been re-established with a greater value of i. We must adjust i by reference to n. As $t = n - 1$,

11. $\quad [[a = x^{i+1}]] \; IF \; i < t \; THEN \; [[a = x^{i+1} \; and \; i < n - 1]] \; GOTO \; 9$
12. $\quad [[a = x^{i+1} \; and \; i \geq n - 1]]$

If, in 12, the equality is attained, then

$$a = x^{i+1} \qquad and \qquad i = n - 1$$

giving $a = x^n$, and the program is correct.

We note also that the GOTO instruction of line 11 leads to line 9 with the assertion

$$a = x^{i+1} \qquad and \qquad i < n - 1$$

If we use this assertion, we must have for the preassertion of line 10:

10. $\quad [[a = x^{i+2} \; and \; i < n - 1]] i \leftarrow i + 1 \; [[a = x^{i+1} \; and \; i < n - 1]]; \; t \leftarrow n - 1$
11. $\quad IF \; i < t \; THEN \; [[a = x^{i+1} \; and \; i < n - 1]] \; GOTO \; 9$
12. $\quad [[a = x^{i+1} \; and \; i = n - 1 \; thus \; a = x^n]]$

Thus we shall arrive at line 12 with the correct assertion if we can reach line 9 with

$$a = x^{i+1} \quad and \quad i < n - 1$$

But by the initialisation

$$a = x \quad and \quad i = 0$$

We must therefore have $0 < n - 1$ or $n > 1$. We have the result we have been looking for—the program computes $a = x^n$ for $n > 1$ only.

It is not very easy to correct this. It appears likely that the author has chosen his terminating condition badly and that he has sought to correct it by introducing the variable t, computed in line 10, whose value is thereafter constant. Its computation inside the loop is abnormal.

We have said that situations have primacy over actions. To re-edit the program, we must first describe a general situation. Suppose that we had done part of the work and had calculated $a = x^i$ for a value of $i \leq n$ (it would be absurd to suppose $i > n$, for that would mean that the computation had gone too far):

9. *comment*: we have computed $a = x^i$ and $i \leq n$

If $i = n$, we have finished:

10. IF $i = n$ THEN GOTO 12

If not, we must get nearer to the solution by incrementing i:

11. $a \leftarrow a * x$; $i \leftarrow i + 1$; GOTO 9

It remains to find values of a and i such that hypothesis 9 is verified for all n, positive and zero. We must take $i = 0$ and then $a = x^0 = 1$. Hence the new, correct, program:

```
3   PRINT "this program calculates x to the power n"
4   PRINT "give me x please:"; READ x
5   PRINT "give me n please:"; READ n
6   IF n < 0 THEN BEGIN PRINT "n positive, please"; GOTO 5 END
7
8   a ← 1; i ← 0
9   comment: a = xⁱ and i ≤ n
10  IF i = n THEN GOTO 12; comment: a = xⁱ and i = n gives x = aⁿ
11  a ← a * x; i ← i + 1; GOTO 9
12  PRINT a
13  FINISH
```

1.5   Recurrent Construction of Iterative Programs

The exercise we have just carried out may appear difficult to the reader. Indeed, there are many who think that the proof *a posteriori* of a program already written is a labour at the limit of what is possible. The only way to arrive at a soundly based program is to construct it on a foundation of its assertions. We have established, above, a methodology of programming [AR1], [AR2].

A program describes the set of transformations which must be executed by a computer for it to pass from the situation of its initial state (the data) to that of its final state (the results). If the way from one to the other is not direct, we must mark it by means of intermediate situations.

The iterative solution of a problem rests upon the loop instruction, characterised by the invariance of its situations. The construction of a loop depends on the choice of the invariant situation with which it is associated. To construct a loop, a good method is the following:

–specify a general situation, invariant for the loop, which might be called a "recurrence hypothesis";
–see whether it is finished (and if so leave the loop);
–if not, move towards the solution while maintaining the recurrence hypothesis (or by re-establishing it, for one will in general be obliged temporarily to discard it);
–begin the process by finding initial values compatible with the problem and satisfying the recurrence hypothesis.

Rather than remain at a pseudotheoretical level, we shall present this through a well-known example in order to show how one can choose such a recurrence hypothesis and the consequences of this choice. Suppose we have to sort a vector a of n elements $a[1 \dots n]$. We wish to find a permutation of this vector by transposition of its elements such that each element of the resultant vector is less than or equal to that which follows it (its successor):

$$a[i] \leq a[i + 1] \text{ for all } i \text{ such that } 1 \leq i < n$$

The most usual way to formulate a recurrence hypothesis is to suppose that we have done part of the work. Suppose that we have sorted by transpositions part of the vector; that is, $a[1 \dots i]$ has been sorted, where $i \leq n$, by transposition. The work is finished if all of the vector has been sorted; that is, if $i = n$. If not, we must extend the sorted part. For this we bring $x = a[i + 1]$ to its proper place in the sorted part of the array, also by transposition. Hence the program

```
i := 1;
DO
    [[a[1...i] sorted by transposition]]
    IF i = n THEN EXIT FI;
    x := a[i + 1];
    put x into its proper place in a[1...i + 1] by transposition;
    i := i + 1;
OD
```

Any implementation of the action "put x into its proper place in $a[1...i + 1]$ by transposition" gives a sorting program. One might either

–first find the place for x and then put x into this place by transpositions, or
–realise the operation directly by recurrence.

In the former case, the search can be done linearly or by using dichotomy. We give here a program based on a linear search:

```
i := 1;
DO
    [[a[1,...,i] sorted by transposition]]
    IF i = n THEN EXIT FI;
    x := a[i + 1];
    j := i + 1;
    DO
        [[the place for x is at j or below]]
        IF j = 1 THEN EXIT FI;
        IF a[j − 1] ≤ x THEN EXIT FI;
        j := j − 1
    OD;
    k := i + 1;
    DO [[the elements above k have been moved up]]
        IF k = j THEN EXIT FI;
        a[k + 1] := a[k]; k := k − 1
    OD;
    a[k] := x;
    i := i + 1
OD
```

One remark is needed. We have written the assertions in plain language. This has the effect of simplicity and allows this method of working to be put within the reach of those without a strong mathematical background. But there are hidden snags too. Thus, for example, the assertion

        [[the place for x is at j or below]]

means that the place for x cannot be above j

   –either because j is the highest position which it can take, $j = i + 1$;
   –or because the elements above j belonging to $a[1 \ldots i]$ are greater than x,

all of which can be written as

$$j \leq i \text{ implies for all } j \text{ such that } j < j' \leq i, x < a[j']$$

The reader concerned for rigour will work with such assertions. Our intention is not to give a course in mathematics. We make use of mathematics here as physicists and chemists have always done. But it is as well to remain clear, to know that perhaps these assertions in plain language can become a source of ambiguity, and not hesitate to have recourse to a more rigorous formalism.

    The program we have just written contains two successive loops inside a larger enclosing loop. The second internal loop causes k to run through the same values as are taken by j in the first. One may wish to combine these two loops into one. This is a problem in program transformation, which will be dealt with in later chapters.

    We leave as exercises for the reader the problems of realising the sorting program (a) through the method of dichotomy, and (b) by putting x at each stage directly into its place by successive transpositions with preceding elements.

1.6   Partial Correctness

    To resolve a problem there is not in general a unique recurrence hypothesis. For each hypothesis there is a corresponding program (if the hypothesis is acceptable!). The effect of the choice of hypothesis on the form of the resultant program is difficult to predict. We shall develop some other sorting programs to illustrate this point.

    We have taken as a recurrence hypothesis "$a[1 \ldots i]$ has been sorted by transposition". Let us now take a weaker hypothesis. We cannot abandon the affirmation that we have only made transpositions; that is part of the statement of the problem. Thus there remains as recurrence hypothesis

[[only transpositions have been made]]

It appears unlikely that we should be able to proceed on such a feeble hypothesis. But, nonetheless, it is true that we have worked towards the object of the sorting; that is, we have reduced the disorder of the vector. If we apply the proposed method strictly, we must now test whether it is finished. In the absence of precise information on the state of the vector, one cannot decide this by a simple test. To know if it is finished, that is to say if the vector has been sorted, we return to the definition of the sort: the result is a permutation of the initial vector (which is assured by the fact that we have only done transpositions) such that for all i less than n

$$a[i] \leq a[i + 1]$$

The work is not finished if this condition is false, and there is a value of i less than n such that $a[i] > a[i + 1]$.

If we find such an i, the sorting is not finished. We must go back to the recurrence hypothesis (that is to say, that only transpositions are done) to reduce the disorder of the vector. We know that a pair of consecutive elements is badly ordered. We transpose these two elements. At the beginning, we take the vector as it is; having done nothing, we have satisfied the recurrence hypothesis

```
DO
    [[we have made only transpositions]]
    see whether there is a value of i such that a[i] > a[i + 1];
    IF none such THEN EXIT FI;
    interchange a[i] and a[i + 1]
OD
```

We shall deal later in detail with the three parts of this program, simple enough in other respects, which are here suggested in informal language. We have here a simple program, "partially correct"—and that remark may seem not particularly interesting. If the program stops, it gives the right result. We can be sure of this because it will not leave the loop, through EXIT, unless and until the vector has been sorted. It is this which is meant by "partial correctness"—a program which gives the right result if it stops, but it is not yet certain that it does stop.

The program above is meaningless if it does not stop. To prove that it does, we make use of an integral value which measures in some way how far the program is from the solution. If we can show that this value decreases at each step of the loop, then termination is certain. It will not be necessary to believe that it will always be reached. However, here is a very short program operating on a natural integer n:

```
READ n;
WHILE n ≠ 1
    DO IF even(n) THEN n := n/2
                  ELSE  n := 3 * n + 1
        FI
    OD
```

No one knows whether this always stops. Its termination has been verified by computer for values of n up to a very large number. It is conjectured that it does always stop, but this has not been demonstrated.

We return to our sorting program. It is not difficult to show that it stops. In the following, an "inversion" means any pair of elements $a[i] > a[j]$ with $i < j$. The interchange of two adjacent elements initially in inversion reduces by one the total number of inversions. This does not change the number of inversions due to elements other than i and $i + 1$. If there is an inversion involving i, or $i + 1$, and another element j other than i and $i + 1$, it is not affected by the interchange, for the relative positions of the elements concerned remain the same.

The number of inversions in the vector is taken as a measure of the remoteness of the solution. When it is zero, the vector has been sorted. It is reduced by one at each step of the loop. Therefore the program terminates. We know, moreover, the cost of this; the number of steps of the loop is equal to the number of inversions in the original vector. If there are few, the program may be acceptable. In the worst case, that of a vector in reverse order, there are $n(n - 1)/2$ inversions (each element is in inversion with respect to every element which follows it). We must expect therefore that the number of steps of the loop will be of the order of n^2. As it contains an inner loop for seeking an inverse adjacent pair of elements, requiring a number of steps of order n, this program will be of order n^3, which is very bad.

But we have learnt a result of general significance—that any sorting program which operates by interchange of neighbours is of order n^2 (it removes the inversions one by one).

Let us finish the program. The development of the instructions needs no explanation:

```
DO
        i := 1;
        DO
                [[no inversion of neighbours until i]]
                IF i = n THEN EXIT FI;
                IF a[i] > a[i + 1] THEN EXIT FI;
                i := i + 1
        OD;
        IF i = n THEN EXIT FI;
        x := a[i]; a[i] := a[i + 1]; a[i + 1] := x
OD
```

We notice in this program that one test is repeated. If we leave the inner loop with $i = n$, we test again for $i = n$ before leaving the outer loop. In other words, for $i = n$ we leave two loops. If now we leave the inner loop with $i \neq n$, the test which follows has no effect. The program can be shortened by the introduction of an instruction EXIT(2) which leaves two nested loops:

```
DO
    i := 1;
    DO
        IF i = n THEN EXIT(2) FI;
        IF a[i] > a[i + 1] THEN EXIT FI;
        i := i + 1
    OD;
    x := a[i]; a[i] := a[i + 1]; a[i + 1] := x
OD
```

1.7   Strengthening the Recurrence Hypothesis

The programming process is not necessarily complete when a program is correct. The program must be examined to see if it can be improved. We have already discussed this. We shall show here how a study of the program can reveal properties which can be used to save instructions.

In the earlier form of the program, without EXIT(2), the first loop can be interpreted in a more refined way as:

search for the first inversion of adjacent elements of *a*.

At the exit from the loop:

−if $i = n$, the vector has been sorted;
−if $i < n$, there is an inversion between i and $i + 1$, and this is the first. In other words, the vector has been sorted up to i.

This gives us a new program identical with the old except that the first loop has been replaced by an indication of its effect, and we have added the newly discovered assertion:

```
DO
    i := 1;
    search for the first inversion of neighbours after i;
    IF i = n THEN EXIT FI;
    [[a sorted up to i]]
    interchange a[i] and a[i + 1]
OD
```

The interchange affects the elements i and $i + 1$ and leaves the lower part of the vector unchanged. If it is not empty, it remains sorted. There are thus two possibilities:

–if $i = 1$, the part $1, 2$ of a has been sorted;
–if $i > 1$, the part from 1 to $i - 1$ has been sorted.

> [[a sorted up to i]]
> interchange $a[i]$ and $a[i + 1]$
> [[a sorted up to if $i = 1$ then 2 else $i - 1$]]

This assertion, true before OD, is also true at the beginning of the loop. We have strengthened the initial assertion. Having started with "only transpositions have been made", we now have "by transpositions only, a has been sorted up to if $i = 1$ then 2 else $i - 1$". With such an assertion, the search for the first inversion of adjacent elements need not begin at 1 but at 2 or $i - 1$.

We note also that the initialisation must be modified if we wish this assertion to be true at the entry to the loop. To simplify matters, we shall change the value "if $i = 1$ then 2 else $i - 1$" to i before OD, in order to affirm that a has been sorted up to i at the entry to the loop and that i is initialised to 1 before the loop. We have again reached the recurrence hypothesis of Section 1.5, but through a different strategy of progression. The two programs are not very different. That which we have obtained here is a little less efficient and involves more comparisons than that of Section 1.5. We leave it as an exercise to the reader to say why.

```
i := 1;
DO
      [[by transpositions, a sorted up to and including i]]
      DO
          IF i = n THEN EXIT FI;
          IF a[i] > a[i + 1] THEN EXIT FI;
          i := i + 1
      OD;
      IF i = n THEN EXIT FI;
      x := a[i]; a[i] := a[i + 1]; a[i + 1] := x;
      i := IF i = 1 THEN 2 ELSE i - 1 FI
OD
```

1.8   The Effect of the Choice of the Recurrence Hypothesis

We have seen that the weakening of the recurrence hypothesis is expressed in a degradation of the program. The use of a new property has improved the program but enriched the recurrence hypothesis. Can we see here an indication of a general phenomenon linking the performance of the program to the richness of the recurrence hypothesis? This is a question that we cannot always answer in the affirmative, although it appears to be very often so.

Let us enrich the hypothesis of Section 1.5 by supposing that not only is there a part of the vector already sorted, but that we know also that this part is in its proper place. For convenience, let us suppose that this place is at the top of the vector:

$a[m + 1 \ldots n]$ is sorted, and in place, by transpositions

It is finished if $m = 0$, for then a is sorted from 1 to n. But this takes no account of the affirmation that the upper part is in its proper place. If $m = 1$, the part from 2 to m is sorted and in place. Trivially, the first element is also in place. Sorting is thus finished if $m = 1$ also. If it is not finished, to reach the solution we must extend the part which is sorted and in place. To do this, we put the element m in its proper place. This is necessarily the greatest element in the part 1 to m, whence the program

```
m := n ;
DO
    [[a[m + 1 ... n] sorted, in place, by transpositions]]
    IF m = 1 THEN EXIT FI ;
    move by transpositions the greatest of 1 ... m to m ;
    m := m − 1
OD
```

The innermost operation

move by transpositions the greatest of $1 \ldots m$ to m

can be effected in either of two ways:

−directly, by recurrence (left as an exercise for the reader), giving the well-known "bubble sort" with its variants;
−by partition into two—

search for the position k of the greatest of $1 \ldots m$
interchange the elements $a[k]$ and $a[m]$

We give this version in detail without further comment:

```
m := n ;
DO
    [[a[m + 1 ... n] sorted, in place, by transpositions]]
    IF m = 1 THEN EXIT FI ;
    j := 1 ; k := 1 ;
    DO
```

$$[[a[1 \ldots j] \le a[k]]]$$
IF $j = m$ THEN EXIT FI;
$j := j + 1$;
  IF $a[j] > a[k]$ THEN $k := j$ FI
OD;
$x := a[k]$; $a[k] := a[m]$; $a[m] := x$;
$m := m - 1$
OD

This is a very well-known sorting procedure, but one not without interest. The outer loop is executed $n - 1$ times. There are thus exactly $n - 1$ interchanges in the program. The inner loop is done $m - 1$ times. There are thus $n(n - 1)/2$ comparisons. But comparisons are cheaper than interchanges.

The program can be improved. We note that in fact the search for the greatest element in the inner loop is done by selecting elements of the vector of increasing size. We are sorting into increasing order; we keep only the last element of the increasing sequence. Let us now try keeping the last but one as well. When we modify k, let us keep as p its previous value:

$$\text{IF } a[j] > a[k] \text{ THEN } p := k; k := j \text{ FI}$$

At the time of that operation, k was the greatest element in $1 \ldots j - 1$, and so p is the position of the greatest element in $1 \ldots k - 1$.

As before, let us enrich the recurrence hypothesis of the inner loop. (It will be necessary in consequence to modify the initialisation. We shall see this later.)

DO
  $$[[a[1 \ldots k - 1] \le a[p] \quad a[1 \ldots j] \le a[k]]]$$
  IF $j = m$ THEN EXIT FI;
  $j := j + 1$;
    IF $a[j] > a[k]$ THEN $p := k; k := j$ FI
  OD;
  $$[[a[1 \ldots k - 1] \le a[p] \text{ and } a[1 \ldots m] \le a[k]]]$$
  interchange $a[k]$ and $a[m]$;
  $$[[a[1 \ldots k - 1] \le a[p]]]$$

We thus have an assertion at the end of the loop much stronger than that taken as invariant. We must try to make use of this. It is interesting because the invariant of the inner loop is k is the position of the greatest element in $1 \ldots j$. So at the end of a step of the loop we have the information that p is the position of the greatest element in $1 \ldots k - 1$. Rather than carrying on with $k = 1$, the position of the greatest element of a vector of length 1, we take $k = p$, the position of the greatest of $k - 1$ elements.

But p is not defined unless there exists j such that $a[j] > a[k]$. We have to clarify the assertion. It is of use only if p exists. Let us denote by a recognisable particular value, for example $p = 0$, the case where p is undefined. {If p is defined, then $p > 0$}. Writing $\rightarrow$ for implication,

$$P \rightarrow Q \text{ stands for}$$
IF P THEN Q ELSE TRUE FI

The above piece of program becomes

> DO
> $$[[p \neq 0 \rightarrow a[1 \ldots k - 1] \leq a[p] \quad a[1 \ldots j] \leq a[k]]]$$
>   IF $j = m$ THEN EXIT FI;
> $j := j + 1$;
>   IF $a[j] > a[k]$ THEN $p := k$; $k := j$ FI
> OD;
> $$[[p \neq 0 \rightarrow a[1 \ldots k - 1] \leq a[p] \quad a[1 \ldots m] \leq a[k]]]$$
> interchange $a[k]$ and $a[m]$;
> $$[[p \neq 0 \rightarrow a[1 \ldots k - 1] \leq a[p]]]$$

We can take this as a new invariant of the loop, provided that the initialisation is modified so that this hypothesis is realised at the entry to the loop. It is sufficient to take $p = 0$.

Taking account of this invariant, the inner loop can be entered with the best values when p is non-zero. As, moreover, $p \leq k - 1$ and $k \leq m$, we have $p \leq m - 1$:

> $m := n$; $p := 0$;
> DO
>   [[$a[m + 1 \ldots n]$ sorted, in place, by transpositions
> $p \neq 0 \rightarrow a[1 \ldots k - 1 \leq a[p]]]]$
>   IF $m = 1$ THEN EXIT FI;
>   IF $p = 0$ THEN $j := 1$; $k := 1$
>   ELSE $j := k - 1$; $k := p$; $p := 0$
>   FI;
>   DO
> $$[[p \neq 0 \rightarrow a[1 \ldots k - 1] \leq a[p] \quad a[1 \ldots j] \leq a[k]]]$$
>   IF $j = m$ THEN EXIT FI;
> $j := j + 1$;
>   IF $a[j] > a[k]$ THEN $p := k$; $k := j$ FI
>   OD;
>   interchange $a[k]$ and $a[m]$;
> $m := m - 1$
> OD

This program still takes $n - 1$ steps of the outer loop, but the inner loop has been accelerated. If p is non-zero, it has fewer than $m - 1$ steps. We can do better. Let us suppose that at the end of the inner loop we had $k = m$ and $p \neq 0$. The interchange of the elements k and m is useless, because $k = m$. Moreover, we have the greatest element in $1 \ldots m - 1$ and we can immediately do the interchange in the next step of the loop. In other words, we skip one step of the outer loop by doing

$$k := p; m := m - 1$$

But then m decreases by two, and we can expect $m = 0$. We must change the test $m = 1$ to $m \leq 1$. With this modification, we can never have $j = m$ at the entry to the inner loop. This is not possible at the first entry, through the initialisation, if n is greater than 1, which is what we will suppose. If at the exit from the inner loop, $k - 1 = m - 1$, then p must be reset to 0 (we have made use of the greatest element in $1 \ldots m - 1$). We cannot then obtain $k = m$ unless k has been defined in the inner loop, and then $p \neq 0$. Thus we obtain a new version where not only the number of comparisons has been reduced, but even the number of interchanges and of steps of the outer loop. The performance of this program depends on the data. By tests with vectors whose elements have been taken at random over an interval with a uniform distribution of values, we have obtained an improvement of the order of 20 to 30% over the program not making use of the variable p:

```
m := n; p := 0;
DO
        [[a[m + 1 ... n] sorted, in place, by transpositions
          p ≠ 0 → a[1 ... k − 1] ≤ a[p] and k − 1 < m]]
        IF m < 1 THEN EXIT FI;
        IF p = 0 THEN j := 1; k := 1
                 ELSE j := k − 1; k := p; p := 0
        FI;
        DO
              [[p ≠ 0 → a[1 ... k − 1] ≤ a[p],   a[1 ... j] ≤ a[k]]]
              IF j = m THEN EXIT FI;
              j := j + 1;
              IF a[j] > a[k] THEN p := k; k := j FI;
        OD;
        IF k = m THEN m := m − 1; k := p; p := 0 FI;
        x := a[k]; a[k] := a[m]; a[m] := x;
        m := m − 1
OD
```

It will be noticed that what we have gained in efficiency we have lost in simplicity. This program is much more difficult to explain, and it seems hardly possible for it to have been written by any other method than that which we have followed.

1.9 "Heap Sort"

We can go still further along the path of the enrichment of the recurrence hypothesis in pursuit of improved performance. There is no question of our reinventing, through more or less convincing reasoning, the algorithm of J. W. Williams [WIL]. That is often considered as delicate and difficult of presentation [WIR]. We wish only to show that it has its place in the set of sorting algorithms which we have just been studying.

We have progressed by enriching the recurrence hypothesis. Can we do more? We have supposed the existence of an upper part of the vector sorted and in its proper place. We can add nothing to that. Rather it is to the lower part that we must turn our attention. We cannot suppose that to have been sorted—for the sorting would have been finished. Let us say then that it is arranged in a way to be defined—not yet sorted, but not entirely in disorder. This must prepare us for the following action: namely, to find the position of the greatest element in $1 \ldots m$. We cannot suppose that this greatest element is at m, for by recurrence we could then show that the vector has already been sorted. We must therefore suppose that the greatest element is at 1, the only other easily accessible place.

The organisation of the first part implies that its greatest element is at its head. We know from other work—and this is brilliantly presented by Hopcroft [HOP]—that if an algorithm has a computing time of the order of n^2 and if the problem can be partitioned into two sub-problems of measure $n/2$ and of time dependence linear in n, then we can find an algorithm requiring a time of the order of $n \log n$. The organisation of the lower part of the vector must thus depend on such a partitioning. The idea of J. W. Williams was to arrange it as a binary tree with the greatest element as the vertex. Each sub-tree has the same arrangement. The tree is represented linearly in the vector by the convention that the sub-trees of the element i have vertices $2i$ and $2i + 1$. We call a section of the vector organised in this way a "heap". (The author uses the French word "epi", an ear of corn. The word "tas", heap, hardly conveys the idea of orderly arrangement; "epi" sounds a little like "heap", but it also means the stock from which spring the shoots carrying the grains.)

We shall say that $a[j \ldots k]$ is a heap when:

—for all i such that $j \leq i$ and $2i + 1 \leq k$,

$$a[i] \leq a[2i + 1] \quad and \quad a[i] \leq a[2i]$$

—there exists an i such that $j \leq i$ and $2i = k$, $a[i] \leq a[2i]$

The recurrence hypothesis is now

[[$a[m + 1 \ldots n]$ is sorted, in place, by transpositions
$a[1 \ldots m]$ is a heap]]

The condition at the end of the loop is the same as in Section 1.8. There is no need to find the position of the greatest element in $1 \ldots m$—that is already known to be 1. The interchange of the elements at 1 and m extends the part sorted and in place, but it also disorganises the heap in $1 \ldots m$. First, this heap has been shortened, the element m no longer being part of it. Next, its first element is no longer the greatest. But since only the element 1 has been modified, the sub-heaps with vertices 2 and 3 are unchanged. We have to reorganise a heap whose head is "aberrant".

The initialisation is a problem in itself:

> make a heap in $1 \ldots n$; $m := n$;
> DO
>> [[$a[m + 1 \ldots n]$ sorted, in place, by transpositions
>> $a[1 \ldots m]$ is a heap]]
>> IF $m = 1$ THEN EXIT FI;
>> interchange the elements at 1 and m; $m := m - 1$;
>> reorganise the heap $1 \ldots m$ with aberrant head
> OD

Let us assume that we know how to reorganise a heap with aberrant head. The initial construction of a heap on $1 \ldots n$ can proceed from that. But first we note that for all the elements of the second half of the vector there are no possible sub-heaps—for $i > n/2$ means $2i > n$—and these elements are themselves heaps. It is thus sufficient to go back again from $n : 2$ (integral part of $n/2$) to 1, reorganising those heaps of which only the head is aberrant. The initialisation is thus

> $i := n : 2$;
> DO
>> reorganise the heap from i to n with aberrant head;
>> IF $i = 1$ THEN EXIT FI;
>> $i := i - 1$
> OD

We denote by reorg(i, j) the reorganisation of a heap on $a[i \ldots j]$. The heap sort program is

> $i := n : 2$;
> DO
>> reorg(i, n);
>> IF $i = 1$ THEN EXIT FI;
>> $i := i - 1$;

```
OD;
m := n;
DO
    IF m = 1 THEN EXIT FI;
    x := a[1]; a[1] := a[m]; a[m] := x;
    m := m − 1;
    reorg(i, m)
OD
```

It remains for us to reorganise a heap i, j with aberrant head. If the vertex i has no sub-heaps $(2i > j)$, there is nothing to do. If it has two sub-heaps $(2i + 1 \leq j)$, we must take that one of these which has the larger head (in fact, the new head must be the greatest element in this heap—the sub-heaps are correctly organised, and the head of each is its greatest element). Then we interchange the vertex i with this head, thus putting the right value in i but disorganising the sub-heap in giving it an aberrant head. We continue with this heap:

reorg(i, j):

```
DO
    k := 2 * i; IF k > j THEN EXIT FI;
    IF k + 1 ≤ j THEN
        IF a[k + 1] > a[k] THEN k := k + 1 FI
    FI;
    IF a[i] ≥ a[k] THEN EXIT FI;
    x := a[i]; a[i] := a[k]; a[k] := x;
    i := k
OD
```

This procedure runs through the elements of a from i to j inclusive, doubling, at least, the index each time. Its execution time is thus proportional to the logarithm of the length of the vector. The heap sort thus consists of two parts: the initialisation and the sort itself, each of which requires an execution time of the same order proportional to $n \log n$. This algorithm needs to make far fewer comparisons than that which we have been studying but, in general, more interchanges.

Exercises

E.1.1   Under what conditions can the two assignments $x := 1$; $y := 2$ be permuted to give $y := 2$; $x := 1$? Same question for $a[i] := 1$; $a[j] := 2$.

E.1.2 When may we permute $x := f$; $y := g$? Consider the cases

f, g constants with respect to x and y,
     dependent on one only of these two variables,
     dependent on both variables.

E.1.3 When may we combine $x := 3$; $x := 4$ into $x := 4$? Same question for $a[i] := 3$; $a[i] := 4$; $a[a[i]] := 3$; $a[a[i]] := 4$.

E.1.4 When may we combine $x := f$; $y := g$ in each of the cases listed in Exercise E.1.2?

E.1.5 Double assignment. The notation

$$x, y := f, g$$

is to be read as: compute the values of f and g; assign the first of these to x and the second to y: Thus

$x, y := y, x$ interchanges the values of x and y;

$x, y := x + y, x - y$ puts into x, y their sum and difference. How can the double assignment

$$x, y := f, g$$

be replaced by a sequence of single assignments? Examine all the cases listed in Exercise E.1.2.

E.1.6 Sorting by insertion with dichotomic search. Go through the sorting strategy of Section 1.6 again, but find the place of x in $a[1 \ldots i]$ by dichotomy—that is, by partitioning the area of search at each stage into two. Evaluate the complexity of the algorithm—that is, the number of comparisons and of transpositions.

E.1.7 Use the strategy of paragraph 1.6 for sorting by insertion to achieve the operation which puts x into its correct place by a single loop. Show the connection with the program of paragraph 1.6.

E.1.8 Sorting. Compare the program of paragraph 1.7 with that of paragraph 1.6. Say why it is slower. Can it be improved?

E.1.9 Bubble sort. Use the strategy of paragraph 1.8 to effect in a single loop the action of moving by transposition the maximum element of $1 \ldots m$ to position m. Compute the number of comparisons and transpositions in this program. Investigate the possible improvements to this program.

E.1.10 Write a program to find whether a character string C is an anagram of given string D (that is, it has the same characters though possibly in a different order; for example, "paul sernine" is an anagram of "arsene lupin", the space counting as a character). Repeat for the same problem but with the spaces ignored.

E.1.11   Write a program which compares two character strings apart from any spaces.

E.1.12   Given a vector $a[1 \ldots n]$ and an integer p, $1 \leq p < n$, write a program which exchanges the parts $1, \ldots p$ and $p + 1, \ldots n$ of the vector a without making use of an auxiliary vector. Take care that the order of elements within each of the two parts is maintained.

E.1.13   A vector $a[1 \ldots n]$ and a vector defining an ordering of a are given. The first element has as index in a the value of the variable d. The successor of the element of rank i in a is the element of rank $c[i]$. Permute the elements of a so that they appear in this order in a, without using any auxiliary vector (apart from a and c).

E.1.14   Make a sorting program taking as recurrence hypothesis that $a[m + 1 \ldots n]$ is in place.

Chapter 2

Recursive Programming

2.1 Recursivity Recalled

In Chapter 1, we have shown how to construct an iterative program; that is to say one whose underlying computing strategy is based on the use of recurrence. To avoid vagueness, let us return to a specific example—the computation of x^n.

Suppose we have done part of the work and have already computed x^i. We have finished if $i = n$. Otherwise, by multiplying this result by x, we obtain x^{i+1}. By changing from i to $i + 1$, we go back to the initial hypothesis. To start, we can take $i = 1$ and $x^i = x$. The recurrence works as follows:

–if I have been able to compute x^i, I can compute x^{i+1},
–and I can compute x^1.

Without changing anything in this form of reasoning, we can construct a "recursive" algorithm. We shall use the symbol $\simeq$ as sign of definition. Let $\exp(x, n)$ be the function x^n:

$$\exp(x, n) \simeq \text{IF } n = 1 \text{ THEN } x \text{ ELSE } x * \exp(x, n - 1) \text{ FI}$$

Such a definition embodies precisely the above notion of recurrence: if I can compute $\exp(x, n - 1)$, I can compute

$$\exp(x, n) = x * \exp(x, n - 1)$$

and I can compute $\exp(x, 1) = x$.

We shall discuss later the significance of what we have just done, the differences between recursive and iterative definitions, the transition from one to the other. For the moment, we shall consider further examples of recursive definitions and say a few words on how to find them. Although a recursive definition may be considerably simpler than an iterative definition, experience

27

shows in fact that many programmers do not know how to make use of them, perhaps because they are too much accustomed to the writing of iterative programs. Certain school teachers have tried to persuade me that, in a sense, recursive definition is "more abstract" than the iterative. It could be...

In the writing of the recursive definition of $\exp(x, n)$, we have used the well-known property

$$x^n = x * x^{n-1}$$

We have been able to use this relation, but at the same time it has obscured perhaps more profitable relations. We are about to try a method of operation which is often useful and simple, and which has the advantage of being usable even by programmers with little knowledge of the properties of the function to be computed.

2.2   The Construction of Recursive Definitions

2.2.1   The Factorial Function

The function $n!$, written here as $\mathrm{fac}(n)$, is defined by

$$\mathrm{fac}(n) = n * (n - 1) * (n - 2) * \ldots * 2 * 1$$

We mark off the right-hand terms

$$\mathrm{fac}(n) = n * \boxed{(n - 1) * (n - 2) * \ldots * 2 * 1}$$

The boxed expression is $\mathrm{fac}(n - 1)$. We have the required relation

$$\mathrm{fac}(n) = n * \mathrm{fac}(n - 1)$$

We must find a particular case to stop the recurrence. As a working rule we should first resolve the general case and not look for a specific value for which there is an explicit definition until later, just as we have done for iteration; the initialisation is dealt with at the end. We choose the special value to prevent the recursive definition leading into difficulties. Here, $\mathrm{fac}(n)$ is defined in terms of $\mathrm{fac}(n - 1)$, which in turn must be defined. We can stop at $\mathrm{fac}(1) = 1$.

$$\mathrm{fac}(n) \simeq \text{IF } n = 1 \text{ THEN } 1$$
$$\text{ELSE } n * \mathrm{fac}(n - 1)$$
$$\text{FI}$$

Some writers propose the extension of the definition to include

$$\mathrm{fac}(0) = 1$$

This is a pointless convention.

2.2.2   The Exponential Function

We return to the computation of x^n:

$$\exp(x, n) = x * x * x * \ldots * x \qquad (n \text{ factors in this expression})$$

We mark off the $n - 1$ right-most factors

$$\exp(n) = x * \boxed{x * x * \ldots * x} \qquad (n - 1 \text{ factors in the box})$$

This is the familiar relation

$$\exp(x, n) = x * \exp(x, n - 1)$$

As a special case, we can take $\exp(x, 1) = x$ or $\exp(x, 0) = 1$ (the latter has the advantage of extending the definition to the case $n = 0$):

$$\exp 1(x, n) \simeq \text{IF } n = 0 \text{ THEN } 1 \text{ ELSE } x * \exp 1(x, n - 1) \text{ FI}$$

The complexity of this will be discussed later. There are other ways of grouping the factors x in $\exp(x, n)$. Suppose n is even. We might partition the factors in two equal sets

$$\exp(x, n) = (x * x * \ldots * x) * (x * x * \ldots * x)$$

with $n/2$ factors in each set. In this case,

$$\exp(x, n) = \exp(x, n/2)^2$$

or, by writing $y = \exp(x, n/2)$,

$$\exp(x, n) = y * y$$

If, however, n is odd, we can still do the same thing having first separated one of the factors

$$\exp(x, n) = (x) * (x * x * \ldots * x) * (x * x * \ldots * x)$$

We obtain thus a second definition of $\exp(x, n)$:

$$\exp2(x, n) \simeq \text{IF } n = 0 \text{ THEN } 1$$
$$\text{ELSE IF even}(n) \text{ THEN } y * y$$
$$\text{ELSE } x * y * y$$
$$\text{FI}$$
$$\text{FI}$$
$$\text{WHERE}(y = \exp2(x, n:2))$$

In this definition, the clause $\text{WHERE}(y = \exp2(x, n:2))$ gives the meaning of an intermediate variable introduced for the convenience of the computation.

When n is even we can group the factors in another way, by taking them two at a time:

$$\exp(x, n) = (x * x) * (x * x) * (x * x) * \ldots (x * x)$$

There are $n/2$ groups, each of two factors:

$$\exp3(x, n) \simeq \text{IF } n = 0 \text{ THEN } 1$$
$$\text{ELSE IF even}(n) \text{ THEN } \exp3(x * x, n : 2)$$
$$\text{ELSE } x * \exp3(x * x, n : 2)$$
$$\text{FI}$$
$$\text{FI}$$

It is too early to compare these three versions. They are not equivalent. It is clear that the second and third forms make n decrease more rapidly and so must require fewer operations than the first. We shall return to this point later.

2.2.3   Reverse of a String

We wish to define the function which gives the reverse of a string: that is, a string formed of the same characters but in reverse order. Thus the string ABCD has as its reverse DCBA. As before we isolate a part of each string:

$$A(BCD) \qquad \text{gives} \qquad (DCB)A$$

The string in the result box is the reverse of the string in the initial box. We have to isolate the first character of c, the given string. The function $\text{sbs}(c, 1, 1)$ gives the left-most sub-string of length 1. The rest of the string is given by $\text{sbs}(c, 2, \text{" "})$. It remains to decide on the special case. The isolation of a part of the string in a box is useless if this part is null; thus if the length of the string is less than 2,

$$\text{rev}(c) \simeq \text{IF length}(c) < 2 \text{ THEN } c$$
$$\text{ELSE rev}(\text{sbs}(c, 2, \text{" "}))\,!\,\text{sbs}(c, 1, 1)$$
$$\text{FI}$$

Clearly, this is not the only way to partition the given string. We could isolate the right-most character instead of the left-most. That would make little or no difference. We could cut the string into two pieces at any point:

$$\text{rev2}(c) \simeq \text{IF length}(c) < 2 \text{ THEN } c$$
$$\text{ELSE rev2}(\text{sbs}(c, z + 1, \text{" "}))\,!\,\text{rev2}(\text{sbs}(c, 1, z))$$
$$\text{FI}$$
$$\text{WHERE}(z = \text{length}(c) : 2)$$

This definition contains two occurrences of the function rev2. It is much more complex than before. We shall investigate this further.

2.2.4   *Expression of an Integer in Base b*

Given a natural integer n, and a number base b (natural integer greater than 1), it is required to form the string of characters which represents n in base b. There is no simple way of setting out the result, unless the generalisation of the case $b = 10$ is accepted without demonstration. (This demonstration is quite easily done.) The figure on the right of the representation of n in base 10 is the remainder in the division of n by 10. The rest of the figures, to the left, are the representation of the quotient, n divided by 10.

The only difficulty comes from the requirement not to write non-significant leading zeros. Only the number 0 is written with 0 as its first figure. We have said that there is an advantage in beginning with the general case:

$$\text{rep}(n, b) = \text{rep}(n : b, b) \,!\, \text{fig}(\text{mod}(n, b))$$

where $\text{mod}(n, b)$ is the remainder in the division of n by b and $\text{fig}(x)$ the character which represents x in base b $(0 \leq x < b)$. To avoid having leading non-significant zeros, we need $n : b$ to be non-zero. Then, by recurrence, it does not begin with a zero. We have $n : b$ non-zero for $n > b$. The special case is thus $n < b$:

$$\text{rep}(n, b) \simeq \textbf{IF } n < b \textbf{ THEN } \text{fig}(n)$$
$$\textbf{ELSE } \text{rep}(n : b, b) \,!\, \text{fig}(\text{mod}(n, b))$$
$$\textbf{FI}$$

That $\text{rep}(n, b)$ does not begin with 0 if n is not itself 0 can be seen by following the form of reasoning by recurrence which we have used before.

2.2.5   *Fibonacci Numbers*

Fibonacci numbers are defined by recurrence by

$$\text{fib}(0) = 1$$
$$\text{fib}(1) = 1$$
$$\text{fib}(i) = \text{fib}(i - 1) + \text{fib}(i - 2)$$

There is nothing to add to this except the formulation

$$\text{fib}(n) \simeq \textbf{IF } n < 2 \textbf{ THEN } 1$$
$$\textbf{ELSE } \text{fib}(n - 1) + \text{fib}(n - 2)$$
$$\textbf{FI}$$

As with the procedure rev2, there are two calls of fib within fib. This gives rise here to considerable complexity of computation. We shall discuss this point further.

2.2.6   The Product of Two Integers

If n is even, $n = 2 * (n:2)$. If n is odd, $n = (n:2) + (n:2 + 1)$. From this it is easy to deduce the following definition:

$$\text{prod}(n, a) \simeq \text{IF } n = 1 \text{ THEN } a$$
$$\text{ELSE IF even}(n) \text{ THEN } 2 * \text{prod}(n:2, a)$$
$$\text{ELSE prod}(n:2, a) + \text{prod}(n:2 + 1, a)$$
$$\text{FI}$$
$$\text{IF}$$

We have given this procedure, of very limited practical interest, as an example of a mixed case: if n is even, there is only one recursive call; if it is odd, there are two. (See Section 4.8.1.)

2.3   Computation of a Recursively Defined Function

2.3.1   Monadic Definition

A definition which contains only one recursive call on the function itself is called monadic. We take as an example the computation of exp3(2, 13).

We have, taking again the notation of Section 2.2.2,

$$x = 2 \qquad n = 13$$

As $n \neq 0$ and n is odd,

$$\text{exp3}(2, 13) = 2 * \text{exp3}(2 * 2, 13:2) = 2 * \text{exp3}(4, 6)$$

We must now compute exp3(4, 6). As 6 is even,

$$
\begin{aligned}
\text{exp3}(4, 6) \quad &= \text{exp3}(4 * 4, 6:2) = \text{exp3}(16, 3) \\
\text{exp3}(16, 3) \quad &= 16 * \text{exp3}(16 * 16, 3:2) = 16 * \text{exp3}(256, 1) \\
\text{exp3}(256, 1) \quad &= 256 * \text{exp3}(256 * 256, 1:2) = 256 * \text{exp3}(65536, 0) \\
\text{exp3}(65536, 0) &= 1
\end{aligned}
$$

for this time, the second argument is zero, and there is no recursion. We can substitute the result so obtained in the line above:

$$
\begin{aligned}
\text{exp3}(256, 1) \quad &= 256 * 1 = 256 \\
\text{exp3}(16, 3) \quad &= 16 * \text{exp3}(256, 1) = 16 * 256 = 4096 \\
\text{exp3}(4, 6) \quad &= \text{exp3}(16, 3) = 4096 \\
\text{exp3}(2, 13) \quad &= 2 * \text{exp3}(4, 6) = 2 * 4096 = 8192
\end{aligned}
$$

This method of computation is complex and very badly suited to execution "by hand". That should cause no surprise—a recursive definition is not a description of a computing strategy. It answers the question "Can that function be computed?" rather than "How should that function be computed?".

The computation above was done in two consecutive parts:

–in the first phase, it passed from one recursive call to another until a value of n which stopped the recursion was reached (here $n = 0$),
–in the second phase, results obtained were substituted back to complete the evaluation of partially computed expressions.

We shall see in a later chapter that it is by this method that a computer operates in executing a recursive procedure. There are numerous cases where this method of execution can be simplified.

2.3.2   Dyadic Definition

We shall consider the computation of fib(5) (Section 2.2.5):

$$fib(5) = fib(4) + fib(3)$$
$$fib(4) = fib(3) + fib(2)$$
$$fib(3) = fib(2) + fib(1)$$
$$fib(2) = fib(1) + fib(0)$$
$$fib(1) = 1$$
$$fib(0) = 1$$

From here we can begin the back-substitution. Immediately fib(2) can be computed:

$$fib(2) = 1 + 1 = 2$$

We come back to fib(3):

$$fib(3) = fib(2) + fib(1) = 2 + 1 = 3$$

For fib(4), we now know fib(3) and fib(2):

$$fib(4) = fib(3) + fib(2) = 3 + 2 = 5$$

and, finally,

$$fib(5) = fib(4) + fib(3) = 5 + 3 = 8$$

This process does not appear very complicated. It is quite different on a computer. To compute fib(5), we have used two values previously computed, which are obviously still there on our sheet of paper. A computer would first compute fib(4), that is, 5, and store that value; then fib(3), that is, 3, which it would add to the stored value 5. This means that it will have computed fib(3) twice—first in the computing of fib(4) and second as a term to be added to fib(4). We shall see that on a computer, this process requires a time which increases exponentially with n.

2.4   The Nature of a Recursive Definition

As has just been remarked, a recursive definition gives only a very poor means of computing a function, and yet it offers facilities which are not found in the computer. On the other hand, the writing of a recursive definition does not require the use of the assignment instruction. We may note in every one of the examples presented here the total absence of this instruction. This is not only a syntactic phenomenon. We might have said that the WHERE clause of Section 2.2.2 was a kind of pseudo-assignment. It is nothing of the sort. We insisted in Chapter 1 on the transformational nature of the assignment: it changes the value of a variable, creating a discontinuity in time. There is the time before its execution and the time afterwards. They correspond to different situations.

There is nothing of this in a recursive definition. With every name is associated a value which does not vary in time. Take for example the function rev(c) of Section 2.2.3, with c = "abcd"!

$$\text{rev}(c) = \text{rev}(\text{sbs}(c, 2, \text{" "}))\,!\,\text{sbs}(c, 1, 1)$$

The first term of the concatenation involves a new call on another value of c. This is not a change to the value of c. And this must be so because we are about to use this value in the second term of the concatenation.

A new call of c is in fact a change of context. We no longer work with the preceding c, which keeps its value, but with a new variable, distinct from the preceding one. That is what happens in the computer. The variables of the procedure are local to that procedure. A new activation creates new variables, which have and keep their values as long as they exist.

This being so, a recursive definition is not by nature transformational. It describes relations between values. Recursivity allows functions to be defined and applied to arguments. That is why this form of programming has been given the name FUNCTIONAL PROGRAMMING or APPLICATIVE PROGRAMMING according to which aspect has been emphasised— definition of function or application of a function to its arguments. We have come right out of the domain of transformational programming based on the assignment instruction, sometimes called IMPERATIVE PROGRAM-MING to insist on the "command" aspect of the instructions.

It provides an axiomatic definition of a function rather than a method of computation. This results for the moment from the difficulties of computation which we have stressed. We shall see this in a more precise manner when we show how to pass from recursivity to iteration, thus adding a computational strategy to the recursive definition which it contains only implicitly.

Such a difference between iteration and recursivity may appear surprising when one considers that it is the same reasoning by recurrence which gives rise to both the one and the other. We have no simple explanation for this phenomenon.

What has just been said leads on to two questions:

–if recursive definition is truly closer to the axiom than to the method of computation, it must facilitate the study of the properties of a function;

–is functional programming of practical utility? So far we have presented only "toy problems". Can we not go further?

We shall try to answer these questions by example.

2.5   Properties of a Recursively Defined Function

2.5.1   A Simple Example

Let us return to the definition of the representation of an integer n in base b and show that if $n \neq 0$, the left-most figure of n is different from 0:

$$\text{rep}(n, b) \simeq \text{IF } n < b \text{ THEN fig}(n)$$
$$\text{ELSE rep}(n : b, b) \,! \, \text{fig}(\text{mod}(n, b))$$
$$\text{FI}$$

We operate by recurrence on the computation [VUI]. We suppose the property true for the inner call. We show that it is thus true for the outer call. We show that finally it is true if there is no recursive call. This implies that it is always true, because in order to compute the function, either there is no recursivity and it is proved or the inner call is executed first. In other words, we make use of the order of computation imposed by the recursive definition.

Suppose then $n \neq 0$. If n is less than b, the result is given by fig(n), formed of a single figure, different from 0 since n is non-zero. If now $n \geq b$, we have $n : b \neq 0$; if we suppose the property true for the inner call,

rep($n : b, b$) does not begin with 0, and so nor does
rep($n : b, b$) ! fig(mod(n, b))

We have thus demonstrated the property in which we were interested and proved the validity of our definition.

2.5.2   Computational Precision

We are about to show through an example how a recursive definition allows us to study the precision of a computation. We shall study the definitions of the function x^n, inspired by a study of iterative programs [DUM]. The recursive definitions contain only operations on the integer n, made without error, and multiplications, subject to error. We suppose the computations to be carried out by the computer in "semi-logarithmic" notation (or "scientific" in the terminology of manufacturers of pocket calculators). The numbers are expressed with a mantissa having a constant number of significant figures. Let m be the number of binary digits in each of the mantissae of x and y, the most significant always being a 1. The product of x and y is a number of $2m - 1$ or $2m$ digits, of which we retain the m most significant. This result has a reasonably constant relative error. We denote by δ the mean deviation of a product, that is to say the mean value of the quantity $x * y/xy$. It is a number in the interval

$$1 \leq \delta < 1 + 2^{-m}$$

Let $\theta1(x, n)$ be the deviation of the function $\exp1(x, n)$; that is,

$$\theta1(x, n) = \exp1(x, n)/x^n$$

We shall modify the definition of exp1 slightly by taking $x^1 = x$ as the special case in order subsequently to avoid a multiplication by 1, which does not introduce an error:

$$\exp1(x, n) = \text{IF } n = 1 \text{ THEN } x \text{ ELSE } x * \exp1(x, n - 1) \text{ FI}$$

This gives

$$\theta1(x, n) = \text{IF } n = 1 \text{ THEN } 1 \text{ ELSE } (x * \exp1(x, n - 1))/x^n \text{ FI}$$

We rearrange the second alternative:

$$(x * \exp1(x, n - 1))/x^n$$
$$= (x * \exp1(x, n - 1))/(x * \exp1(x, n - 1))(x \exp1(x, n - 1))/(x x^{n-1})$$
$$= \delta\theta1(x, n - 1)$$

Whence the recursive definition of $\theta1$:

$$\theta1(x, n) = \text{IF } n = 1 \text{ THEN } 1 \text{ ELSE } \delta\theta1(x, n - 1) \text{ FI}$$

$\theta1$ does not depend on x. This is true if $n = 1$. If we suppose it to be true for $n - 1$, then it is also true for n. It may be expressed more simply:

$$\theta1(n) = \text{IF } n = 1 \text{ THEN } 1 \text{ ELSE } \delta\theta1(n - 1) \text{ FI}$$

It can be verified by recurrence that

$$\theta 1(n) = \delta^{n-1}$$

This result is quite as expected. The procedure computes x^n by $n-1$ multiplications. The total deviation is the product of $n-1$ elementary deviations.

Let us do the same for $\exp2(x, n)$. Again, to avoid an unnecessary operation we rewrite $\exp2$:

$\exp2(x, n) \simeq$ IF $n = 1$ THEN x
                      ELSE   IF even(n) THEN $\exp2(x, n:2) * \exp2(x, n:2)$
                                       ELSE $x * \exp2(x, n:2) * \exp2(x, n:2)$
                           FI
      FI

We calculate the deviation in the three cases:

–If $n = 1$, there is no operation, and $\theta 2(x, n) = 1$.
–If n is even,

$$\theta 2(x, n) = (\exp2(x, n:2) * \exp2(x, n:2))/(\exp2(x, n:2))^2$$
$$\cdot (\exp2(x, n:2))^2/(x^{n:2})^2$$

or

$$\theta 2(x, n) = \delta\theta 2(x, n:2)^2$$

–If n is odd,

$$\theta 2(x, n) = (x * \exp2(x, n:2) * \exp2(x, n:2))/(x \exp2(x, n:2)^2)$$
$$\cdot (x \exp2(x, n:2)^2)/(x(x^{n:2})^2)$$
$$= \delta^2 \theta 2(x, n:2)^2$$

Whence the recursive definition of $\theta 2$:

$\theta 2(x, n) =$ IF $n = 1$ THEN 1
                     ELSE IF even(n) THEN $\delta\theta 2(x, n:2)^2$
                                   ELSE $\delta^2 \theta 2(x, n:2)^2$
                       FI
      FI

Here again, $\theta 2$ is independent of x:

$\theta 2(n) =$ IF $n = 1$ THEN 1
                   ELSE IF even(n) THEN $\delta\theta 2(n:2)^2$
                                 ELSE $\delta^2 02(n:2)^2$
                     FI
      FI

As this definition is rather more complicated, a good way to proceed is to compute the first few values. We find easily

$$\theta 2(1) = 1 \qquad \theta 2(2) = \delta \qquad \theta 2(3) = \delta^2 \qquad \theta 2(4) = \delta^3$$

We conjecture that $\theta 2(n) = \delta^{n-1}$. This is verified by recurrence:

$$\theta 2(2n) = \delta \theta 2(n)^2 = \delta(\delta^{n-1})^2 = \delta^{2n-1}$$
$$\theta 2(2n + 1) = \delta^2 \theta 2(n)^2 = \delta^2(\delta^{n-1})^2 = \delta^{2n}$$

Thus, we obtain what is perhaps rather a surprising result. This procedure, although giving rise to fewer multiplications, gives the same precision as that using repeated multiplication.

As an exercise for the reader, we leave the verification of the result for exp3, which is also the same.

The three procedures give the same precision.

2.5.3 Complexity

We shall count the number of multiplications necessary to compute x^n. Let $m1(n)$ be the number of multiplications necessary to compute $\exp1(x, n)$

$$\exp1(x, n) \simeq \text{IF } n = 1 \text{ THEN } 1 \text{ ELSE } x * \exp1(x, n - 1) \text{ FI}$$

If $n = 1$, no operation is necessary, and so $m1(1) = 0$. Otherwise, we must do all the multiplications of $\exp1(x, n - 1)$ plus one:

$$m1(n) = \text{IF } n = 1 \text{ THEN } 0 \text{ ELSE } m1(n - 1) + 1 \text{ FI}$$

This gives immediately,

$$m1(n) = n - 1$$

This result was easily predictable, and it has already been used; $\exp1(x, n)$ computes x^n by $n - 1$ multiplications by x.

Now consider $\exp3(x, n)$:

$$\exp3(x, n) \simeq \text{IF } n = 1 \text{ THEN } x$$
$$\text{ELSE IF even}(n) \text{ THEN } \exp3(x * x, n : 2)$$
$$\text{ELSE } x * \exp3(x * x, n : 2)$$
$$\text{FI}$$
$$\text{FI}$$

Let $m3(n)$ be the number of multiplications necessary. If $n = 1$, no operation is necessary and so $m3(1) = 0$. If n is even, we need one multiplication to compute $x * x$, and then we have to do the operations of $\exp3(x * x, n : 2)$, making thus

$$1 + m3(n:2)$$

If, finally, n is odd, there is one multiplication for the multiplication by x, one for the argument $x * x$, and then those of exp3.

$$m3(n) = \text{IF } n = 1 \text{ THEN } 0$$
$$\text{ELSE } \text{IF } \text{even}(n) \text{ THEN } 1 + m3(n:2)$$
$$\text{ELSE } 2 + m3(n:2)$$
$$\text{FI}$$
$$\text{FI}$$

Consider the binary representation of n. The integer $n:2$ has one less binary digit than does n. The division of n by 2 takes one digit from n and increases m3 by (at least) 1. If the digit taken from n is a 0, then m3 is increased by 1. If it is a 1, m3 is increased by 2. We leave it to the reader to verify that

$$m3(n) = \text{(number of binary digits of } n\text{)}$$
$$+ \text{(number of ones in the binary representation of } n\text{)}$$
$$- 2.$$

Hence we deduce

$$\log_2(n) \le m3(n) < 2\log_2(n)$$

This shows that although exp3 requires far fewer multiplications than exp1, this procedure gives nevertheless the same precision. That is the practical justification for this procedure—we lose nothing in precision, but we gain in computing time. We must beware of jumping too hastily to the conclusion that, because fewer multiplications have been done, the precision is better. That is clearly false in this case.

2.6 The Choice of a Recursive Form

We have seen that one and the same function can have several different recursive definitions. The choice of the form can be important.

2.6.1 The Problem of the Termination

We have defined the factorial on the basis of the property

$$n! = n * (n - 1)!$$

We might have used

$$n! = (n + 1)!/(n + 1)$$

giving

facfalse(n) $\simeq$ IF $n = 1$ THEN 1
                 ELSE facfalse($n + 1$)/($n + 1$)
      FI

Such a definition is unacceptable, because this procedure cannot stop itself. To compute 3! it will try 4! and, if it succeeds, 5!, going further away from the terminating condition instead of getting nearer to it. We have advised the reader to begin with the general case. The computation of $f(x)$ usually gives rise to a new call $f(b(x))$. This in turn gives rise to a sequence of arguments x, $b(x)$, $b(b(x))$, $b(b\ldots b(x)\ldots)$ which must tend towards the terminating value and reach it in a finite number of steps. In other words, there must exist a finite integer k such that $b^k(x)$ satisfies the terminating condition.

2.6.2 Complexity

The number of calculations to be done depends on the speed with which the terminating condition is reached. We have verified it in the case of the exponential. The terminating condition was given by $n = 0$ or $n = 1$. In exp1, n is decreased by 1. In the two other definitions n is divided by 2. They have a lower order of complexity.

But this is not the only way in which the complexity is affected. A dyadic definition is likely to be much more complex than a monadic definition. But the transition from dyadic to monadic form is not always simple.

Let us return to the two definitions of the reverse of a string. The number of concatenations to be done depends only on the length of the string. Let n(length(c)) be the number of concatenations implied by the recursive definition

rev(c) $\simeq$ IF length(c) < 2 THEN c
                   ELSE rev(sbs(c, 2, " "))! sbs(c, 1, 1)
        FI

n(length(c)) = IF length(c) < 2 THEN 0 ELSE n(length(c) $-$ 1) + 1 FI

which gives n(length(c)) = length(c) $-$ 1. Now take the second definition,

rev2(c) $\simeq$ IF length(c) < 2 THEN c
                    ELSE rev2(sbs(c, $z + 1$, " "))! rev2(sbs(c, 1, z))
      FI
        WHERE (z = length(c) : 2)

We now have

$n(\text{length}(c)) = \text{IF length}(c) < 2 \text{ THEN } 0$
$$\qquad\qquad\qquad \text{ELSE } n(\text{length}(c) - z) + n(z) + 1$$
$$\qquad \text{FI}$$
$$\qquad\quad \text{WHERE } (z = \text{length}(c) : 2)$$

If the length of c is even, say length$(c) = 2m$, then

$$z = m \qquad \text{length}(c) - z = m$$

and

$$n(2m) = n(m) + n(m) + 1$$

If it is odd,

$$\text{length}(c) = 2m + 1 \qquad z = m$$
$$n(2m + 1) = n(m + 1) + n(m) + 1$$

Since $n(1) = 0$, we have as solution $n(z) = z - 1$, and so this procedure is of the same complexity as the other. We need to beware of hasty conclusions as to the number of operations on the sole basis of the monadic or dyadic forms. We shall treat the case of the Fibonacci numbers in more detail.

2.7   Transformation of Recursive Definitions

First let us evaluate the number of operations necessary to compute a Fibonacci number starting with the definition

$$\text{fib}(n) \simeq \text{IF } n < 2 \text{ THEN } 1 \text{ ELSE fib}(n - 1) + \text{fib}(n - 2) \text{ FI}$$

Let fa(n) be the number of additions or subtractions needed to compute fib(n).
If n is less than 2, there is nothing to do:

$$\text{fa}(1) = 0$$

Otherwise, two subtractions are needed to compute $n - 1$ and $n - 2$, then what is needed to compute fib$(n - 1)$ and fib$(n - 2)$, and finally one addition to combine them together:

$$\text{fa}(n) = \text{fa}(n - 1) + \text{fa}(n - 2) + 3$$

This is a recurrence relation of the same form as that for the Fibonacci sequence itself.

Writing fa$(n) = x \text{ fib}(n) + y$ and substituting in the recurrence relation

$$x \text{ fib}(n) + y = x \text{ fib}(n - 1) + y + x \text{ fib}(n - 2) + y + 3$$

which gives $y = -3$.

We now have

$$fa(n) = x\,fib(n) - 3$$

From $fa(0) = fa(1) = 0$ and $fib(0) = fib(1) = 1$ we see that $x = 3$, and so the number of additions needed to compute $fib(n)$ is $3 * (fib(n) - 1)$. Now $fib(n)$ increases exponentially with n. Therefore the recursive procedure which we have been considering requires a computation time which increases exponentially with n. (The reader should, as an exercise, verify that the increase is exponential.)

We will change the recursive definition. The difficulty here arises because there are two recursive calls. To avoid that, we shall write a procedure which computes simultaneously two successive values of fib. Let this be the function $fib2(n)$ whose value is a pair of integers:

$$fib2(n) = fib(n), fib(n - 1)$$

As $fib2(0)$ is undefined, we begin with

$$fib2(1) = fib(1), fib(0) = 1, 1$$

Now

$$fib2(n) = fib(n), fib(n - 1) = fib(n - 1) + fib(n - 2), fib(n - 1)$$

So $fib2(n)$ is expressed in the same terms as

$$fib2(n - 1) = fib(n - 1), fib(n - 2)$$

$$fib2(n) = \text{IF } n = 1 \text{ THEN } 1, 1$$
$$\text{ELSE } x + y, x$$
$$\text{FI}$$
$$\text{WHERE } (x, y = fib2(n - 1))$$

This definition is monadic. Its complexity is no longer the same. Let $fa2$ be the number of additions and subtractions necessary to compute $fib(n)$. If $n = 1$, no operation is necessary. If $n \neq 1$, we need one subtraction to compute $n - 1$ and one addition for $x + y$:

$$fa2(n) = \text{IF } n = 1 \text{ THEN } 0 \text{ ELSE } fa2(n - 1) + 2 \text{ FI}$$

from which we see that

$$fa2(n) = 2(n - 1)$$

The computation is linear in n.

This is somewhat disturbing. A few modifications, amounting to very little, in the recursive definition can have considerable effect on the computation time. How can we generalise this? Are there general rules? With some dyadic definitions, we can expect multiple computations of the function for one and the same argument, resulting in an evident loss of efficiency.

But the transformation enabling this to be avoided is not always so simple. The following example is taken from the book by Dijkstra, *A Discipline of Programming* [D13]. It is concerned with numbers whose only prime factors are 2, 3, and 5; that is to say, with numbers of the form $2^p3^q5^r$ where p, q, r are natural integers. The problem posed is to compute these numbers as a monotonically increasing sequence. The problem is solved if it is known how to find the successor of a number in the sequence. Let $s(x)$ be the successor of x. We extend the definition by saying that $s(x)$ is the smallest member of the sequence greater than x.

A number in the sequence is divisible by 2, or by 3, or by 5, and by at least one of these numbers. The result of the division has itself no other prime divisors than 2, 3, or 5. It is thus also a member of the sequence. Suppose $s(x)$ to be divisible by 2. It is of the form 2 * (a member of the sequence). This number is itself greater than $x : 2$. There cannot be a member of the sequence between $x : 2$ and $s(x) : 2$, for then its double could be $s(x)$. So, if $s(x)$ is divisible by 2, it is $2 * s(x : 2)$. Thus, $s(x)$ can only be one of

$$2 * s(x : 2) \qquad 3 * s(x : 3) \qquad 5 * s(x : 5)$$

As the sequence is in increasing order, it is the smallest of these three.

We have to find a simple case not involving recursion. The first few numbers of the sequence are 2 3 4 5 6:

$$s(x) \simeq \text{IF } x < 6 \text{ THEN } x + 1$$
$$\text{ELSE } \min(2 * s(x : 2), 3 * s(x : 3), 5 * s(x : 5))$$
$$\text{FI}$$

There are three calls on s. Some of these will give rise to repeated computations. There is no clear way of avoiding these redundant operations [BER].

2.8   The Proper Use of Recursion

When it is written simply and based on a well-established property of the function to be computed, a recursive definition presents no problems and can be very effective. Its execution by computer requires, in general, the use of a stack (realised by the compiler) and so stack-management time and store space. If the depth of recursion (number of nested calls) is kept small, this time and space requirement will be small. To avoid this requirement an iterative procedure will be needed. But the management of iteration also involves implicit operations which can cost as much as for recursion. We shall see some examples of this in the case of recursive sub-programs.

It also takes time to construct an iterative form which will be at least as efficient as the recursive form. How much does that cost? We must reject absolutely the myth that recursion is always inefficient and should always be avoided. That is true only to a very variable extent. Only by a careful study in each case can we say whether recursion ought to be rejected as inefficient. It is in the analytical stage so much more simple that it must be regarded as a normal programming tool. That being so, the initial statement of a recursive definition may conceal some dangerous traps. To the same extent as recourse to recursion must be a normal aspect of programming, so must prudence in the face of the uncommented statement of a recursive procedure. Here are some classic examples of such traps.

2.8.1   Function 91

The following function is due to MacCarthy:

$$f(n) \simeq \text{IF } n > 100 \text{ THEN } n - 10$$
$$\text{ELSE } f(f(n + 11))$$
$$\text{FI}$$

For n greater than 100, $f(n) = n - 10$.

We note that the inner call $f(n + 11)$ does not itself give rise to recursion if $n + 11 > 100$; that is if $n > 89$. For such a value,

$$f(n + 11) = n + 11 - 10 = n + 1$$

$89 < n \leq 100$ gives $f(n) = f(n + 1)$, which implies that within this interval f is constant:

$$f(100) = f(f(111)) \qquad f(111) = 101 \qquad f(101) = 91$$

For $89 < n \leq 100$, $f(n) = 91$.

We can now extend this result. For $78 < n \leq 89$, $f(n) = f(f(n + 11)) = f(91) = 91$. So step by step we obtain the value of f:

$$f(n) = \text{IF } n > 100 \text{ THEN } n - 10 \text{ ELSE } 91 \text{ FI}$$

There is no longer recursion or iteration. The recursive definition was dyadic and complex. Let cf(n) be the number of additions and subtractions needed to compute f. To compute $f(n)$ with $n > 100$ requires one subtraction. For other values of n, one addition is needed for $n + 11$, then cf$(n + 11)$ operations to compute $f(n + 11)$, and finally cf$(f(n + 11))$ operations more:

$$\text{cf}(n) = \text{IF } n > 100 \text{ THEN } 1$$
$$\text{ELSE } 1 + \text{cf}(n + 11) + \text{cf}(f(n + 11))$$
$$\text{FI}$$

We can replace $f(n + 11)$ by its value:

cf$(n) = $ IF $n > 100$ THEN 1
                      ELSE $1 + $ cf$(n + 11) + $ cf(IF $n + 11 > 100$ THEN $n + 1$
                                                                    ELSE 91 FI)
      FI

This distinguishes the case $n > 89$:

cf$(n) = $ IF $n > 100$ THEN 1
                      ELSE IF $n > 89$ THEN $2 + $ cf$(n + 1)$
                                          ELSE cf$(n + 11) + $ cf$(91) + 1$
                  FI
      FI

For $89 < n \leq 100$,

$$\text{cf}(n) = \text{cf}(n + 1) + 2 \quad \text{and} \quad \text{cf}(100) = 2 + \text{cf}(101) = 3$$

giving cf$(n) = 203 - 2n$ and then cf$(91) = 21$. For $n \leq 89$,

$$\text{cf}(n) = \text{cf}(n + 11) + 22$$

After further calculations, we find cf$(n) = 203 - 2n$:

$$\text{cf}(n) = \text{IF } n > 100 \text{ THEN 1 ELSE } 203 - 2n \text{ FI}$$

Thus, we have a function whose value is simple to compute—we have an explicit definition for it—but whose recursive definition has the double inconvenience of not showing clearly this simple value and of demanding considerable computing time.

The definition of $f(n)$ can be modified to avoid the double call $f(f(n + 11))$. We remark that the recursion leads to the nesting of an increasing number of calls on f. We define a new function:

$$g(n, i) = f^i(n)$$

Thus,

$$g(n, i) = g(f(n), i - 1)$$
$$g(n, 1) = f(n)$$

For $n \leq 100$,

$$g(n, i) = g(f(f(n + 11)), i - 1) = g(n + 11, i + 1)$$

For $n > 100$, $f(n) = n - 10$. The result depends on i. We thus obtain

$g(n, i) \simeq $ IF $n > 100$ THEN IF $n = 1$ THEN $n - 10$ ELSE $g(n - 10, i - 1)$ FI
                      ELSE $g(n + 11, i + 1)$
      FI

This hardly changes the complexity of the computation.

What do we learn from this example? That a recursive definition can hide a simple result. Care is needed. To write a recursive definition for computing a function is in general a simple and reasonably efficient solution, as can often be demonstrated. To say what a given recursive definition will compute can be difficult.

2.8.2   Call by Need

Let $f(n, p)$ be the function of two integers n, p defined by

$$f(n, p) \simeq \text{IF } n = 0 \text{ THEN } 1 \text{ ELSE } f(n - 1, f(n - p, p)) \text{ FI}$$

Suppose we wish to compute $f(1, 0)$. Since n is non-zero, there is a recursive call of

$$f(0, f(1, 0))$$

The first argument being zero, the result does not depend on the second argument, and it is 1.

Most computers would go about this differently. There is a recursive call of f. First of all, the arguments of the function are computed, then the function is called. Here the first argument is a constant and immediately available, but the second argument is

$$f(1, 0)$$

which is precisely the final object of the computation.

There is thus an infinite loop, and the computation will not terminate.

The call by value, in which the values of the arguments are computed before the function is entered, is not safe [MAN]. It can make a correct recursive definition impossible to compute. The only safe call is the call by need — not to compute the value of an argument unless and until that is indispensible to the continuation of the computation. We shall resume this matter in Chapter 3.

2.9   Functional Programming

The examples developed in this chapter may leave the impression that recursivity is meant for the definition of elementary functions, not for the programming of real problems. That is why we shall present here a more complex example. The reader already convinced may omit this section, at his own risk.

We shall see in the program transformations an operation of simplification of nested tests:

$$\text{IF } t \text{ THEN IF } t \text{ THEN } a \text{ ELSE } b \text{ FI ELSE } c \text{ FI}$$

In the THEN branch of the outer structure, t has the value *true*. It is therefore pointless to evaluate it again. It is certain, if there are no side effects in the computation of t, that it will be found *true*, and so a will be executed. This instruction thus simplifies to

$$\text{IF } t \text{ THEN } a \text{ ELSE } c \text{ FI}$$

We shall make a function SIMPL(c), which simplifies the character string c, if c is such as to allow simplification:

$$\text{SIMPL}(c) \simeq \text{IF } t = \text{“ ” THEN } c$$
$$\text{ELSE}$$
$$\text{“IF” } ! t ! \text{“THEN” } ! \text{RED}(f, t, \text{TRUE})$$
$$! \text{“ELSE” } ! \text{RED}(g, t, \text{FALSE}) ! h$$
$$\text{FI}$$
$$\text{WHERE}(t, f, g, h = \text{DEC}(c))$$

This definition is based on the dissection of c into the parts of a selection instruction by the function DEC. If c does not begin with a selection instruction, t is empty, and so c is unchanged. Otherwise, there is the recomposition of a selection instruction with the reduced forms of the two alternatives, where t has a known value. The reduction is defined recursively:

$$\text{RED}(c, u, b) \simeq \text{IF } t = \text{“ ” THEN } c$$
$$\text{ELSE IF } t = u \text{ THEN}$$
$$\text{IF } b \text{ THEN RED}(f, u, b) \text{ ELSE RED}(g, u, b) \text{ FI}$$
$$\text{ELSE}$$
$$\text{“IF” } ! t ! \text{“THEN” } ! \text{RED}(f, u, b) !$$
$$\text{“ELSE” } ! \text{RED}(g, u, b) ! h$$
$$\text{FI}$$
$$\text{FI}$$
$$\text{WHERE}(t, f, g, h = \text{DEC}(c))$$

There is no reduction unless c begins with a selection instruction. Unless this has the test u, each of the branches is reduced. If it has u, the TRUE or FALSE branch following b is retained, and then reduced. Note that t and u are character strings representing the tests. For simplicity, it is considered that reduction will take place if the strings representing the tests are identical. This is a sufficient, but not a necessary, condition.

The function DEC(c) puts c into the form

$$\text{“IF” } t \text{ “THEN” } f \text{ “ELSE” } g h$$

where h begins with "FI":

$$\text{DEC}(c) \simeq \text{IF sbs}(c, 1, 3) \neq \text{"IF" THEN " ", " ", " "}, c$$
$$\text{ELSE}$$
$$\text{sbs}(c, 3, i - 3), \text{sbs}(c, i + 6, j - i - 6),$$
$$\text{sbs}(c, j + 6, k - j - 6), \text{sbs}(c, k, \text{" "})$$
$$\text{FI}$$
$$\text{WHERE} (i = \text{pos}(c, 3, \text{"THEN"}),$$
$$j = \text{POSLIB}(c, i + 6, \text{"ELSE"}),$$
$$k = \text{POSLIB}(c, j + 6, \text{"FI"}))$$

POSLIB(c, i, d) gives the position within c, starting at i, of the sub-string d not included in a selection instruction within c. Let j be the first occurrence of d starting at i. If there is no "IF" between i and j, that is the result. Otherwise, j must be sought after the corresponding FI:

$$\text{POSLIB}(c, i, d) \simeq \text{IF } k = 0 \text{ OR } k > j \text{ THEN } j$$
$$\text{ELSE}$$
$$\text{POSLIB}(c, \text{POSASS}(c, k + 3), d)$$
$$\text{FI}$$
$$\text{WHERE} (j = \text{pos}(c, i, d),$$
$$k = \text{pos}(c, i, \text{"IF"}))$$

The FI associated with IF in i is the first following FI, if there is no IF in the interval. Otherwise, we must go to the corresponding FI and look for the result after that:

$$\text{POSASS}(c, i) \simeq \text{IF } k = 0 \text{ OR } k > j \text{ THEN } j$$
$$\text{ELSE POSASS}(c, \text{POSASS}(c, k + 3))$$
$$\text{FI}$$
$$\text{WHERE} (j = \text{pos}(c, i, \text{"FI"})$$
$$k = \text{pos}(c, i, \text{"IF"}))$$

This example gives quite a good idea of the way functional programming works. The functions are defined and then applied to the arguments. The program, if it can be called a program, is reduced to the call of a function. The iterative programming of the same example is far from trivial. We leave it as an exercise for the reader.

It must be recognised that the example invokes recursion. It deals with a character string parenthesised by the words IF...FI. The parenthetic structure is recursive. There is a strong connection between the processed structure and the form of programming. That is, moreover, why the iterative form leads either to the management of a stack or to repeated scans.

Exercises

E.2.1 Real division: Let a, b be real positive numbers, $0 \le a < b$, and d a precision factor, all given. The quotient q of a, b to precision d satisfies

$$|q(a, b, d) - a/b| < d$$

Give a recursive definition of $q(a, b, d)$, involving

$$q(2a, b, 2d) \qquad \text{or} \qquad q(2a - b, b, 2d)$$

E.2.2 Logarithm to base b: Let a, b, d be given real numbers, such that $1 < b$, $1 \le a < b$, and $0 < d$. As in E.2.1, d is a precision factor. Using the same method, find a recursive definition of

$$\log(b, a, d) \qquad \text{such that} \qquad |\log(b, a, d) - \log_b(a)| < d$$

E.2.3 Euclidean division of integers: Let a and b be natural integers, with b non-zero. Let q and r be the quotient and remainder of the euclidean division of a by b

$$a = b * q + r \qquad 0 \le r < b$$

Find the quotient and remainder of the division of q by 2:

$$q = 2 * q' + q''$$

and hence deduce a recursive algorithm for integer division.

E.2.4 Error in computing x^n: Carry out the computation of the deviation for $\exp3(x, n)$, Section 2.5.2.

E.2.5 Error in computing the logarithm: Following the methods of Section 2.5.2, evaluate the precision obtained in the computation of the logarithm to base b, Exercise E.2.2.

E.2.6 Complexity of the computation of the logarithm: Evaluate the complexity of the recursive definition of the logarithm to base b, Exercise E.2.2.

E.2.7 Value of a Roman numeral: Give a recursive definition of the value of a Roman numeral, taken as a character string of the alphabet of signs

$$\text{M D C L X V I}$$

E.2.8 Give a recursive algorithm for deciding whether a character string is a palindrome (is equal to its reverse).

E.2.9 Define recursively a boolean function, true if two character strings are equal, false otherwise. Do the same for the comparison $<$ or $\le$ for the lexicographic ordering of the two strings. Can you write a single recursive procedure to examine the strings, to be used by three procedures for $=$, $<$, $\leq$, so that these three do not make any pass along the strings?

E.2.10   Give a recursive procedure which decides whether one word is an anagram of another. *Note:* if the two words are not of the same length, the answer is already known. But to put this in the recursive definition is in a certain sense stupid. Why, and what can be done?

Chapter 3

Recurrent Programming

3.1   Direct Algorithms

Consider the following little problem: say on what day of the week Christmas Day falls in a given year a; as a point of reference, Christmas Day 1900 was a Tuesday. We shall keep a in the interval

$$1900 \leq a < 2100$$

It is a simple problem. Christmas falls one day later in the week (for 1 year is 365 days or 52 weeks and one day) every year except in leap years when it comes 2 days later in the week than in the year before. The total shift is thus

$$t = d + b$$

where d is the number of years between 1900 and a, and b is the number of these which are leap years:

$$d = a - 1900$$

As the date of the reference year, 1900, is a multiple of 4 (it is not itself a leap year, but that does not matter as Christmas is after 28 February);

$$b = \text{int}(d/4)$$

Denoting the days of the week by numbers: 0 for Sunday, 1 for Monday, etc., and Christmas 1900 being on a Tuesday, the result required is

$$\text{day } t + 2 \text{ of the week}$$

which is a day j, where

$$j = \text{mod}(t + 2, 7)$$

$\text{mod}(a,b)$ denoting the remainder when a is divided by b.

Let us put all this together in the form of an algorithm. The heading gives the names of the algorithm, the result, and the data:

$$j = \text{CHRISTMAS}(a) \qquad a \text{ INTEGER} \qquad 1900 \le a < 2100$$
$$t = d + b$$
$$d = a - 1900$$
$$b = \text{int}(d/4)$$
$$j = \text{mod}(t + 2, 7)$$

(*Remark*: The year 2000 is a leap year, which is necessary to the validity of the algorithm. But 2100 is not a leap year, which is why 2100 has been excluded from the domain of validity.)

We have just given a way of computing j given a. But this is not a program constructed on the basis of the assignment instruction. The several lines of the algorithm are definitions of variables. There is no change in the value of a variable. Each variable is defined once and only once in the algorithm (except for that data). Every definition is explicit; that is, the variable defined does not appear in the expression defining it.

Let us execute the algorithm for the year 1983:

$$d = 1983 - 1900 = 83$$
$$b = \text{int}(d/4) = \text{int}(83/4) = 20$$
$$t = d + b = 83 + 20 = 103$$
$$j = \text{mod}(t + 2, 7) = \text{mod}(105, 7) = 0$$

(Christmas Day 1983 is a Sunday.)

Once a is given, the values of the other variables are known. The order of computation results not from the will of the writer of the algorithm but from the fact that, to compute the value of a variable, the values of those variables on which it depends must be known. In other words, the algorithm is not changed merely by changing the order of the definitions.

There is no assignment, and so there is nothing essential in the written order of the definitions of the algorithm. We have insisted on the transformational nature of assignment instructions; it is that which is responsible for the need to order these instructions, a sequence of transformations not being in general commutative. When assignments disappear, the need for ordering disappears with them.

Because there are no longer any assignments, each name in the algorithm is associated with a unique value. We can therefore always replace a variable by its value, for that is uniquely defined. We thus have regained the possibility of "substitution" in the mathematical sense. An algorithm is not changed if a variable is replaced by its value (and in consequence the definition of an unused variable is removed). So, for example, b can be replaced in t by its value and its definition deleted:

$$t = d + \text{int}(d/4)$$
$$d = a - 1900$$
$$j = \text{mod}(t + 2, 7)$$

Again, we can take t into j, and delete its definition:

$$j = \text{CHRISTMAS}(a) \qquad a \text{ INTEGER} \qquad 1900 \leq a < 2100$$
$$j = \text{mod}(d + \text{int}(d/4) + 2, 7)$$
$$d = a - 1900$$

This algorithm is equivalent to the previous one (in the sense of an equivalence relation), differing from it only by substitutions and suppression of unused definitions of variables.

In the most general case, a definition may include conditional expressions. For example, consider the algorithm that gives Christmas Day up to 2199. The year 2100 is not a leap year. If, then, $a \geq 2100$, the computed number of leap years must be reduced by 1:

$$j = \text{CHRISTMAS}(a) \qquad a \text{ INTEGER} \qquad 1900 \leq a < 2200$$
$$t = d + b$$
$$d = a - 1900$$
$$b = \text{int}(d/4) - \text{IF } a \geq 2100 \text{ THEN 1 ELSE 0 FI}$$
$$j = \text{mod}(t + 2, 7)$$

3.2   Construction of Algorithms

In a definition of an algorithm, a value resulting from the execution of another algorithm may be used. To illustrate this, we shall write an algorithm to give a perpetual calendar. A date being given by a day of the month d, a month m ($1 \leq m \leq 12$), and a year a ($1900 < a < 2100$), on what day of the week does it fall?

For this we shall need the number of days between 1st January of year a and the given date. We may use a table showing the number of days from the beginning of the year to the first of each month m. The 1st January in year a falls on the same day of the week as Christmas Day in year $a - 1$:

$$r = \text{CALPER}(j, m, a) \qquad j, m, a \text{ DATE} \qquad 1900 < a < 2100$$
$$\text{num} = c[m] + j + \text{cor}$$
$$\text{cor} = \text{IF mod}(a, 4) = 0 \text{ AND } m > 2 \text{ THEN 1 ELSE 0 FI}$$
$$r = \text{mod}(\text{num} + p - 1, 7)$$
$$p = \text{CHRISTMAS}(a - 1)$$

$$c[1] = 0 \qquad c[2] \; = 31 \qquad c[3] \; = 59 \qquad c[4] \; = 90$$
$$c[5] = 120 \quad c[6] \; = 151 \quad c[7] \; = 181 \quad c[8] \; = 212$$
$$c[9] = 243 \quad c[10] = 273 \quad c[11] = 304 \quad c[12] = 334$$

The domain of validity of this algorithm is given in the heading. The year must be in the interval 1900 to 2100 (exclusive), and j, m, a must constitute a valid date. The month must be in the range 1 to 12 (inclusive) and the day between 1 and the number of days in that month (inclusive).

The algorithm can be modified to make this clearer. The validity of a and m is given with reference to an interval and so is easy to verify; that of j is computed in the algorithm, the result being -1 for an invalid date.

$$r = \text{CALPERV}(j, m, a) \qquad 1 \leq m \leq 12 \qquad 1900 < a < 2100$$
$$v = j \leq c[m + 1] - c[m] + \text{IF mod}(a, 4) = 0 \text{ AND } m = 2 \text{ THEN } 1$$
$$\text{ELSE} \quad 0 \text{ FI}$$

$$\text{num} = c[m] + j + \text{cor}$$
$$\text{cor} = \text{IF mod}(a, 4) = 0 \text{ AND } m > 2 \text{ THEN } 1 \text{ ELSE } 0 \text{ FI}$$
$$r = \text{IF } v \text{ THEN mod}(\text{num} + p - 1, 7) \text{ ELSE } -1 \text{ FI}$$
$$p = \text{CHRISTMAS}(a - 1)$$
$$c[1] = 0 \qquad c[2] \; = 31 \qquad c[3] \; = 59 \qquad c[4] \; = 90$$
$$c[5] = 120 \quad c[6] \; = 151 \quad c[7] \; = 181 \quad c[8] \; = 212$$
$$c[9] = 243 \quad c[10] = 273 \quad c[11] = 304 \quad c[12] = 334 \quad c[13] = 365$$

Intuitively, the call on the algorithm CHRISTMAS gives p the value of the number for Christmas Day in the year $a - 1$. We can deal formally with this call by means of the so-called "copy rule". The call

$$p = \text{CHRISTMAS}(a - 1)$$

is replaced by a copy of the body of the algorithm, with the following changes:
−the names of data are replaced by the expressions appearing in the call,
−the name of the result is replaced by that appearing in the call,
−the names of variables of the algorithm which already occur in the calling algorithm are replaced by new, as yet unused, names.

We obtain thus a new algorithm, equivalent to the preceding one, but no longer containing a sub-algorithm:

$$r = \text{CALPERV}(j, m, a) \qquad 1 \leq m \leq 12 \qquad 1900 < a < 2100$$
$$v = j \leq c[m + 1] - c[m] + \text{IF mod}(a, 4) = 0 \text{ AND } m = 2 \text{ THEN } 1$$
$$\text{ELSE} \quad 0 \text{ FI}$$

$$\text{num} = c[m] + j + \text{cor}$$
$$\text{cor} = \text{IF mod}(a, 4) = 0 \text{ AND } m > 2 \text{ THEN } 1 \text{ ELSE } 0 \text{ FI}$$
$$r = \text{IF } v \text{ THEN mod}(\text{num} + p - 1, 7) \text{ ELSE } -1 \text{ FI}$$
$$t = d + b$$
$$d = (a - 1) - 1900$$

$$b = \text{int}(d/4)$$
$$p = \text{mod}(t + 2, 7)$$

$c[1] = 0$	$c[2] = 31$	$c[3] = 59$	$c[4] = 90$
$c[5] = 120$	$c[6] = 151$	$c[7] = 181$	$c[8] = 212$
$c[9] = 243$	$c[10] = 273$	$c[11] = 304$	$c[12] = 334$ $c[13] = 265$

This new algorithm is no clearer than the previous one. It has been given solely to illustrate the treatment of the subalgorithm. We shall need this technique later.

3.3   The Precedence Relation

A precedence relation is defined over the variables of an algorithm. We say that the variable x precedes the variable y if x occurs at least once in the definition of y. It follows that the value of y depends on the value of x, and it is not possible to compute y unless x has already been computed. The relation "x precedes y" may thus be read as "the computation of x must precede the computation of y".

This relation is a partial ordering of the variables of the algorithm. Thus, for example, in the last algorithm there is no precedence between j, v, and num.

The data (or the constants—the constants c have not been shown in the accompanying graph associated with the algorithm) are the only entry points of the graph, the only points without predecessors. The data do not depend on

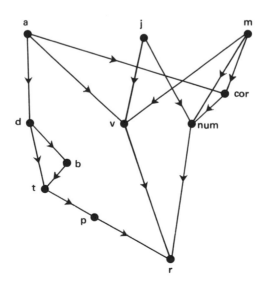

any variable, and they are immediately available. Only a result can be an exit point of the graph, a point without a successor. If an intermediate variable were without successor, it would not belong to any definition; its value would not be used, and so its computation would be needless. If a vertex of the graph is an exit point without being a result, it can be erased from the graph and the corresponding definition deleted without changing the algorithm. However, a result need not be an exit point; its value may be used in the computation of some other result. Note that no circuits are to be found in the graph.

3.4   Transformation into a Program

To obtain a program in the ordinary sense of the term, that is to say with assignment instructions, the definitions have to be changed into assignments and put in order. A total ordering of the definitions must be found, compatible with the partial ordering represented by the precedence relations. It is achieved by what is called a "topological sort".

The algorithm is simple:

–take any exit point of the graph, and write the corresponding assignment at the head of the program being developed;
  –erase this vertex from the graph;
  –repeat as long as the graph is not yet entirely erased.

At certain stages, several vertices will be exit points; any one of these vertices may be chosen for the next step.

Let us apply this to the algorithm developed at the end of Section 3.2. There is only one exit point, r. We write the corresponding assignment and erase r from the graph. There are now three exit points: $p, v.$ num.

Suppose we take v. There will then be in the program, and in this order, assignments to v and then r. Removing v from the graph, there remain p and num as exit points. Take num and then cor. Only p now remains as an exit point. We take in order p, t, b, d and obtain the program:

$$d := a - 1901;$$
$$b := \text{int}(d/4);$$
$$t := d + b;$$
$$p := \text{mod}(t + 2, 7);$$
$$\text{cor} := \text{IF } \text{mod}(a/4) = 0 \text{ AND } m > 2 \text{ THEN } 1 \text{ ELSE } 0 \text{ FI};$$
$$\text{num} := c[m] + j + \text{cor};$$
$$v := j \le c[m + 1] - c[m] + \text{IF } \text{mod}(a, 4) = 0 \text{ AND } m = 2 \text{ THEN } 1$$
$$\text{ELSE} \quad 0 \text{ FI};$$
$$r := \text{IF } v \text{ THEN } \text{mod}(\text{num} + p - 1, 7) \text{ ELSE } -1 \text{ FI}$$

This is a correct program, which effectively computes the required result. There is assignment, but with the choice of names here there is only one assignment to each variable. There is no case of a change of value of a variable. Every variable is in one or other of two possible states:

–undefined, because not yet computed;

–defined, with a value which is not going to be changed by any subsequent assignment.

The difference between assignment and definition is rather subtle. That is why reference has been made to "single assignment" [CHA][TES][ROU].

Let us return to the topological sort. The first exit point is r, and the last assignment of the program is thus that to r. After that, there is a choice between three variables: p, v, num. We have chosen one of these arbitrarily. In fact, a choice corresponds to the existence of independent sub-graphs. These may be computed in any order. They may also be computed in parallel. Let us try to show this. The program can be represented by

Compute in parallel:

BEGIN $d := a - 1901$; $b := \text{int}(d/4)$; $t := d + b$;
        $p := \text{mod}(t + 2, 7)$
END,
BEGIN cor $:= $ IF $\text{mod}(a, 4) = 0$ AND $m > 2$ THEN 1 ELSE 0 FI;
        num $:= c[m] + j + $ cor
END,
$v := j \leq c[m + 1] - c[m] + $ IF $\text{mod}(a, 4) = 0$ AND $m = 2$ THEN 1
                                                                                        ELSE   0 FI

End of parallel computation;

        $r := $ IF v THEN $\text{mod}(\text{num} + p - 1, 7)$ ELSE -1 FI

It is for the detection of parallelism in computations that the idea of single assignment has been put forward. Where there is no assignment, there is no complete ordering of a computation, only a partial ordering. Any complete ordering compatible with the partial ordering corresponds to a possible program, but there are then redundancies in this complete ordering. The form of an algorithm without assignment, or with only single assignment, imposes no ordering. There is only that associated with the precedence relations.

We must return to the program obtained by the topological sort. Whether the date is valid or not, it computes p and num. If the date is valid (v true), the value associated with num and p is assigned to the variable r. If it is not valid, r is assigned the value -1, and the computation has been carried out in vain.

This can be avoided by taking precautions in writing. Let us make a new algorithm CALPER2, isolating the effective computation in a sub-algorithm

CALPEREF:

$r = \text{CALPER2}(j, m, a) \qquad 1 \le m \le 12 \qquad 1900 < a < 2100$
$r = \text{IF } v \text{ THEN CALPEREF}(j, m, a) \text{ ELSE } -1 \text{ FI}$
$v = j \le c[m + 1] - c[m] + \text{IF mod}(a, 4) = 0 \text{ AND } m = 2 \text{ THEN } 1$
$\qquad\qquad\qquad\qquad\qquad\qquad\qquad\qquad\qquad\qquad\qquad \text{ELSE} \quad 0 \text{ FI}$

$r = \text{CALPEREF}(j, m, a)$
$\text{num} = c[m] + j + \text{cor}$
$\text{cor} = \text{IF mod}(a, 4) = 0 \text{ AND } m > 2 \text{ THEN } 1 \text{ ELSE } 0 \text{ FI}$
$p = \text{mod}(t + 2, 7)$
$t = d + b$
$b = \text{int}(d/4)$
$d = a - 1901$

In the first algorithm, r depends only on v. Thus, v will be computed. If it is false, the result is -1; otherwise, the second algorithm is executed. But here one must work delicately; it is the responsibility of the author of the algorithm to discover that there may be a problem, and consequently to anticipate it by a cleverly contrived structure. That, however, does not resolve all the difficulties.

3.5 "Lazy" Evaluation

Consider the following algorithm:

$x = \text{SQRTABS}(t) \qquad t \text{ REAL}$
$x = \text{IF } t > 0 \text{ THEN } u \text{ ELSE } v \text{ FI}$
$u = \text{SQRT}(t)$
$v = \text{SQRT}(-t)$

x depends on t, on u, and on v. By topological sorting, we are led to compute first u and v, and then t:

$u := \text{SQRT}(t); v := \text{SQRT}(-t);$
$x := \text{IF } t > 0 \text{ THEN } u \text{ ELSE } v \text{ FI}$

For any non-zero t, the program tries to compute the square root of a negative number and so produces a run-time error; but the algorithm is properly constructed. For positive t, x has the value of u which is the square root of a positive number. For negative t, x has the value of v, the square root of a positive number.

It is all the more unsatisfactory that an equivalent algorithm is obtained by replacing u and v by their values and suppressing the intermediate variables:

$x = \text{SQRTABSP}(t)$
$x = \text{IF } t > 0 \text{ THEN SQRT}(t) \text{ ELSE SQRT}(-t) \text{ FI}$

The difficulty is exactly that which we have already met in the case of recursive procedures. A variable should not be computed unless and until there is need of it. This algorithm calls only that one of the variables u and v which is computable. Following a topological sort, to force systematically the computation of all the variables leads to an error if any of them is not computable. We must operate the "call by need"; a variable is computed if and only if it is needed.

We have said that, in view of the uniqueness of definition of each variable, substitution can be used, that is, the replacement of the name of a variable at each of its right-hand occurrences by the expression defining that variable. This is exactly the copy rule for procedures. We are led to consider each definition as the definition of a procedure. We can rewrite the algorithm CHRISTMAS:

$$\text{INTEGER PROCEDURE } t; t := d + b;$$
$$\text{INTEGER PROCEDURE } d; d := a - 1900;$$
$$\text{INTEGER PROCEDURE } b; b := \text{int}(d/4);$$
$$\text{INTEGER PROCEDURE } j; j := \text{mod}(t + 2, 7);$$

A program reading the value of a and printing the result j is thus

$$\text{READ } a; \text{ PRINT } j; \text{ FINISH}$$

How does it work? It reads a. Suppose it is given 1983. It tries to print j. That is a function procedure. It enters the body of the procedure and begins to evaluate $\text{mod}(t + 2, 7)$. But t is a function procedure. It has to leave the body of j and enter that of t. It begins to evaluate $d + b$. But d is a function procedure. It leaves the body of t to enter that of d. The computation of d is possible as a is known. It obtains $d = 83$. It returns to the body of t with $t := 83 + b$. As b is a function procedure, it leaves the body of t again to execute that of b. It must evaluate $\text{int}(d/4)$. As d is a function procedure, it leaves the body of b to execute d (a second time). As a has not changed, it recomputes the value 83; it can then achieve the result $b = \text{int}(83/4) = 20$. Then it computes t

$$t = 82 + 20 = 102$$

and j,

$$j = \text{mod}(102 + 2, 7) = 6$$

and finally it prints $j = 6$.

There is a relation between this mechanism and the topological sort. It is required to print the result, exit point of the graph. The evaluation depends on certain variables, which are necessarily predecessors of this vertex in the graph (variables occurring in the definition are called). The graph is thus retraced to an entry point (constant or data value), but only necessary branches are traced.

For SQRTABS(t), x has to be printed. As t is given, one of u, v is called, depending on the sign of t; only that which is defined is computed.

As in the case of recursion, only the call by need is safe [HOO].

There is another phenomenon. The value associated with a name in an algorithm without assignments is unique. Every call of a function procedure associated with a variable will produce the same value (at least for one given execution). Thus in the algorithm CHRISTMAS, the two calls of d produce the same value each time.

We have remarked that the difference between definition and assignment in this kind of algorithm is subtle. In fact, each variable can be in one of only two states:

−not yet computed;
−computed, and then its value remains constant.

This leads us to refine the method of computation, following the technique called "lazy evaluation" [AR2][HOO]. With every variable there is associated a boolean state variable, taking the values "defined" or "undefined". When the name of a variable is encountered in an expression, there are two possibilities:

−the variable is in the "defined" state; its value is known and can be used;
−the variable is in the "undefined" state. Its value is computed, from its definition, and the associated boolean variable is put in the "defined" state.

By this means an efficient method of computation is obtained, which computes only necessary values. The only extra time required, in comparison with an ordinary program, is that for the manipulation of the boolean variables.

We could easily construct an interpreter for a language without assignment based on the idea of lazy evaluation. But we shall now see the limitations of this technique when it is seen to be the equivalent of recursion or recurrence.

3.6   Recurrent Algorithm

3.6.1   An Example

We shall develop an algorithm for multiplication based on the same idea as the exponentiation algorithm of Section 2.2.2. The real a is to be multiplied by the natural integer b. We represent b in base 2;

$$b = \sum_1^n c(j)2^{j-1} \qquad c(n) = 1 \qquad c(j) \in \{0, 1\}$$

The required result r is

$$r = a * b = \sum_{1}^{n} c(j) * (a2^{j-1})$$

Writing $u(i) = a2^i$, we can define u by recurrence:

(1) $u(i) = 2 * u(i - 1)$

(2) $u(0) = a$

whence,

$$r = \sum_{1}^{n} c(j) * u(j - 1)$$

Again, we can define r by recurrence, introducing the variable

$$v(i) = \sum_{1}^{i} c(j) * u(j - 1)$$

(3) $v(i) = v(i - 1) + c(i) * u(i - 1)$

(4) $v(0) = 0$

The required result is $r = v(n)$, but n is not known:

(5) $r = v(n)$

We now have to define $c(i)$ and n. The $c(i)$ are successive binary digits of b. It is known that they can be found by successive division of b by 2. We write

$$w(i) = \sum_{i+1}^{n} c(j)2^{j-1-i}$$

We obtain

$$w(i - 1) = 2 * w(i) + c(i)$$

or, finally,

(6) $w(i) = w(i - 1):2$

(7) $c(i) = w(i - 1) - 2 * w(i)$

(8) $w(0) = b$

Now for all i less than n, $w(i)$ is non-zero, because $c(n) = 1$. Thus, $w(n)$ is the first zero term in the sequence of w. In order to be able to use this as a definition of n, we introduce the operator MU:

(9) $n = \text{MU } i : w(i) = 0$

which is read as

n is the smallest positive or zero i such that $w(i) = 0$

We combine all this into one recurrent algorithm:

$$r = \text{PROD}(a, b) \qquad a\ \text{REAL} \qquad b\ \text{INTEGER}$$
$$u(i) = 2 * u(i - 1)$$
$$u(0) = a$$
$$v(i) = v(i - 1) + c(i) * u(i - 1)$$
$$v(0) = 0$$
$$w(i) = w(i - 1) : 2$$
$$w(0) = b$$
$$c(i) = w(i - 1) - 2 * w(i)$$
$$n = \text{MU}\ i : w(i) = 0$$
$$r = v(n)$$

We can improve this algorithm a little by noting that $c(i)$ can take only the values 0 and 1. Thus

$$v(i) = v(i - 1) \quad \text{if} \quad c(i) = 0; \qquad \text{that is, if} \quad w(i - 1) = 2 * w(i)$$

and

$$v(i) = v(i - 1) + u(i - 1) \qquad \text{otherwise}$$

The variable c can be eliminated:

$$r = \text{PRODA}(a, b) \qquad a\ \text{REAL} \qquad b\ \text{INTEGER}$$
$$u(i) = 2 * u(i - 1)$$
$$u(0) = a$$
$$v(i) = \text{IF}\ w(i - 1) = 2 * w(i)\ \text{THEN}\ v(i - 1)\ \text{ELSE}\ v(i - 1) + u(i - 1)\ \text{FI}$$
$$v(0) = 0$$
$$w(i) = w(i - 1) : 2$$
$$w(0) = b$$
$$n = \text{MU}\ i : w(i) = 0$$
$$r = v(n)$$

Such an algorithm contains several recurrence relations. The first two lines define an infinite sequence, that of the multiples of a by the powers of 2. The sequences of v and w move on together, because the computation of $v(i)$ must make use of $w(i)$. We shall examine later, and in detail, the problem of the execution of such an algorithm, but we can already suggest one way of executing it.

Suppose $a = 7$ and $b = 13$:

$u(0) = 7$	$v(0) = 0$	$w(0) = 13$
$u(1) = 14$	$v(1) = 7$	$w(1) = 6$

$$u(2) = 28 \qquad v(2) = 7 \qquad w(2) = 3$$
$$u(3) = 56 \qquad v(3) = 35 \qquad w(3) = 1$$
$$u(4) = 112 \qquad v(4) = 91 \qquad w(4) = 0$$

3.6.2   The General Form

In the following, an overbar, such as $\bar{x}$, will denote a "tuple" of values; that is to say, the set of values, possibly of different types, which make up the data and results of an algorithm. The most general recurrent algorithm is given by

$$\bar{r} = \mathrm{A}(\bar{d}) \qquad \bar{d} \in \mathscr{D}$$
$$\bar{v}(i) = \mathrm{R}(\bar{v}(i-1), i, \bar{d})$$
$$\bar{v}(0) = \mathrm{I}(\bar{d})$$
$$k = \mathrm{MU}\, i : t(i)$$
$$t(i) = \mathrm{T}(\bar{v}(i), i, d)$$
$$\bar{r} = \mathrm{F}(\bar{v}(k), \bar{d}, k)$$

where R, I, F, T are algorithms, simple or recurrent, and t is a boolean variable. The reader should verify that the algorithm PRODA is indeed of this form. It will be seen that $\bar{v}$ denotes the triplet ("3-tuple") u, v, w. The initial algorithm is

$$u(0), v(0), w(0) = a, 0, b$$

In PRODA, the algorithms R, I, F, T are all direct. In the most general case, they may themselves be recurrent. If I or F is recurrent, then we have a system of successive "loops". If R or T is recurrent, then we have nested loops. It can be shown [AR2] that this form allows all the algorithms to be expressed as Markov algorithms.

In this algorithm, the variable i has a very special role. Unlike the other variables, i is not defined in the algorithm, and it can be imagined as taking a succession of values and thus being outside the rule that a unique value is associated with each name. Another way of presenting this algorithm is to regard it as an abbreviation for the infinite sequence of computations:

$$\bar{v}(0) = \mathrm{I}(\bar{d}) \qquad\qquad t(0) = \mathrm{T}(\bar{v}(0), 0, \bar{d})$$
$$\bar{v}(1) = \mathrm{R}(\bar{v}(0), 1, \bar{d}) \qquad t(1) = \mathrm{T}(\bar{v}(1), 1, \bar{d})$$
$$\bar{v}(2) = \mathrm{R}(\bar{v}(1), 2, \bar{d}) \qquad t(2) = \mathrm{T}(\bar{v}(2), 2, \bar{d})$$
$$\bar{v}(i) = \mathrm{R}(\bar{v}(i-1), i, \bar{d}) \qquad t(i) = \mathrm{T}(\bar{v}(i), i, \bar{d})$$

k is the smallest i for which $t(i)$ has the value TRUE.

The restricted forms of the index of the recurrent variables will be noted:

0 in the definition of the initial values,
i and $i - 1$ in R, i in T,
k in the final algorithm F.

3.6.3   Deep Recurrences

We have said that this general form allows the expression of all algorithms. This may, however, appear to be untrue in some simple cases. Consider, for example, the computation of the Fibonacci numbers, defined by the recurrence relation

$$f(i) = f(i - 1) + f(i - 2)$$

We have no means of investigating recurrences of depth 2. We can avoid this by using a technique comparable to that which is used to replace a second difference by two first differences.

We define a variable $g(i)$ by

$$g(i) = f(i - 1)$$

From this

$$f(i) = g(i) + g(i - 1)$$

There is a risk of difficulties in the initialisation. We have

$$f(1) = 1 \qquad f(0) = 1$$

By the definition of g,

$$g(0) = f(-1), \quad \text{which is undefined}$$

But by the above relations,

$$g(1) = f(0) = 1$$
$$f(1) = g(1) + g(0) = 1 + g(0) = 1, \qquad \text{giving} \quad g(0) = 0$$

Finally,

$$g(i) = f(i + 1)$$
$$f(i) = g(i) + g(i - 1)$$
$$g(0) = 0$$
$$f(0) = 1$$

Now we try to write an algorithm to compute $f(n)$. We have to define the final value of the index by minimisation. It is very simple:

$$r = \text{FIB}(n) \qquad n \text{ INTEGER}$$
$$g(i) = f(i - 1)$$
$$f(i) = g(i) + g(i - 1)$$
$$g(0) = 0$$
$$f(0) = 1$$
$$r = f(k)$$
$$k = \text{MU}i : i = n$$

3.7   Execution of a Recurrent Algorithm

We have said, in connection with direct algorithms, that only the call by need is safe. Let us try to use this in computing

$$\text{PRODA} \, (3, 20)$$

The result is r. Its value

$$r = v(n)$$

depends on n. Thus, n must be evaluated. It is given by a minimisation

$$n = \text{MU} \, i : w(i) = 0$$

The sequence of w must be computed beginning with $i = 0$, up to the first zero value:

$$w(0) = b = 20$$
$$w(1) = w(0) : 2 = 10$$
$$w(2) = w(1) : 2 = 5$$
$$w(3) = w(2) : 2 = 2$$
$$w(4) = w(3) : 2 = 1$$
$$w(5) = w(4) : 2 = 0$$

and so $n = 5$. We now have

$$r = v(5)$$

We must compute $v(5)$:

$$v(5) = \text{IF} \, w(4) = 2 * w(5) \, \text{THEN} \, v(4) \, \text{ELSE} \, v(4) + u(4) \, \text{FI}$$

$v(5)$ depends on $v(4)$ which depends on $v(3)$ and so we have to compute the sequence of v beginning with $v(0)$:

$$v(0) = 0$$
$$v(1) = \quad \text{IF} \, w(0) = 2 * w(1) \, \text{THEN} \ldots$$

Since $w(0) = 2 * w(1)$,

$$v(1) = v(0) = 0$$

And since $w(1) = 2 * w(2)$,

$$v(2) = v(1) = 0$$

Now

$$v(3) = \text{IF} \, w(2) = 2 * w(3) \, \text{THEN} \, v(2) \, \text{ELSE} \, v(2) + u(2) \, \text{FI}$$

We need first $u(2)$, then $u(1)$, and the recurrence with u must be restarted at 0.

We have here a very heavy-handed mechanism, very difficult to put effectively to work. It is moreover contrary to the very idea of recurrence; if we have been able to compute the variables up to the step $i - 1$, then they can be computed up to i. That implies the idea of a slope, based on increasing indices i, up to the critical value which stops the recurrence because a condition is finally satisfied.

The execution mechanism is thus simplified by forcing the computation of all the recurrent variables at each step of the algorithm. That is what we have done in Section 3.6.1. Some undesirable effects can come out of this if certain values of a recurrent variable are not necessary, or worse, not computable. There is no simple way of detecting this [HOO], and it may be seen as a severe restriction on the use of languages without assignment—either the mechanism of execution is very complicated, and so inefficient, or there is the danger of errors in execution which are not errors of the algorithm, without this being decidable.

We should be tempted to say that a "well-constructed" algorithm could not give rise to such errors; that after all they are no more serious than those which are generated by the majority of compilers which do not use the call by need for recursion and so cause errors of execution in well-constructed recursive procedures. The problem is not of current interest; there is no language of the type presented here in actual use, perhaps because of these difficulties. It is not our purpose to promote their use. We wish to show to the programmer means of expressing algorithms without using the assignment instruction. On the other hand, it is possible easily to translate an algorithm expressed in this way into a program with assignments "by hand". This suggests a programming method:

first find a recurrent algorithm,
then transform this into an iterative program.

For the general algorithm given in Section 3.6.2, the following schematic program is obtained:

$$\bar{v}(0) := I(\bar{d});$$
$$i := 0;$$
DO
$$\quad t(i) := T(\bar{v}(i), i, \bar{d});$$
$$\quad \text{IF } t(i) \text{ THEN EXIT FI};$$
$$\quad i := i + 1;$$
$$\quad \bar{v}(i) := R(\bar{v}(i - 1), i, \bar{d})$$
OD;
$$k := i;$$
$$r := F(\bar{v}(k), \bar{d}, k)$$

This form shows very clearly the recurrence mechanism, and so the way in which the recurrent variables are computed. It must be noted that if there are variables local to the algorithm R, itself not recurrent, then, the call by need still being used in R, their values are computed only when necessary. This form reduces the call by value to the control of the recurrence. In fact, this replacement of the call by need by the call by value is a complex problem which has not yet been resolved [MYC].

3.8 Transformation into an Iterative Program

3.8.1 The General Case

The form just given ensures an iterative execution of the recurrence. A control mechanism which organises the computation according to the increasing values of i is superimposed on the recurrent definition. But it is not yet an iterative program, for the uniqueness of value for each name is still maintained. In a language without assignment, this property is not preserved. The assignment instruction, in its nature, modifies the values of the variables of the program.

We rely on the fact that the recurrence is always of depth 1 (we have seen how to achieve this). The computation of $v(i)$ requires only that we know $v(i-1)$. Thus at any time we make use of only two values of v, the old and the new. We obtain the following schematic program:

$$\bar{v} := \mathrm{I}(\bar{d});$$
$$i := 0;$$
$$\mathrm{DO}$$
$$\quad t := \mathrm{T}(\bar{v}, i, \bar{d});$$
$$\quad \mathrm{IF}\ t\ \mathrm{THEN\ EXIT\ FI};$$
$$\quad i := i + 1;\ \bar{v}' := \bar{v};$$
$$\quad \bar{v} := \mathrm{R}(\bar{v}', i, \bar{d})$$
$$\mathrm{OD};$$
$$k := i;\ \bar{r} := \mathrm{F}(\bar{v}, \bar{d}, k)$$

We can save one of the variables i, k. For example, it is enough to change i into k throughout and to delete the assignment $k := i$ at the exit from the loop.

If the final algorithm F does not use the variable k, and if the algorithms T and R do not use i, both variables i and k can be suppressed, giving a much simpler form:

$$\bar{v} := I(\bar{d});$$
$$\text{DO}$$
$$\qquad t := T(\bar{v}, \bar{d});$$
$$\qquad \text{IF } t \text{ THEN EXIT FI};$$
$$\qquad \bar{v}' := \bar{v};$$
$$\qquad \bar{v} := R(\bar{v}', \bar{d})$$
$$\text{OD};$$
$$\bar{r} := F(\bar{v}, \bar{d})$$

There are other possible simplifications, but they cannot be selected and applied without further examination as to the form of R.

3.8.2 An Example

We take as an example the algorithm PRODA of Section 3.6.1. The algorithm T which gives the terminating condition reduces to

$$w(i) = 0$$

and so does not depend directly on i.

The final algorithm F reduces to

$$r := v(n)$$

and does not depend directly on n.

It is thus useless to make i and n appear in the program. The recurrent variables are u, v, w. We shall use first the general scheme:

$$u := a; v := 0; w := b;$$
$$\text{DO}$$
$$\qquad \text{IF } w = 0 \text{ THEN EXIT FI};$$
$$\qquad u' := u; v' := v; w' := w;$$
$$\qquad \text{compute } u, v, w$$
$$\text{OD};$$
$$r := v$$

The computation of u, v, w remains to be worked out. It follows from the three definitions

$$u = 2 * u'$$
$$v = \text{ IF } w' = 2 * w \text{ THEN } v' \text{ ELSE } v' + u' \text{ FI}$$
$$w = w' : 2$$

The u', v', w' are the data of this algorithm. Since w precedes v (there is an occurrence of w in v), w must be computed before v. The computation of u can be done at any time.Hence the more explicit form

$u := a; v := 0; w := b;$
DO
$\quad$ IF $w = 0$ THEN EXIT FI;
$\quad u' := u; v' := v; w' := w;$
$\quad w := w' : 2;$
$\quad v := \quad$ IF $w' = 2 * w$ THEN v' ELSE $v' + u'$ FI;
$\quad u := 2 * u'$
OD;
$r := v$

In this form we note that the variables v' and u' are redundant, for v' only appears in the definition of v and u' in those of u and v. If they are suppressed, the definition of v becomes

$$v := \text{IF } w' = 2 * w \text{ THEN } v \text{ ELSE } v + u \text{ FI}$$

which simplifies to

$$\text{IF } w' \neq 2 * w \text{ THEN } v := v + u \text{ FI}$$

We thus obtain a new program:

$u := a; v := 0; w := b;$
DO
$\quad$ IF $w = 0$ THEN EXIT FI;
$\quad w' := w;$
$\quad w := w' : 2;$
$\quad$ IF $w' \neq 2 * w$ THEN $v := v + u$ FI;
$\quad u := 2 * u$
OD;
$r := v$

3.8.3   The Reduction of the Number of Variables

Let us generalise this. Suppose that in the general form of Section 3.8.1 it is decided to use only one variable to represent $v(i)$ and $v(i - 1)$.

Let x and y be two recurrent variables. If $x(i)$ occurs in the definition of $y(i)$, then $x(i)$ must be computed before $y(i)$ and so x precedes y.

The computation of $y(i)$ destroys the value $y(i - 1)$. As long as there is need of $y(i - 1)$, $y(i)$ must not be computed. The computation of $x(i)$ must precede that of $y(i)$ if $x(i)$ depends on $y(i - 1)$. There are thus two precedence relations: x precedes y if

$-x(i)$ occurs in the definition of $y(i)$;
$-y(i - 1)$ occurs in the definition of $x(i)$.

These relations are not necessarily compatible. Thus in the algorithm PRODA:

$$w(i) \qquad \text{occurs in } v(i) \text{ and so } w \text{ precedes } v$$
$$w(i-1) \text{ occurs in } v(i) \text{ and so } v \text{ precedes } w$$

Because of this contradiction, an auxiliary variable w' must be used. As $u(i-1)$ occurs in $v(i)$, v precedes u. Hence the order w', w, v, u.

If there is no incompatibility in the precedence relations, a single variable can be used for each recurrent variable, and the topological sort can be applied.

3.9   The Use of Recurrence in the Writing of a Program

In a recurrent algorithm, we make use of mathematical substitution. We can thus transform it by normal algebraic means. We know how to transform a recurrent algorithm into an iterative program. We thus have a method of writing a program:

–find a recurrent algorithm,
–improve it algebraically,
–transform it into an iterative program,
–if possible, reduce the number of variables in this program.

It is a powerful method. The example which we give of it is well known. We shall return to this method in Chapter 4, with some less conventional examples.

The integral part of the square root of the integer n is the integer r such that

$$r^2 \leq n < (r+1)^2$$

Note that for all $i < r$, $i^2 < r^2 \leq n$ and $(i+1)^2 \leq r^2 \leq n$.

Thus r is the smallest integer such that $(r+1)^2$ is greater than n. The required algorithm reduces to

$$r = \text{SQRT}1(n) \qquad n \text{ INTEGER}$$
$$r = \text{MU } i:(i+1)^2 > n$$

This algorithm is that of looking up a table of squares. It seeks to enclose n between two successives squares in the table, and then it takes the first square greater than n. The trouble is that if there is no table of squares in the machine, the table has to be recomputed each time. That makes very heavy going. We try to reduce the number of squares required. For this, suppose that for each i we have access to the quantity

$$t(i) = (i+1)^2$$

r is then given by

$$r = \mathrm{MU}\, i : t(i) > n$$

The $t(i)$ must be computed by recurrence. We form

$$t(i) - t(i - 1) = (i + 1)^2 - i^2 = 2 * i + 1$$

Initialisation is simple:

$$t(0) = 1^2 = 1$$

$$r = \mathrm{SQRT2}(n) \qquad n \text{ INTEGER}$$
$$t(i) = t(i - 1) + 2 * i + 1$$
$$t(0) = 1$$
$$r = \mathrm{MU}\, i : t(i) > n$$

There are no more squares but still a lot of computing. Suppose we have

$$s(i) = 2 * i + 1$$

By recurrence

$$s(i) - s(i - 1) = 2 * i + 1 - 2 * (i - 1) - 1 = 2$$
$$s(0) = 1$$

$$r = \mathrm{SQRT3}(n) \qquad n \text{ INTEGER}$$
$$t(i) = t(i - 1) + s(i)$$
$$s(i) = s(i - 1) + 2$$
$$t(0) = 1$$
$$s(0) = 1$$
$$r = \mathrm{MU}\, i : t(i) > n$$

This algorithm is somewhat special in that the result is the value of the minimisation. It requires the computation of *i* to be iterative. We can avoid this by noting that

$$s(r) = 2 * r + 1$$

which gives

$$r = (s(r) - 1) : 2$$

We thus obtain the algorithm

$$r = \mathrm{SQRT4}(n) \qquad n \text{ INTEGER}$$
$$t(i) = t(i - 1) + s(i)$$
$$s(i) = s(i - 1) + 2$$
$$t(0) = 1$$
$$s(0) = 1$$
$$k = \mathrm{MU}\, i : t(i) > n$$
$$r = (s(k) - 1) : 2$$

The transformation of this algorithm into a program is simple. Since $s(i)$ occurs in $t(i)$, s precedes t. This is the only precedence relation. The variable i is not used in the recurrence, nor is the variable k used in the computation of the result. Thus they are not needed in the iterative progam:

$$t := 1; s := 1;$$
$$\text{WHILE } t \leq n \text{ DO}$$
$$s := s + 2;$$
$$t := t + s$$
$$\text{OD};$$
$$r := (s - 1):2$$

The algorithm we have just written is derived from a linear look-up of the table of squares (sequential pass through the table), seeking the first square greater than n. A binary search of the table would have given the result a lot more quickly. Suppose that at some stage n has been found to lie between two squares in the table

$$q(i)^2 \leq n < (q(i) + p(i))^2$$

If $p(i) = 1$, the required result is $q(i)$; otherwise we divide the interval by 2 and place n by reference to

$$(q(i) + (p(i):2))^2$$

In this way we obtain a recurrent definition of p and q:

$$p(i) = p(i - 1):2$$
$$q(i) = \text{IF } (q(i - 1) + p(i))^2 \leq n \text{ THEN } q(i - 1) + p(i)$$
$$\text{ELSE } q(i - 1) \text{ FI}$$
$$k = \text{MU } i : p(i) = 1$$
$$r = q(k)$$

There is a problem in starting. We need an interval within which n is known to lie. We have $0 \leq n$, so $q(0) = 0$, but we also need $p(0)$ such that

$$n < p(0)^2$$

Moreover, as $p(i)$ will be divided by 2, it is desirable for it to be even, and so for $p(0)$ to be a power of 2. Therefore we choose as $p(0)$ the smallest power of 2 whose square is greater than n:

$$r = \text{SQRTD1}(n) \qquad n \text{ INTEGER}$$
$$p(i) = p(i - 1):2$$
$$q(i) = \text{IF } (q(i - 1) + p(i))^2 \leq n \text{ THEN } q(i - 1) + p(i)$$
$$\text{ELSE } q(i - 1) \text{ FI}$$

$$k = \text{MU } i : p(i) = 1$$
$$r = q(k)$$
$$l = \text{MU } j : (2^j)^2 > n$$
$$p(0) = 2^l$$
$$q(0) = 0$$

We have here an example of an algorithm where the computation of the initial value of a recurrent variable it itself achieved by recurrence.

This algorithm is awkward for two reasons: the computation of $p(0)$ is based on raising values to the power j; and the computation of $q(i)$ is based on squaring. Applying the same technique again, we shall first suppose those quantities whose computation is long to be known and then define them by recurrence:

$$(q(i - 1) + p(i))^2 = q(i - 1)^2 + 2 * p(i) * q(i - 1) + p(i)^2$$

We note that, $p(i - 1)$ being even,

$$p(i) = p(i - 1) : 2 \qquad \text{implies} \qquad p(i - 1) = 2 * p(i)$$

and thus

$$(q(i - 1) + p(i))^2 = q(i - 1)^2 + p(i - 1) * q(i - 1) + p(i)^2$$

Writing,

$$x(i) = q(i)^2 \qquad z(i) = p(i) * q(i) \qquad c(i) = p(i)^2$$

we have

$$(q(i - 1) + p(i))^2 = x(i - 1) + z(i - 1) + c(i)$$

whence

$$q(i) = \text{IF } x(i - 1) + z(i - 1) + c(i) \le n \text{ THEN } q(i - 1) + p(i)$$
$$\text{ELSE } q(i - 1) \text{ FI}$$

We must compute $x(i) = q(i)^2$:

$$x(i) = \text{IF } x(i - 1) + z(i - 1) + c(i) \le n \text{ THEN } (q(i - 1) + p(i))^2$$
$$\text{ELSE } q(i - 1)^2 \text{ FI}$$

To simplify the writing, we introduce a new variable:

$$u(i) = x(i - 1) + z(i - 1) + c(i)$$
$$x(i) = \text{IF } u(i) \le n \text{ THEN } u(i) \text{ ELSE } x(i - 1) \text{ FI}$$
$$q(i) = \text{IF } u(i) \le n \text{ THEN } q(i - 1) + p(i) \text{ ELSE } q(i - 1) \text{ FI}$$

It remains to compute $z(i) = p(i) * q(i)$:

$$z(i) = \text{IF } u(i) \le n \text{ THEN } (q(i - 1) + p(i)) * p(i) \text{ ELSE } q(i - 1) * p(i) \text{ FI}$$

Since $p(i) = p(i - 1):2$,

$$q(i - 1) * p(i) = q(i - 1) * p(i - 1):2 = z(i - 1):2$$
$$z(i) = \text{IF } u(i) \leq n \text{ THEN } z(i - 1):2 + c(i) \text{ ELSE } z(i - 1):2 \text{ FI}$$

The initial values are

$$x(0) = 0 \qquad z(0) = 0 \qquad c(0) = p(0)^2$$

We must compute $c(0)$ in the algorithm which produces $p(0)$. We write

$$w(j) = 2^j \qquad w'(j) = 4^j$$

and obtain, finally,

```
r = SQRTD2(n)        n INTEGER
w(j) = w(j − 1) * 2        w(0) = 1
w'(j) = w'(j − 1) * 4        w'(0) = 1
l = MU j : w'(j) > n
p(0) = w(1)
c(0) = w'(1)
x(0) = 0
z(0) = 0
q(0) = 0
u(i) = x(i − 1) + z(i − 1) + c(i)
c(i) = c(i − 1):4
p(i) = p(i − 1):2
x(i) = IF u(i) ≤ n THEN u(i) ELSE x(i − 1) FI
q(i) = IF u(i) ≤ n THEN q(i − 1) + p(i) ELSE q(i − 1) FI
z(i) = IF u(i) ≤ n THEN z(i − 1):2 + c(i) ELSE z(i − 1):2 FI
k = MU i : p(i) = 1
r = q(k)
```

This can be simplified a little. The result is given by $q(k)$, and the variable q is not used for the computation of any other recurrent variable. If then r could be deduced from another recurrent variable, the computation of q would not be needed:

$$z(k) = p(k) * q(k) \qquad \text{and} \qquad p(k) = 1 \quad \text{give} \quad z(k) = q(k)$$

We note that since $c(i) = p(i)^2$, $p(i) = 1$ is strictly equivalent to $c(i) = 1$. The variable $p(i)$ can thus be suppressed and the minimisation condition replaced by $c(i) = 1$:

$$k = \text{MU } i : c(i) = 1$$

Next, $p(i)$ becomes redundant and can be suppressed. This in turn means that w is no longer used and can disappear. We thus obtain a new algorithm, simpler than the preceding one and with less work to do:

$$r = \text{SQRTD3}(n) \qquad n \text{ INTEGER}$$
$$w'(j) = 4 * w'(j - 1)$$
$$l = \text{MU} j : w'(j) > n$$
$$w'(0) = 1$$
$$c(0) = w'(1)$$
$$x(0) = 0$$
$$z(0) = 0$$
$$u(i) = x(i - 1) + z(i - 1) + c(i)$$
$$c(i) = c(i - 1) : 4$$
$$x(i) = \text{IF } u(i) \leq n \text{ THEN } u(i) \text{ ELSE } x(i - 1) \text{ FI}$$
$$z(i) = \text{IF } u(i) \leq n \text{ THEN } z(i - 1) : 2 + c(i) \text{ ELSE } z(i - 1) : 2 \text{ FI}$$
$$k = \text{MU } i : c(i) = 1$$
$$r = z(k)$$

This algorithm can be expressed as a program without difficulty. The program contains two successive loops. The first of these achieves the recurrence on $w'(j)$; one variable is enough. The final value of w' is passed as initial value to c. Thus one variable called c is used to represent w' in the first loop and c in the second.

In the second loop, $c(i)$ must be computed first. The computation of $z(i)$ requires at every instance that of $z(i - 1) : 2$. There is first the assignment

$$z := z : 2$$

after which, if and only if $u < n$, x and z are modified. Here is the resultant program:

```
c := 1;
WHILE c ≤ n DO c := 4 * c OD;
x := 0;   z := 0;
WHILE c ≠ 1 DO
        c := c : 4; u := x + z + c;
        z := z : 2;
        IF u ≤ n THEN x := u; z := z + c FI
OD;
r := z
```

The first program obtained is very well known, and there are many ways of achieving it without the need of recourse to recurrence. This one is much less familiar. The reader should try to reach it by a more direct method.

3.10   Giving a Meaning to a Program

We have remarked that the assignment instruction was a cause of obscurity in programs. To make a program easier to understand, the replacement of iteration by recurrence is a good thing to do. We effect the inverse of compilation by re-establishing the recurrence relations which bind the successive values of a variable, after having changed the names of the variables in such a way that distinct names correspond to distinct values.

The example here is not one of the simplest. It illustrates the power of the system well, and at the same time shows the different phases of the work.

Consider the following program, where n and b are natural integers, with b greater than 1:

$$t := 1; b2 := b * b;$$
$$\text{WHILE } t \leq n \text{ DO } t := t * b2 \text{ OD};$$
$$s := 0;$$
$$\text{WHILE } t \neq 1 \text{ DO}$$
$$\qquad t := t/b2; s := s/b + t;$$
$$\qquad \text{WHILE } n \geq s \text{ DO}$$
$$\qquad\qquad n := n - s; s := s + 2 * t$$
$$\qquad \text{OD};$$
$$\qquad s := s - t$$
$$\text{OD};$$
$$\text{result} := s/2$$

This program is complex, containing three loops. We isolate the inner loop, calling it A:

$$n, s := A(n, s, t)$$
$$\qquad s := s + t;$$
$$\qquad \text{WHILE } n \geq s \text{ DO}$$
$$\qquad\qquad n := n - s; s := s + 2 * t$$
$$\qquad \text{OD};$$
$$\qquad s := s - t$$

The second loop of the program becomes

$$\text{WHILE } t \neq 1 \text{ DO}$$
$$\qquad t := t/b2; s := s/b;$$
$$\qquad n, s := A(n, s, t)$$
$$\text{OD}$$

Let us write the function A without assignments. The data n, s must be distinguished from the results which we denote by np, sp. The variables n, s in the loop become recurrent sequences which we denote by $n(i), s(i)$, as no ambiguity can arise with n, s:

$$np, sp = A(n, s, t)$$
$$n(i) = n(i - 1) - s(i - 1)$$
$$s(i) = s(i - 1) + 2 * t$$
$$n(0) = n$$
$$s(0) = s + t$$
$$np = n(k)$$
$$sp = s(k) - t$$
$$k = \text{MU } i := n(i) < s(i)$$

We leave it to the reader to show that

$$s(i) = (2 * i + 1) * t + s$$

By summing the relations $n(i) = n(i - 1) - s(i - 1)$ from 1 to k and simplifying, we obtain

$$n(k) = n(0) + \sum_{1}^{k} s(i - 1)$$

We replace $s(i - 1)$ by its value. After simple computations which are left to the reader,

$$n(k) = n(0) - (s + t)k - tk(k - 1)$$

and, finally,

$$np = n - ks - k^2 t$$

Suppose that at entry $0 \leq n$. The algorithm proceeds as long as $n(i) \geq s(i)$, and so does not give any $n(i) < 0$. Certainly, then, $0 \leq n(k)$.

Finally, $n(k) < s(k)$ by the minimisation, and on exit

$$0 \leq np < sp + t$$

As for sp, it is

$$sp = s(k) - t = (2k + 1)t + s - t = 2kt + s$$

From this k can be found

$$k = (sp - s)/(2t)$$

Substituting this in np,

$$np = n - k(s + kt) = n - (sp - s)(sp + s)/(4t) = n - sp^2/4t + s^2/4t$$

We thus have a simple relation between the data and results of A.

$$np + sp^2/4t = n + s^2/4t \qquad 0 \leq np < sp + t$$

Putting this into the second loop:

$$s := 0;$$
WHILE $t \neq 1$ DO
$$t := t/b2; s := s/b;$$
$$[[n + s^2/4t = a]]$$
$$n, s := A(n, s, t)$$
$$[[n + s^2/4t = a \qquad 0 \leq n < s + t]]$$
OD

By the loop mechanism, if one step of the loop has been taken, we have at the entry to the loop the assertion

$$[[n + s^2/4t = a \qquad 0 \leq n < s + t]]$$
$$t := t/b2;$$
$$[[n + s^2/4b2t = a]]$$
$$s := s/b;$$
$$[[n + s^2/4t = a]]$$

We have an invariant for the loop, if it is true at the first entry to the loop. Now, after the initialising loop,

$$t > n \qquad s = 0 \qquad a = n \text{ initial}$$

which establishes the validity of the invariant for the loop.

At the exit from the second loop, we still have

$$n + s^2/4t = n \text{ initial} \qquad 0 \leq n < s + t$$

and besides, $t = 1$ and $r = s/2$:

$$n \text{ initial} = n + r^2 \qquad 0 \leq n < 2r + 1$$

We have thus proved (at least in outline—the reader has been left to fill in the details) that our program computes the integral part of the square root of n. The result does not depend on the value of b, which exists only to reduce the complexity of the computation.

Exercises

E.3.1   Write a recurrent algorithm to compute the value of the polynomial

$$\sum_{i=0}^{n} a_i x^i$$

where n is a natural integer, a the vector of real coefficients, x real, all given.

There are two ways of partitioning the sum. These give two algorithms which should be compared.

E.3.2 Write a recurrent algorithm to compute the greatest common divisor of two non-zero natural integers by Euclid's algorithm.

E.3.3 It is required to compute the logarithm to base b (real) of x (real), verifying that $1 \leq x < b$, to a given precision.

Write a direct algorithm for this, using interpolation in a (little) table.

E.3.4 It is required to compute the logarithm, with the same data as in the preceding exercise. This logarithm is to be represented in base 2:

$$\log(b, x) = \sum a_i/2^i$$

the number of terms in the sum being chosen to give the required precision. Give a recurrent algorithm computing the successive a_i and the corresponding sum.

E.3.5 The same exercise, for the function arc cos, or arc tan, ...

E.3.6 Give a natural integer n, a real vector a, and a real x, it is required to compute the Fourier sum

$$\sum_{p=0}^{n} a_p \cos(px)$$

The cosine is to be computed by recurrence

$$\cos(px) = 2 * \cos((p - 1) * x) * \cos(x) - \cos((p - 2) * x)$$

E.3.7 CAND and COR are non-commutative boolean operators:

$$a\,\text{CAND}\,b = \text{IF } a \text{ THEN } b \text{ ELSE FALSE FI}$$
$$a\,\text{COR}\,b = \text{IF } a \text{ THEN TRUE ELSE } b \text{ FI}$$

Given a natural integer n, a real vector $a[0 \ldots n - 1]$ and a real x, write a recurrent algorithm whose result is n if x is not in the vector a, and the position of the first occurrence of x in a otherwise.

E.3.8 Say whether the vectors a and b are equal.

Chapter 4

From Recursion to Recurrence

4.1 The Recurrent Form Associated with a Recursive Scheme

4.1.1 The Scheme to Be Considered

We shall consider here a monadic recursive scheme generalising the majority of recursive definitions which we have already met:

$$f(x) \simeq \text{IF } c(x) \text{ THEN } a(x) \text{ ELSE } f(b(x)) \circ d(x) \text{ FI}$$

Here x denotes a simple variable or a list of variables; $c(x)$ is a directly computable function of x with a boolean value; $a(x)$ is a directly computable function of x and so are $b(x)$ and $d(x)$. The sign $\circ$ denotes any binary operation, whose properties will be defined in due course.

As defined, $f(x)$ may be a single value or a list of values. We suppose that its definition is well formed and that all the operations invoked have a meaning.

As an example, we construct a recursive definition of the Euclidean division of two integers a and b. The quotient q and the remainder r are given by

$$a = b * q + r \qquad 0 \leq r < b \qquad a, b, q, r \text{ INTEGER}$$

Divide q by 2:

$$q = 2 * q' + q'' \qquad 0 \leq q'' < 2$$

Substituting this in a and rearranging the result,

$$a = (2 * b) * q' + (b * q'' + r)$$

As q'' can take only the values 0 and 1,

$$0 \leq b * q'' + r = r' < 2 * b$$

and so q', r' are the quotient and remainder of the division of a by $2b$; the value of q'' follows from the inequality given above. If

$$q'' = 0 \qquad \text{then} \qquad r' < b \qquad \text{else} \qquad b \leq r'$$

We have a case of direct resolution if $a < b$; for then $q = 0$ and $r = a$ are the quotient and remainder, hence the recursive definition in which $\text{DIV}(a, b)$ has as values the quotient and remainder of the division of a by b:

$$\text{DIV}(a, b) \simeq \text{IF } a < b \text{ THEN } 0, a$$
$$\text{ELSE IF } r' \leq b \text{ THEN } 2 * q', r'$$
$$\text{ELSE } 2 * q' + 1, r' - b$$
$$\text{FI}$$
$$\text{FI}$$
$$\text{WHERE } (q', r' = \text{DIV}(a, 2 * b))$$

In this definition, the variable x is represented by the pair a, b. The function with boolean value $c(x)$ is represented by $a < b$:

$a(x)$ is the pair $0, a$
$b(x)$ the function transforming a, b into $a, 2 * b$
$d(x)$ is the second component of x; that is, b

Finally,

$$(q', r') \circ b = \text{IF } r' < b \text{ THEN } 2 * q', r' \text{ ELSE } 2 * q' + 1, r' - b \text{ FI}$$

This example shows that the recognition of the scheme in a concrete definition can be a rather delicate matter. But it also suggests the very general scope of the scheme. We have already seen in Section 2.7 how dyadic schemes can be reduced to this form, which widens the scope further.

4.1.2　The Associated Recurrent Form

The computation of $f(x)$ is done in one of the following two ways:

−either $c(x)$ is true and $a(x)$ is computed,
−or $c(x)$ is false, and then a new value $f(b(x))$ must be computed.

Usually, the computation of f for a certain argument will invoke the computation of f for a new argument, thus giving rise to a sequence of arguments until a value for which direct computation is possible is reached. Let us examine this sequence. Let $u(i)$ be the general term of the sequence, and

$$y(i) = f(u(i))$$

the associated value of f.

We wish to compute f(x). The first term of the sequence is thus

(1) $u(0) = x$

The required result is f(x); thus f($u(0)$) = $y(0)$,

(2)   result = $y(0)$

If c($u(i - 1)$) is false, $y(i - 1)$ = f($u(i - 1)$) is not directly computable, and there is a recursive call:

$$y(i - 1) = f(b(u(i - 1))) \circ d(u(i - 1))$$

The new argument is

(3) $u(i) = b(u(i - 1))$

from which f($b(u(i - 1))$) = f($u(i)$) = $y(i)$

(4) $y(i - 1) = y(i) \circ d(u(i - 1))$

The computation stops for the first argument satisfying c:

(5) $k = \text{MU} \, i : c(u(i))$

For this value $u(k)$, c being true, f can be calculated directly.

(6) $y(k) = a(u(k))$

Thus, we have completely defined the computation of f(x)—beginning with $u(0) = x$ (relation (1)), the successive values of u are computed by the recurrence (3), as far as that which stops the recurrence (relation (5)).

Having the last argument $u(k)$, $y(k)$ can be computed by relation (6). This done, by relation (4), we return to $y(0)$, which is the required result (2).

This method of operation is in perfect accord with that mentioned in Section 2.3, the first recurrence going from $i = 0$ up to $i = k$ to reach the value of the argument which stops the recursion, then the second recurrence going down, computing the y.

4.1.3 The Iterative Program

To be completely rigorous, it is necessary to put these relations into a rather different form if we wish to obtain a recurrent algorithm in the canonical form of Chapter 3. In particular, the indices in relation (4) have to be changed to give an ascending recurrence, but this can be avoided if we require the corresponding iterative program.

The question of the recurrent variables $u(i)$ is more serious. They are generated in ascending order in the first recurrence, and used in descending order in the second. We cannot therefore use the method of Chapter 3, which associates only two simple variables with each recurrent variable (the previous and current values). Instead, we have to keep all the values of u in a vector. In the program, $u(i)$ (recurrent variable) becomes $u[i]$ (vector). Thus we obtain the following schematic program:

$$u[0] := x; i := 0;$$
WHILE NOT c($u[i]$) DO
$\qquad i := i + 1; u[i] := b(u[i - 1])$
OD;
$y := a(u[i]);$
WHILE $i \neq 0$ DO
$\qquad i := i - 1; y := y \circ d(u[i])$
OD;
result := y

This shows clearly the two loops of the corresponding iterative program and the need to keep the intermediate values in a vector. In fact, the recursive definition hides a complex computing mechanism, and it is hardly surprising that its execution is heavy going. In the most general case, we have to implement an equivalent of what is given here.

4.1.4   Example

In fact, there are few examples justifying such complexity. It is usually possible to effect simplifications, as will be illustrated below. For a recursive definition needing such an iterative program, we should have had to fabricate a special case. Suppose then the function f of the natural integer n to be defined by

$$f(n) \simeq \text{IF } n = 1 \text{ THEN } 1 \text{ ELSE } n - f(\text{INT}(\text{SQRT}(n))^2 \text{ FI}$$

The direct application of what has just been done gives the iterative program:

$$u[0] := n; i := 0;$$
WHILE $u[i] \neq 1$ DO
$\qquad i := i + 1; u[i] := \text{INT}(\text{SQRT}(u[i - 1]))$
OD;
$y := 1;$
WHILE $i \neq 0$ DO
$\qquad i := i - 1; y := u[i] - y * y$
OD;
result := y

The reader should attempt by some other means to write an iterative program for computing this function. I should be interested to know whether there is anything simpler...

4.2   The Stack

We shall look again at the use of the vector u as a means of keeping the results of the first loop until they are required in the second. We note that the successive values are placed in the vector u in the sense of increasing i and removed in the reverse order. The last value placed in u is the first to be taken out. Such a structure is called a "stack"; it is characterised by the fact that the last value in is the first value out. The relation of this structure with the structure of parenthesis is well known; the last parenthesis opened is the first parenthesis closed.

We shall rewrite the program of Section 4.1.2 to show more clearly the fact that every entry to u is preceded by an increment in i, while every withdrawal from u is followed by a decrement in i:

$$i := -1; v := x;$$
$$i := i + 1; u[i] := v;$$
$$\textbf{WHILE NOT } c(v) \textbf{ DO}$$
$$\quad v := b(v); i := i + 1; u[i] := v$$
$$\textbf{OD};$$
$$v := u[i]; i := i - 1; y := a(v);$$
$$\textbf{WHILE } i \neq -1 \textbf{ DO}$$
$$\quad v := u[i]; i := i - 1; y := y \circ d(v)$$
$$\textbf{DO};$$
$$\text{result} := y$$

We give this transformation without justification. The methods to be developed later demonstrate how it can easily be achieved in an almost mechanical way. (We remark only that the instruction $i := i - 1$ having been anticipated before the second loop, the test which controls this loop has become $i \neq -1$.)

We denote by   push(v) the sequence $i := i + 1; u[i] := v$
and by   pop(v) the sequence $v := u[i]; i := i - 1$

The initialisation $i := -1$ defines the stack to be empty. The comparison $i \neq -1$ tests whether the stack is not empty. This leads to another formulation, in a sense more "abstract" (it says nothing as to how the stack is implemented).

We denote schematically by

$$\text{stack} := \text{empty}$$

the initialisation of the stack, and by

$$\text{stack} \neq \text{empty}$$

the test verifying that it is not empty.

```
stack := empty; v := x;
push(v);
WHILE NOT c(v) DO
    v := b(v); push(v)
OD;
pop(v); y := a(v);
WHILE stack ≠ empty DO
    pop(v); y := y ∘ d(v)
OD;
result := y
```

Some redundancy can be seen in this program. The last value of v is pushed, and so made accessible on the stack, but all the time it is also available as v. To improve matters we might, instead of pushing each v as soon as it is computed, decide not to push it until the imminent computation of a new value endangers the old one. Here again we could carry out a systematic transformation. We prefer for the moment to keep to a more "semantic" method, trusting our understanding as to the correct operation:

```
stack := empty; v := x;
WHILE NOT c(v) DO
    push(v); v := b(v)
OD;
y := a(v);
WHILE stack ≠ empty DO
    pop(v); y := y ∘ d(v)
OD;
result := y
```

This is the most general form of an iterative program computing the function f defined in Section 4.1.1. It requires a stack and two loops. We shall examine the possibilities of simplification later. For the moment we shall go on a little with the problem of the exchange of values between the two loops. So far we have operated first by using a vector, then with its abstraction the mechanism of stack management. It is true that, for most programmers, a stack is implemented with a vector and a pointer, as we have just done. But this is a very specific implementation, which can conceal the true nature of the stack mechanism, and makes it difficult to find more suitable forms when that is what is required.

In the specification of abstract types [MEB], the operation "push" is characterised as an application of the cartesian product to sets of stacks and of elements in the set of stacks

$$\text{stack} * \text{element} \to \text{stack}$$

We can say that one way of keeping the elements $u[i]$ is to group them into a single value so that they can be retrieved. We rewrite the recurrent system of Section 4.1.2:

$$
\begin{aligned}
u(0) &= x \\
\text{result} &= y(0) \\
u(i) &= b(u(i-1)) \\
y(i-1) &= y(i) \circ d(u(i-1)) \\
k &= \text{MU}\, i : c(u(i)) \\
y(k) &= a(u(k))
\end{aligned}
$$

We form a recurrent sequence $p(i)$ by

$$p(i) = g(p(i-1), u(i-1))$$

choosing g such that g^{-1} exists:

$$p(i-1), u(i-1) = g^{-1}(p(i))$$

We initialise p with an initial value e such that for all i, $p(i) \neq e$:

$$p(0) = e$$

We obtain the new iterative program

```
p := e; v := x;
WHILE NOT c(v) DO
      p := g(p, v); v := b(v)
OD;
y := a(v);
WHILE p ≠ e DO
      p, v := g⁻¹(p); y := y ∘ d(v)
OD;
result := y
```

It differs from the previous version only in notation. The operation push(v) has been replaced by an instruction

$$p := g(p, v)$$

with the same significance—the new stack is obtained by combining the element v and the old stack, this combination being reversible.

There is only a change of notation. But this new form suggests other stacking modes. Thus, in a language with good primitives for the manipulation of character strings, we might take a character string as a stack. To push v, concatenate it at the head of the string with a suitable separator. To pop, take off the head of the string, up to the first separator.

We shall give a different example. But first we note that $d(v)$ could have been pushed rather than v, since in fact it is this value which is used in the second loop. This can be an important point, if the values $d(v)$ are easier to push than are the values v:

$$p := e; v := x;$$
$$\text{WHILE NOT } c(v) \text{ DO}$$
$$\quad p := g(p, d(v)); v := b(v)$$
$$\text{OD};$$
$$y := a(v);$$
$$\text{WHILE } p \neq e \text{ DO}$$
$$\quad p, w := g^{-1}(p); y := y \circ w$$
$$\text{OD};$$
$$\text{result} := y$$

To illustrate the interest of this form, we return to the recursive definition of Section 2.2.2:

$$\exp2(x, n) \simeq \text{IF } n = 0 \text{ THEN } 1$$
$$\qquad\qquad\qquad \text{ELSE IF even}(n) \text{ THEN } y * y$$
$$\qquad\qquad\qquad\qquad\qquad\qquad \text{ELSE } x * y * y$$
$$\qquad\qquad\qquad\qquad \text{FI}$$
$$\qquad \text{FI}$$
$$\qquad\qquad \text{WHERE}(y = \exp2(x, n:2))$$

This is easily translated into the recurrent scheme

$$u(i) = u(i - 1):2$$
$$u(0) = n$$
$$y(i - 1) = \text{IF even}(u(i - 1)) \text{ THEN } y(i)^2 \text{ ELSE } x * y(i)^2 \text{ FI}$$
$$k = \text{MU } i : u(i) = 0$$
$$y(k) = 1$$
$$\text{result} = y(0)$$

The second recurrence does not use $u(i - 1)$ but only

$$\text{even}(u(i - 1))$$

The division of $u(i - 1)$ by 2 produces a remainder which can be interpreted as giving the parity of $u(i - 1)$. Thus,

$$u(i), d(i) = \text{div}(u(i - 1), 2)$$

The $d(i)$ have to be "pushed" to be used in the recurrence on y. Thus a number 0 or 1 has to be combined with p in a way which can be reversed. This number could be concatenated as rightmost digit in the binary representation of p. We then take a natural integer for p, and for the function $g(p, d)$

$$2 * p + d$$

We obtain the new system

$$u(i), d(i) = \text{div}(u(i - 1), 2)$$
$$p(i) = 2 * p(i - 1) + d(i) \text{ equivalent to } p(i - 1), d(i) = \text{div}(p(i), 2)$$
$$y(i - 1) = \text{IF } d(i) = 0 \text{ THEN } y(i)^2 \text{ ELSE } x * y(i)^2 \text{ FI}$$
$$u(0) = n$$
$$k = \text{MU } i : u(i) = 0$$
$$y(k) = 1$$
$$\text{result} = y(0)$$

We cannot take $e = 0$ as initial value of p; for then

$$p(1) = 2 * p(0) + d(0)$$

would still be equal to 0 for $d(0) = 0$. Thus we take

$$p(0) = 1$$

There is no difficulty in transforming this into an iterative program. A single variable is enough for each of the recurrent variables:

```
u := n; p := 1;
WHILE u ≠ 0 DO
        u, d := div(u, 2); p := 2 * p + d
OD;
y := 1;
WHILE p ≠ 1 DO
        p, d := div(p, 2);
        y := IF d = 0 THEN y * y ELSE x * y * y FI
OD;
result := y
```

Make no mistake—in this program the variable p is really a stack. In the first loop, the rightmost binary digit of u is concatenated to the right of p. This means that the binary representation of p is obtained by placing a 1 (initial value of p) at the head (to the left) of the mirror image of the binary representation of n. Thus for $n = 13$, represented in binary as 1101, p is represented by 1 1011 and so has the value 27 at the exit from the first loop.

Thus the first loop has as its only effect that of returning the binary representation of n.The second loop extracts the binary digits from this, from right to left. We thus have a new interpretation of the program:

y is initialised to the value 1
the successive bits of n are extracted, from left to right for each bit, y is
squared, and multiplied by x if the bit is 1

It is left as an exercise for the reader to write the corresponding program.

There is also the relation between the two definitions exp2 and exp3 of
Section 2.2.2. These are both based on the binary representation of n; but exp2
scans n from left to right, while exp3 scans it from right to left (which is simpler).
It is important to remember that the two definitions give rise to the same
number of multiplications and the same precision. This is why the program we
have just developed is rarely used.

Later we shall meet other examples of the representation of stacks.

4.3   Programs without Stacks

We have several times indicated that the general iterative scheme can often
be simplified. We consider here the case where the stack is not needed, leaving
an iterative program with two loops.

The stack is used to transmit the values $u(i)$ from ascending recurrence to
descending recurrence. This is unnecessary if the values u can be recomputed.
The ascending recurrence is given by

$$u(0) = x$$
$$u(i) = b(u(i-1))$$

The recurrence on y arises from

$$k = \text{MU}\, i : c(u(i))$$

We need to be able to recomput the values of u, in reverse order beginning with
$u(k)$. *This is possible if the function* b *has an inverse:*

$$u(i-1) = b^{-1}(u(i))$$

We will then have the following recurrent scheme:

$$u(0) = x \qquad u(i) = b(u(i-1)) \qquad \text{ascending recurrence}$$
$$k = \text{MU}\, i : c(u(i))$$
$$y(k) = a(u(k))$$
$$y(i-1) = y(i) \circ d(u(i-1)) \qquad \text{descending recurrence}$$
$$u(i-1) = b^{-1}(u(i))$$
$$\text{result} := y(0)$$

$$u := x;$$

$$\text{WHILE NOT } c(u) \text{ DO}$$
$$u := b(u)$$
$$\text{OD};$$
$$y := a(u);$$
$$\text{WHILE } u \neq x \text{ DO}$$
$$u := b^{-1}(u); y := y \circ d(u)$$
$$\text{OD};$$
$$\text{result} := y$$

The termination problem of the second loop has been resolved without recourse to a counter. The first recurrence runs from 0 to k and the second from k to 0, but we can also say that the first recurrence causes u to run through the values $u(0) = x$ to $u(k)$. It is certain that, for all i such that $1 \leq i \leq k$, $u(i) \neq u(0) = x$.

If indeed it were otherwise, the sequence u would be periodic, and the exit condition would never be reached.

The second recurrence causes u to run through the values $u(k)$ to $u(0) = x$. The division algorithm given in Section 4.1.1 is of this type. The function b changes the pair a, b to $a, 2 * b$. Its inverse changes the pair a, b (where b is even) to $a, b : 2$.

The transformation to the recurrent scheme is simple. The pair a, b is replaced by the recurrent pair $u(i), v(i)$:

$$u(i) = u(i - 1)$$
$$v(i) = v(i - 1) * 2 \qquad \text{giving} \quad v(i - 1) = v(i) : 2$$
$$q(i - 1) = \text{IF } r(i) < v(i - 1) \text{ THEN } 2 * q(i) \text{ ELSE } 2 * q(i) + 1 \text{ FI}$$
$$r(i - 1) = \text{IF } r(i) < v(i - 1) \text{ THEN } r(i) \text{ ELSE } r(i) - v(i - 1) \text{ FI}$$
$$k = \text{MU } i : u(i) < v(i)$$
$$u(0) = a \qquad v(0) = b$$
$$q(k) = 0 \qquad r(k) = u(k)$$

We have here an additional simplification (which reduces the program without affecting its complexity—it still involves two recurrences). The sequence u is constant, equal to a.

The iterative form is easily deduced from this scheme. We have first computed $2 * q(i)$ in the second loop, to shorten the text.

$$v := b;$$
$$\text{WHILE } v \leq a \text{ DO } v := 2 * v \text{ OD};$$
$$q := 0; r := a;$$
$$\text{WHILE } v \neq b \text{ DO}$$
$$v := v : 2; q := 2 * q;$$
$$\text{IF } r \geq v \text{ THEN } q := q + 1; r := r - v \text{ FI}$$
$$\text{OD};$$

This is the well-known algorithm for division in base 2. Operating on the binary representations, the first loop shifts the divisor to the left to make it greater than the dividend. The second loop shifts to the right, and, whenever possible, the divisor is subtracted from what remains of the dividend, and 1 is added to the right of the quotient; otherwise, 0 is added to the right.

4.4 A Program with Only One Loop

A new simplification is seen in the scheme when the value $u(k)$ which causes exit is known in advance. If then

$$c(x) \quad \text{is equivalent to} \quad x = x_0$$

the first loop

$$
\begin{aligned}
&u := x; \\
&\text{WHILE } u \neq x_0 \text{ DO} \\
&\qquad u := b(u) \\
&\text{OD};
\end{aligned}
$$

is not needed. Its only effect is to give u the value x_0. The value then taken by f is a(x). But since $x = x_0$ is a constant, $a(x_0)$ is also a constant which we denote simply by a:

$$f(x) \simeq \text{IF } x = x_0 \text{ THEN } a \text{ ELSE } f(b(x)) \circ d(x) \text{ FI}$$

The associated iterative scheme is

$$
\begin{aligned}
&u := x_0; y := a; \\
&\text{WHILE } u \neq x \text{ DO} \\
&\qquad u := b^{-1}(u); y := y \circ d(u) \\
&\text{OD}; \\
&\text{result} := y
\end{aligned}
$$

The best known example of this is the factorial:

$$
\begin{aligned}
&\text{fac}(n) \simeq \text{IF } n = 0 \text{ THEN } 1 \text{ ELSE } n * \text{fac}(n - 1) \text{ FI} \\
&b(n) = n - 1 \text{ has as inverse } b^{-1}(n) = n + 1
\end{aligned}
$$

The corresponding iterative program is

$$
\begin{aligned}
&u := 0; y := 1; \\
&\text{WHILE } u \neq n \text{ DO} \\
&\qquad u := u + 1; y := y * u \\
&\text{OD}; \\
&\text{result} := y
\end{aligned}
$$

We shall see some other cases of simplification.

4.5   Interpretation of the Recursive Scheme

We return to the recurrent form of the recursive scheme:

$$u(0) = x$$
$$\text{result} = y(0)$$
$$y(i - 1) = y(i) \circ d(u(i - 1))$$
$$u(i) = b(u(i - 1))$$
$$k = \text{MU } i : c(u(i))$$
$$y(k) = a(u(k))$$

We can replace $y(0)$ by its value

$$\text{result} = y(1) \circ d(u(0))$$
$$y(1) = y(2) \circ d(u(1))$$

which gives

$$\text{result} = (y(2) \circ d(u(1))) \circ d(u(0))$$

Repeating this process,

$$\text{result} = ((\dots(y(k) \circ d(u(k - 1))) \circ d(u(k - 2))) \circ \dots) \circ d(u(0))$$

To simplify the writing, we shall suppress the parentheses while emphasising always that the computation is to be done from left to right. Moreover, $y(k) = a(u(k))$, so

$$\text{result} = a(u(k)) \circ d(u(k - 1)) \circ \dots \circ d(u(0))$$

We thus have a clear interpretation as to what the recursive scheme considered here will compute, if in addition we note that

$$u(i) = b^i(x)$$

There is "accumulation" of the operation $\circ$ over the values $d(b^i(x))$. It is a generalisation of the factorial, which accumulates multiplication over the successors of 1.

4.6   Other Simplifications

4.6.1   Associativity

First let us suppose that the operation $\circ$ is associative:

$$(a \circ b) \circ c = a \circ (b \circ c)$$

This means that we can reverse the order of computation within an expression, taking it from right to left. This has an enormous advantage—the values u are used in the sense of increasing index. We form a recurrent sequence by the accumulation of operations ∘ from the right:

$$\text{result} = a(u(k)) \circ d(u(k-1)) \circ d(u(k-2)) \circ \ldots$$

$$\underbrace{\phantom{a(u(k)) \circ d(u(k-1)) \circ \underbrace{d(u(k-2)) \circ \ldots}_{w(k-2)}}}_{w(k)}$$

Then,

$$\text{result} = a(u(k)) \circ w(k)$$
$$w(i) = d(u(i-1)) \circ w(i-1)$$

For $i = 1$,

$$w(1) = d(u(0)) \circ w(0)$$

Now $d(u(0))$ is the rightmost term of the expression, so $w(0)$ must be defined in such a way that

$$d(u(0)) \circ w(0) = d(u(0))$$

which implies that $w(0)$ must be the neutral element to the right of the operation ∘.

If so:

the operation is associative
it has an element neutral to the right, denoted by e and such that, for all x,
$x \circ e = x$

f is computed by the recurrent scheme:

$$u(i) = b(u(i-1))$$
$$w(i) = d(u(i-1)) \circ w(i-1)$$
$$u(0) = x$$
$$w(0) = e$$
$$k = \text{MU}\, i : c(u(i))$$
$$\text{result} = a(u(k)) \circ w(k)$$

The corresponding iterative program is very simple:

```
u := x; w := e;
WHILE NOT c(u) DO
    w := d(u) ∘ w;
    u := b(u)
OD;
result := a(u) ∘ w
```

It will be noted that this program differs profoundly from that given previously. It operates in the sense of "increasing" u [$u := b(u)$], and w occurs as a right operand of $\circ$ ($w := d(u) \circ w$ in the place of $y := y \circ d(u)$).

Applying this to the factorial,

$$u := n; w := 1;$$
$$\text{WHILE } u \neq 0 \text{ DO}$$
$$\qquad w := u * w;$$
$$\qquad u := u - 1$$
$$\text{OD};$$
$$\text{result} := w$$

Remark. The initialisation $w := 1$ is due to the fact that 1 is the neutral element for multiplication and not because of the constants appearing in the recursive definition. The result is given by

$$\text{result} := a(x) * w$$

but $a(x) = 1$ (constant appearing in the definition).

In this program u runs from n to 0, rather than from 0 to n as in the preceding program. The operation $*$ being commutative, the change from

$$y := y * w \qquad \text{to} \qquad w := u * w$$

has no effect.

4.6.2 Permutability

Suppose the operation $\circ$ is "permutable",

$$(a \circ b) \circ c = (a \circ c) \circ b$$

as in the case of subtraction,

$$(a - b) - c = (a - c) - b$$

In the general expression of the result, we can now permute any two terms of the sequence (except the first)

$$\text{result} = (((\ldots) \circ d(u(p))) \circ d(u(p - 1))) \circ \ldots$$
$$= (((\ldots) \circ d(u(p - 1))) \circ d(u(p))) \circ \ldots$$

By repeated application of this operation we can effect any desired permutation of the sequence $d(u(k - 1)), \ldots, d(u(0))$ and in particular,

$$\text{result} = a(u(k)) \circ d(u(0)) \circ \ldots \circ d(u(k - 1))$$

the computation being done always from left to right. Nothing is gained by this if a depends in fact on $u(k)$, not known in advance.

If a is a constant, then the result can be computed by ascending recurrence:

$$w'(0) = a$$
$$w'(1) = w'(0) \circ d(u(0))$$

and more generally,

$$w'(i) = w'(i - 1) \circ d(u(i - 1))$$
$$w'(0) = a$$
$$u(0) = x$$
$$u(i) = b(u(i - 1))$$
$$k = \text{MU } i : c(u(i))$$
$$\text{result} = w'(k)$$

The iterative program is thus

$$u := x; w' := a;$$
$$\textbf{WHILE NOT } c(u) \textbf{ DO}$$
$$\qquad w' := w' \circ d(u);$$
$$\qquad u := b(u)$$
$$\textbf{OD};$$
$$\text{result} := w'$$

This can be applied to the factorial function, for

$$(a * b) * c = (a * c) * b$$

The constant a is 1:

$$u := n; w' := 1;$$
$$\textbf{WHILE } u \neq 0 \textbf{ DO}$$
$$\qquad w' := w' * u;$$
$$\qquad u := u - 1$$
$$\textbf{OD};$$
$$\text{result} := w'$$

This is the program already obtained, but where this time w' is initialised to 1—not the neutral element of multiplication but a constant in the recursive definition.

4.7 A Degenerate Form of the Recursive Scheme

4.7.1 The Degenerate Form

We consider now a degenerate case of the recursive scheme where there is no binary operation

$$f(b(x)) \circ d(x)$$

but only a unary function which we denote by h:

$$f(x) \simeq \text{IF } c(x) \text{ THEN } a(x) \text{ ELSE } h(f(b(x))) \text{ FI}$$

The writing of the associated recurrent algorithm is very simple. We follow the same method as above. We obtain

$$u(i) = b(u(i - 1))$$
$$y(i - 1) = h(y(i))$$
$$u(0) = x$$
$$y(k) = a(u(k))$$
$$k = \text{MU } i : c(u(i))$$
$$\text{result} = y(0)$$

There are still two recurrences: one ascending for u, the other descending for y. But the recurrence for y does not use u, and there is no need of a stack. The ascending recurrence is stopped by the condition $c(u)$. The descending recurrence for y is not stopped by a condition on y, so a counter i has to be used. In the most general case, the associated iterative scheme is thus

```
u := x; i := 0;
WHILE NOT c(u) DO
        i := i + 1; u := b(u)
OD;
y := a(u);
WHILE i ≠ 0 DO
        y := h(y); i := i − 1
OD;
result := y
```

We have no simple example of such a scheme. Two forms of simplification are often possible.

4.7.2   When a Is Constant

In this case the recurrence on y can be turned around. With

$$w(i) = y(k - i)$$

we have

$$w(0) = y(k) = a$$
$$\text{result} = y(0) = w(k)$$

We have a new recurrent scheme:

$$u(i) = b(u(i - 1))$$
$$w(i) = h(w(i - 1))$$

$$u(0) = x$$
$$w(0) = a$$
$$k = \text{MU } i : c(u(i))$$
$$\text{result} = w(k)$$

and the corresponding simple program:

$$u := x; w := a;$$
$$\text{WHILE NOT } c(u) \text{ DO}$$
$$u := b(u);$$
$$w := h(w)$$
$$\text{OD};$$
$$\text{result} := w$$

Here is a simple example of this.

We define add(a, b) by

$$\text{add}(a, b) \simeq \text{IF } b = 0 \text{ THEN } a \text{ ELSE } s(\text{add}(a, p(b))) \text{ FI}$$

p is the predecessor function, s the successor function, and a is a constant through the algorithm. We obtain easily

$$u := b; w := a;$$
$$\text{WHILE } u \neq 0 \text{ DO}$$
$$u := p(u);$$
$$w := s(w)$$
$$\text{OD};$$
$$\text{result} := w$$

This is the well-known algorithm for the addition of integers. The fact that

$$p(u) = u - 1 \qquad s(w) = w + 1$$

plays no part in it.

4.7.3 When h is the Identity Operation

If $h(x) = x$, the general scheme simplifies further. The recurrence on y becomes

$$y(i - 1) = h(y(i)) = y(i)$$

that is, the sequence y is constant. We then have

$$\text{result} = y(0) = y(k) = a(u(k))$$

The recurrent scheme associated with the recursive definition

$$f(x) \simeq \text{IF } c(x) \text{ THEN } a(x) \text{ ELSE } f(b(x)) \text{ FI}$$

is thus

$$u(i) = b(u(i-1))$$
$$u(0) = x$$
$$k = \text{MU } i : c(u(i))$$
$$\text{result} = a(u(k))$$

which gives the following iterative scheme:

```
u := x;
WHILE NOT c(u) DO
        u := b(u)
OD;
result := a(u)
```

A simple example of this is another form of the recursive definition of addition:

$$\text{add}(a, b) \simeq \text{IF } b = 0 \text{ THEN } a \text{ ELSE add}(s(a), p(b)) \text{ FI}$$

The iterative program is obtained directly:

```
u := a; v := b;
WHILE v ≠ 0 DO
        u := s(u); v := p(v)
OD;
result := u
```

4.8   Special Cases

We have just identified a certain number of schemes for which there are simplified forms of iterative program. But this cannot exhaust the cases where such a simplification is possible. Just as in mathematics, certain forms of differential equations are known for which there is a general method of solution (Lagrange, Clairaut,...) without in any way exhausting the cases where an explicit solution is possible, so here recursive definitions will be encountered which will allow simplification without falling into any of the cases treated above. We shall give two examples of this, which it is believed are representative of numerous other cases.

4.8.1   A Dyadic Scheme

We have already shown how the dyadic scheme for the Fibonacci numbers can be reduced. Here is an example, apparently more complex, of a definition comprising one monadic branch and one dyadic. (See Section 2.2.6.)

When I want to do by hand the division of two integers with a large number of significant figures, I first construct a multiplication table of the divisor with the first nine non-zero integers. This can be done by succesive addition, but then the divisor has to be copied out each time to minimise the risk of error, and this is hardly practical. I operate as follows:

To compute the product by $2k$, I double the product by k.

To compute the product by $2k + 1$, I add the products by k and $k + 1$, already computed and written in successive lines, thus well placed for addition.

This is a recursive definition of the product:

$$f(k, x) \simeq \text{IF } k = 1 \text{ THEN } x$$
$$\text{ELSE IF even}(k) \text{ THEN } 2 * f(k:2, x)$$
$$\text{ELSE } f(k:2, x) + f((k:2) + 1, x)$$
$$\text{FI}$$
$$\text{FI}$$

As has already been done for the Fibonacci numbers, the functions f are taken in pairs, writing

$$g(k, x) = f(k, x), f(k + 1, x)$$

We thus obtain

$$g(2k, x) = f(2k, x), f(2k + 1, x)$$
$$= 2 * f(k, x), f(k, x) + f(k + 1, x)$$

which can be expressed in terms of the components of $g(k, x)$:

$$g(2k + 1, x) = f(2k + 1, x), f(2k + 2, x)$$
$$= f(k, x) + f(k + 1, x), 2 * f(k + 1, x)$$

which again can be expressed in terms of the components of $g(k, x)$, whence the definition of g, using the fact that $f(0, x) = 0$:

$$g(k, x) \simeq \text{IF } k = 0 \text{ THEN } 0, x$$
$$\text{ELSE IF even}(k) \text{ THEN } 2 * u, u + v$$
$$\text{ELSE } u + v, 2 * v$$
$$\text{FI}$$
$$\text{FI}$$
$$\text{WHERE } (u, v = g(k:2, x))$$

This is a function whose definition has exactly the same form as that of the
function exp2 considered in Section 4.2. We give the iterative program without
developing the computations:

$$q:= k; p:= 1;$$
$$\text{WHILE } q \neq 0 \text{ DO}$$
$$\quad q, d:= \text{div}(q, 2);$$
$$\quad p:= 2*p + d$$
$$\text{OD};$$
$$u:= 1; v:= x;$$
$$\text{WHILE } p \neq 1 \text{ DO}$$
$$\quad p, d:= \text{div}(p, 2);$$
$$\quad \text{IF } d = 0 \text{ THEN } v:= u + v; u:= 2*u$$
$$\quad\quad\quad\quad\quad\quad \text{ELSE } u:= u + v; v:= 2*v$$
$$\quad \text{FI}$$
$$\text{OD}$$

4.8.2   Non-Associativity

Suppose we wish to express a number n in base b, where $b < 10$. We can form
a character string to represent it, but this string can also be considered as the
representation in base 10 of another integer $f(n, b)$. We give a recursive
definition of this.

We obtain f(n, b) by writing the figure representing mod(n, b) to the right of
the representation of f$(n:b, b)$. Now, to write a figure x at the right of the
number y is to form a new number:

$$10*y + x$$

The recurrence can be stopped by taking $n = 0$, which has the same
representation in all bases:

$$\text{f}(n, b) \simeq \text{IF } n = 0 \text{ THEN } 0$$
$$\quad\quad\quad\quad\quad \text{ELSE } 10*\text{f}(n:b, b) + \text{mod}(n, b)$$
$$\quad\quad \text{FI}$$

The law $y \circ x = 10*y + x$ is neither associative nor permutative, and so this
scheme falls into none of the cases which we have studied as giving rise to
simplification. None the less we form the recurrence relations. The base b is a
constant for the algorithm. We denote by $u(i)$ the first argument of f, by $y(i)$ the
associated value of f. We give the recurrence relations without redeveloping
the computations;

$$y(i - 1) = 10*y(i) + \text{mod}(u(i - 1), b)$$
$$u(i) = u(i - 1):b$$

$$u(0) = n$$
$$k = \text{MU}\, i : u(i) = 0$$
$$y(k) = 0$$
$$r = y(0)$$

We cannot apply the methods proposed for the cases where the operation denoted by ∘ has specific favourable properties, but we can keep to the general idea which led to these methods. The result has to be expressed as a function of the several values appearing in the recurrence; in other words, $r = y(0)$ has to be computed by accumulation of the recurrence relations:

$$y(0) = 10 * y(1) + \text{mod}(u(0), b)$$

Replacing $y(1)$ by its value

$$y(0) = 100 * y(2) + 10 * \text{mod}(u(1), b) + \text{mod}(u(0), b)$$

If we reiterate this process, $10^i * y(i)$ will appear, which suggests the introduction of a new variable

$$z(i) = 10^i * y(i)$$

We have then

$$z(i - 1) = 10^{i-1} * y(i - 1) = 10^{i-1} * (10 * y(i) + \text{mod}(u(i - 1), b))$$
$$= 10^i * y(i) + 10^{i-1} * \text{mod}(u(i - 1), b)$$

and, finally,

$$z(i - 1) = z(i) + 10^{i-1} * \text{mod}(u(i - 1), b)$$

For the extreme values,

$$r = y(0) = 10^\circ * y(0) = z(0)$$
$$z(k) = 10^k * y(k) = 0$$

and, finally, we have a new system (we write $s(i) = 10^i$):

$$z(i - 1) = z(i) + s(i - 1) * \text{mod}(u(i - 1), b)$$
$$s(i) = 10 * s(i - 1)$$
$$u(i) = u(i - 1) : b$$
$$u(0) = n$$
$$s(0) = 1$$
$$k = \text{MU}\, i : u(i) = 0$$
$$r = z(0)$$
$$z(k) = 0$$

This time the law in question is addition, and it has all the desired favourable properties. We can use the results of Section 4.6.1. By adding together the relations involving z for i from 1 to k, we obtain

$$r = z(0) = \sum_{i=1}^{k} s(i-1) * \mathrm{mod}(u(i-1), b)$$

The sum is computed by recurrence, giving the new scheme

$w(i) = w(i-1) + s(i-1) * \mathrm{mod}(u(i-1), b)$
$w(0) = 0$ (neutral element for addition)
$u(i) = u(i-1) : b$
$u(0) = n$
$s(i) = 10 * s(i-1)$
$s(0) = 1$
$k = \mathrm{MU}\, i : u(i) = 0$
$r = w(k)$

From this we deduce the required iterative program:

$$w := 0; s := 1; u := n;$$
$$\text{WHILE } u \neq 0 \text{ DO}$$
$$u, q := \mathrm{div}(u, b);$$
$$w := w + s * q;$$
$$s := 10 * s$$
$$\text{OD};$$
$$\text{result} := w$$

We could try to generalise what has just been done and devise a schematic model. There seems no point, however, in extending the catalogue of schemes for which there is a simple iterative transformation. When the work is done "by hand", the recognition of an abstract scheme in a concrete definition is by no means easy, and a lot of time can be spent searching through the catalogue for the applicable scheme. It seems preferable to follow systematically the general method:

–form the recurrence relations (this is usually done very quickly);

–reorganise them to obtain if possible a single ascending recurrence. To do this, a good way to proceed is to write the explicit form of the result as a combination of the recurrence relations, as we have been doing.

"Artificial intelligence" operates otherwise [BD1]. The system of R. Burstall and J. Darlington indeed searches through a catalogue for a known, applicable, theoretical scheme. If one is found, the transformation takes place; otherwise the system is stranded. The function given here leaves such a system high and dry.

For the human being relying on natural intelligence, recourse to a catalogue is likely seriously to impede progress (bring it to a full stop if the catalogue is insufficiently rich, or drag it to a crawl if it is too thick). It is much better to work steadily with a method of general application.

Exercises

E.4.1 Give the recurrent form, then the iterative program, associated with the recursive definition exp3(x, n), Section 2.2.2.

E.4.2 Give first the recurrent, then the iterative, forms associated with the recursive definition of the expression of an integer in base b, Section 2.2.4.

E.4.3 The same, for the recursive definition of the real numbers of Exercise E.2.1.

E.4.4 The same, for the recursive definition of the logarithm, Exercise E.2.2.

E.4.5 Construct an iterative program to compute the value associated with a Roman numeral using the recursive definition found in Exercise E.2.7.

E.4.6 Construct the iterative programs for comparison of strings by lexicographic order (Exercise E.2.9).

E.4.7 Exercise E.3.1 asked for the construction of two recurrent algorithms for the evaluation of a polynomial. Each is the translation of a recursive definition. What are these definitions?

E.4.8 In Section 2.8.1, a recursive definition of a function was given, of which it was shown that it computed a very simple function, given in the same section. We have shown that the dyadic definition can be replaced by a monadic definition $g(n, i)$.

Form the recurrent algorithm associated with the recursive definition $g(n, i)$. Show from these recurrences that the value is 91 for $n \leq 100$.

Chapter 5

From Recursion to Iteration

5.1 An Example of Direct Transformation

5.1.1 Invariance in a Loop

We have based the writing of an iterative program on the choice of an invariant situation. We would be able to pass directly from recursion to iteration if we could deduce this invariant from the recursive definition. Returning to the general scheme of Chapter 4:

$$f(x) \simeq \text{IF } c(x) \text{ THEN } a(x) \text{ ELSE } f(b(x)) \circ d(x) \text{ FI}$$

and supposing that the law of $\circ$ is associative, we have a recurrent system computing f (Section 4.6.1):

$$\begin{aligned}
u(i) &= b(u(i-1)) \\
w(i) &= d(u(i-1)) \circ w(i-1) \\
u(0) &= x \\
w(0) &= e \\
k &= \text{MU } i : c(u(i)) \\
\text{result} &= a(u(k)) \circ w(k)
\end{aligned}$$

The variables w have been introduced to represent the quantities

$$w(i) = d(u(i-1)) \circ d(u(i-2)) \circ \ldots \circ d(u(0))$$

We have also

$$\begin{aligned}
\text{result} &= y(i) \circ d(u(i-1)) \circ d(u(i-2)) \circ \ldots \circ d(u(0)) \\
&= y(i) \circ w(i)
\end{aligned}$$

Thus, the quantity

$$y(i) \circ w(i) = f(u(i)) \circ w(i)$$

is invariant over i and equal to the required result.

105

In the associated iterative program, the recurrent variables $u(i)$ and $w(i)$ are replaced by the simple variables u and w. We thus have as invariant for the loop

$$[[\text{result} = f(u) \circ w]]$$

5.1.2   Construction of the Iterative Program

From this point, the construction of the program is easy. Following the method of Chapter 1, we first examine the condition for termination. Execution finishes if the result is computable, then if $f(u)$ is computed directly, then if $c(u)$ is true. In that case, $f(u) = a(u)$ and the result is

$$\text{result} = a(u) \circ w$$

otherwise, we replace in

$$\text{result} = f(u) \circ w$$

the value of f taken from the recursive definition

$$f(u) = f(b(u)) \circ d(u)$$

We thus have

$$\text{result} = (f(b(u)) \circ d(u)) \circ w$$

The law of $\circ$ being associative,

$$\text{result} = f(b(u)) \circ (d(u) \circ w)$$

To find the invariant of the loop, the argument of f must be replaced by u and the second operand of the operation $\circ$ by w. We then have

$$\begin{aligned}
&\textbf{WHILE NOT } c(u) \textbf{ DO} \\
&\quad u, w := b(u), d(u) \circ w \\
&\textbf{OD}; \\
&\text{result} := a(u) \circ w
\end{aligned}$$

To begin the loop, we need initial values for u and w such that

$$f(x) = f(u) \circ w$$

We take $u = x$ and $w = e$, the neutral element to the right for the operation $\circ$. We then have the program already given:

$$\begin{aligned}
&u := x;\, w := e; \\
&\textbf{WHILE NOT } c(u) \textbf{ DO} \\
&\quad w := d(u) \circ w; \\
&\quad u := b(u)
\end{aligned}$$

$$\text{OD};$$
$$\text{result} := \text{a}(u) \circ w$$

(The double assignment to u, w has been replaced by two single assignments in the correct order.)

5.2 Extension

Let us go through what has been done, pointing out the different stages.

5.2.1 Generalisation

We began with the recursive definition

$$f(x) = f(b(x)) \circ d(x)$$

The invariant for the loop was, in the case of associativity,

$$\text{result} = f(u) \circ v$$

The expression to the right of the equal sign can be considered as a "generalisation" of the recursive definition. It is of the same form, but the argument of f and the second operand of the operator $\circ$ are arbitrary variables, unconstrained by the existence of an x such that

$$u = b(x) \qquad \text{and} \qquad v = d(x)$$

The invariant for the loop thus follows from the recursive definition by generalisation. The form of the definition is preserved, but the several expressions in it are replaced by variables, the same expression being consistently replaced by the same variable.

We shall see that this is not critical. A poor generalisation prevents the realisation of further stages, and the reasons for the stoppage indicate ways of improving the generalisation. We shall give an example of this.

5.2.2 The Test for Exit

The generalised form contains an occurrence of the recursive function f. We have reached the end if this can be computed directly, that is, if the condition for non-recursion in the recursive definition is satisfied.

The test for exit is given by the recursive definition.

5.2.3   Progression

The generalised form must contain an occurrence of the recursively defined function. This is replaced by its value, taken from the recursive definition. This is a simple substitution in the mathematical sense of the term. Because the definition is recursive, the replacement re-establishes an occurrence of the function.

Then the resultant expression is rearranged to give it the form of the invariant for the loop, to within changes of variables. These changes of variables, which restore to the expression obtained the form of the invariant, are sometimes called "unification" (they give the same form to two expressions or transform one of them into the other).

If the unification is impossible, that is to say if there is no change of variables mapping one expression onto the other, then either the generalisation has been poorly done or there is no iterative program of one loop which will compute the recursive function.

5.2.4   Initialisation

There is nothing special here. Initial values have to be found which put the required result $f(x)$ into the form of the invariant for the loop. This is generally a matter of bringing into play the neutral elements of the operations.

This method, very simple and quick to apply, is not constrained to the case of an associative law. We shall present a few examples of it.

5.3   Examples

5.3.1   The Reverse of a String

We gave in Section 2.2.3 a recursive definition of the reverse of a character string:

$$\text{rev}(c) \simeq \text{IF length}(c) < 2 \text{ THEN } c$$
$$\text{ELSE rev}(\text{sbs}(c, 2, \text{""}))\,!\,\text{sbs}(c, 1, 1)$$
$$\text{FI}$$

The recursive definition is

$$\text{rev}(c) = \text{rev}(\text{sbs}(c, 2, \text{""}))\,!\,\text{sbs}(c, 1, 1)$$

We generalise this, overlooking the relation existing between the argument of rev and the second operand of the concatenation,

$$\text{result} = \text{rev}(u)\,!\,v$$

We thus have a program beginning

$$DO$$
$$[[\text{result} = \text{rev}(u)!\,v]]$$
$$\cdots$$

It is finished when rev(u) can be computed directly, that is, by the recursive definition when length(u) is less than 2.

$$DO$$
$$[[\text{result} = \text{rev}(u)!\,v]]$$
$$\text{IF length}(u) < 2 \text{ THEN EXIT FI};$$
$$\cdots\cdots$$
$$OD;$$
$$[[\text{result} = \text{rev}(u)!\,v \text{ AND length}(u) < 2 \text{ gives result} = u!\,v]]$$
$$\text{result} := u!\,v$$

We now see the progression; rev(u) is replaced in the invariant for the loop by its value

$$\text{rev}(\text{sbs}(u, 2, \text{“ ”}))!\,\text{sbs}(u, 1, 1)$$

Thus,

$$\text{result} = \text{rev}(\text{sbs}(u, 2, \text{“ ”}))!\,\text{sbs}(u, 1, 1)!\,v$$

The operation of conacatenation being associative, this is also

$$\text{result} = \text{rev}(\text{sbs}(u, 2, ”\,”))!\,(\text{sbs}(u, 1, 1)!\,v)$$

To return to the form of the invariant, we must take as new u, v,

$$u, v := \text{sbs}(u, 2, \text{“ ”}),\ \text{sbs}(u, 1, 1)!\,v$$

We thus have the required program. The double assignment is linearised, noting that v must be computed first as its value depends on u. Initialisation is done by putting

$$\text{rev}(c) \qquad \text{into the form} \qquad \text{rev}(u)!\,v$$

As there is no concatenation in rev(c), the concatenation to the right in rev(u)!v must have no effect, so v must be the neutral element for concatenation, the empty string:

$$u := c\,;\ v := \text{“ ”};$$
$$DO$$
$$[[\text{result} = \text{rev}(u)!\,v]]$$
$$\text{IF length}(u) < 2 \text{ THEN EXIT FI};$$
$$v := \text{sbs}(u, 1, 1)!\,v\,;$$
$$u := \text{sbs}(u, 2, \text{“ ”})$$
$$OD;$$
$$\text{result} := u!\,v$$

The presentation of this program can be improved. A "WHILE" loop can be used. Also, we have chosen to stop the recursion when length(c) becomes less than 2. We might have asked for c of length zero. That poses no difficulty. If c is of length 1, sbs($c, 1, 1$) is identical to c, and sbs($c, 2, ""$) is empty. The corresponding recursive definition is

$$\text{rev}(c) \simeq \text{IF } c = \text{ "" THEN ""}$$
$$\text{ELSE rev(sbs}(c, 2, "")) ! \text{sbs}(c, 1, 1)$$
$$\text{FI}$$

The generalised form is the same, the recursive form not having changed. The termination is given by $u = ""$. We have then

$$\text{result} = \text{rev}(u) ! v$$

but as u is empty, rev(u) is also empty, and the concatenation reduces to v. Finally, we have

$$u := c \, ; v := "" \, ;$$
$$\text{WHILE } u \neq "" \text{ DO}$$
$$v := \text{sbs}(u, 1, 1) ! v \, ;$$
$$u := \text{sbs}(u, 2, "")$$
$$\text{OD;}$$
$$\text{result} := v$$

Several times people have remarked to me that this program cannot be right; a character is taken from the head of u and placed at the head of v. That is correct; and that is how the string is reversed. Imagine a queue, which people leave to form another; whoever is at the head of the first goes to the head of the second. If you were, at the start, at the head of the first queue, you would be the first to join the second, and one after another, people arriving later would go in front of you in the second queue, and you would be the last, ...

5.3.2   Expression in Base b

We return to the example of Section 2.8.2, which called for a great deal of work in the writing of the iterative program:

$$f(n, b) \simeq \text{IF } n = 0 \text{ THEN } 0$$
$$\text{ELSE } 10 * f(n : b, b) + \text{mod}(n, b)$$
$$\text{FI}$$

We must first generalise the form of the recursive definition. This time we shall deliberately make a bad generalisation. In

$$10 * f(n:b, b) + \text{mod}(n, b)$$

while retaining the factor 10 multiplying a function f of two arguments, we shall include the addition of an extra term:

$$\text{result} = 10 * f(u, w) + v$$

We have then the beginning of the program

```
DO
    [[result = 10 * f(u, w) + v]]
    IF u = 0 THEN [[result = 10 * f(u, w) + v AND u = 0
                        gives f(u, w) = 0
                        gives result = w]]
                    EXIT
FI
```

To proceed, we now take the value of $f(u, w)$ from the recursive definition; that is,

$$10 * f(u:w, w) + \text{mod}(u, w)$$

into the invariant for the loop

$$\begin{aligned} \text{result} &= 10 * (10 * f(u:w, w) + \text{mod}(u, w)) + v \\ &= 100 * f(u:w, w) + 10 * \text{mod}(u, w) + v \end{aligned}$$

This can never be expressed in the form

$$10 * f(\ldots$$

because of the factor 100 at the beginning. We have generalised badly. From $10 * f$ we reach $100 * f$, which shows that the multiplier of f is not constant. Conversely, from $f(u, w)$ we reach $f(u:w, w)$, which shows that the second argument of f is constant. It keeps its initial value, which is b. We thus have a second form of invariant:

$$\text{result} = s * f(u, b) + v$$

If $f(u, b)$ is replaced by its value as given by the recursive definition

$$10 * f(u:b, b) + \text{mod}(u, b)$$

we obtain

$$\begin{aligned} \text{result} &= s * (10 * f(u:b, b) + \text{mod}(u, b)) + v \\ &= (10 * s) * f(u:b, b) + (s * \text{mod}(u, b) + v) \end{aligned}$$

Thus we have the new values of s, u, v:

$$s, u, v := 10 * s, u : b, s * \mathrm{mod}(u, b) + v$$

Since the computation of v makes use of u and s, it must be done first, after which the order of computation of u and s is not significant. To start, s, u, v must be found such that

$$f(n, b) = s * f(u,b) + v$$

We take

$$s = 1 \qquad \text{(neutral element for multiplication)}$$
$$v = 0 \qquad \text{(neutral element for addition)}$$
$$u = n$$

Finally,

```
u := n; v := 0; s := 1;
WHILE u ≠ 0 DO
      v := s * mod(u, b) + v;
      s := 10 * s;
      u := u : b
OD;
result := v
```

This program can be slightly rearranged, noting that $u:b$ and $\mathrm{mod}(u, b)$ are both needed. It is worthwhile computing them together, using a supplementary variable r, in anticipation of the computation of u:

```
u := n; v := 0; s := 1;
WHILE u ≠ 0 DO
      u, r := div(u, b);
      v := s * r + v;
      s := 10 * s
OD;
result := v
```

This example illustrates two points:

–if the generalisation is badly done, the unification cannot be done, and study of the reason for this shows which quantity has in error been taken as constant. Correct it and start again.

–even after such an error and its correction, this method is clearly simpler than that of Chapter 4 and requires less imagination. Unfortunately, it is limited; it can only produce an iterative program with one loop (at least within the framework of what has been done here; see [ARK]).

5.4   Program Synthesis

We have insisted in Chapter 2 on the understanding that a recursive procedure is more a definition, in the limit axiomatic, than the description of a computing strategy. Now we can pass in a systematic way from this definition to an iterative procedure which describes the computing strategy. The example of the reversal of a string is especially typical. The recursive definition says what the reverse of a string is. The transformation of this definition into an iterative program shows us that the head of the given string must be taken and put at the head of the reverse string.

Thus by this transformation we have produced a new result—in this sense, it is legitimate to present the transformation of recursion into iteration as the true "synthesis" of a program. In the most general form, synthesising a program consists of producing a form suitable for the computer from a specification of the problem. In the present case, the recursive definition is the specification from which we start in order to produce the iterative program.

All the same, we still have to produce the recursive definition, which can be complex. The example presented here has something of a history. A team of research workers had implemented a program for the automatic synthesis of iterative programs starting from axiomatic specifications. On the basis of sound axioms, the program had synthesised Euclid's algorithm. I had written to them putting forward the following problem.

Two natural integers x and y, and a natural integer b greater than 1, are given. The integers x and y are written in the base b, each being represented by a string of characters:

$$x \text{ is written} \qquad c_1 c_2 c_3 \ldots c_p \qquad \text{with} \quad c_1 \neq 0 \quad \text{if} \quad x \neq 0$$

and similarly,

$$y \text{ is written} \qquad d_1 d_2 d_3 \ldots d_q$$

We form the longest common prefix (leftmost part) of these two strings. This prefix is empty if $c_1 \neq d_1$.

Otherwise, it is the longest string which is at the same time a leftmost part (that is to say a substring beginning with c_1 or d_1) of x and y. This string represents an integer z in base b. We define z to be zero if this string is empty. As an example, in base $b = 10$, the integers $x = 1357$, $y = 134$ have as longest common prefix $z = 13$.

The reply was the following: This problem is presented as one about natural numbers—given x, y, b find z. But in fact, it has to do with character strings. First, the representations of x and y in base b have to be found—this much can be synthesised from the axioms. Next, the longest common prefix has to be extracted from the two strings. This also can be synthesised. Finally, the integer represented in base b by this string has to be found.

The decision so to treat the problem was not made by the synthesising system but by its users. Now, perhaps surprisingly, this problem is indeed a problem about integers, with a very simple solution. Suppose first that $x = y$. In this case, the strings representing them are identical, and their longest common prefix is identical to these two strings, and thus $z = x = y$. If however the numbers are different, one of them is greater than the other. Suppose this is x. If x is very much greater than y, the string which represents it is longer, the common prefix is shorter than x, and so the rightmost figure of x is not in the prefix. It can be removed from x without this affecting the result. Let us call the required number lcpre(x, y). Taking the rightmost figure from x is the same as replacing x by $x : b$. Consequently, if x is "very much greater" than y

$$\text{lcpre}(x, y) = \text{lcpre}(x : b, y)$$

Suppose now that x is greater than y but that the strings representing these integers have the same length. The longest common prefix cannot include all the figures of x, because they are not all equal to those of y. There is at least one figure of x which is not in the longest common prefix, and since by definition the prefix is at the left, the rightmost figure of x is not in the prefix. Again,

$$\text{lcpre}(x, y) = \text{lcpre}(x : b, y)$$

From this we deduce the recursive definition

$$
\begin{aligned}
\text{lcpre}(x, y) \simeq \text{IF } &x = y \text{ THEN } x \\
&\text{ELSE IF } x > y \text{ THEN lcpre}(x : b, y) \\
&\qquad\qquad \text{ELSE lcpre}(x, y : b) \\
&\qquad\text{FI} \\
\text{FI}&
\end{aligned}
$$

A recursive definition of the greatest common divisor of two integers x and y is

$$
\begin{aligned}
\text{gcd}(x, y) \simeq \text{IF } &x = y \text{ THEN } x \\
&\text{ELSE IF } x > y \text{ THEN gcd}(x - y, y) \\
&\qquad\qquad \text{ELSE gcd}(x, y - x) \\
&\qquad\text{FI} \\
\text{FI}&
\end{aligned}
$$

The iterative forms of these two algorithms are easily obtained. We give a few details of the derivation of the iterative form of lcpre. We have to generalise the recursive definition, which is either

$$\text{lcpre}(x : b, y) \qquad \text{or} \qquad \text{lcpre}(x, y : b)$$

Suppose it is lcpre(u, v). If the generalisation has gone too far, the fact will be obvious. At the beginning, it is enough to take $u = x$, $v = y$. It is finished if $u = v$, and the result is u; otherwise we go to either lcpre($u : b, v$) or lcpre($u, v : b$) as the case may be:

$$u := x; v := y;$$
WHILE $u \neq v$ DO
$\qquad$ [[result $=$ lcpre(u, v)]]
$\qquad$ IF $u > v$ THEN $u := u : b$
$\qquad\qquad\qquad\qquad$ ELSE $v := v : b$
$\qquad$ FI
OD;
result $:= u$

For the greatest common divisor, the same method gives

$$u := x; v := y;$$
WHILE $u \neq v$ DO
$\qquad$ [[result $=$ gcd(u, v)]]
$\qquad$ IF $u > v$ THEN $u := u - v$
$\qquad\qquad\qquad\qquad$ ELSE $v := v - u$
$\qquad$ FI
OD;
result $:= u$

The moral of this story is not that program synthesis is prone to failure but rather that it is extremely sensitive to the manner in which the problem to be solved is specified. The same is true for the construction of iterative programs starting from recursive definitions. A slight change in the form of a recursive definition can considerably modify the process of transformation to the iterative program. For example,

$$f(x) \simeq \text{IF } x = 0 \text{ THEN } 0 \text{ ELSE } f(b(x)) \circ d(x) \text{ FI}$$

is easily transformed into an iterative program if the operation $\circ$ is permutable (Section 4.6.2), while

$$f(x) \simeq \text{IF } x = 0 \text{ THEN } x \text{ ELSE } f(b(x)) \circ d(x) \text{ FI}$$

cannot be so transformed. It is this which led Burstall and Darlington, after they had written their first system for automatic transformation [BD1], to write a second system to transform one recursive procedure into another, thus allowing the second, non-transformable, definition above to be changed into the first, transformable, version. We are a long way from understanding all the ramifications of this problem [BD2].

5.5   A Complex Recursion

It may happen that a very complicated recursive scheme will lead to a very simple iterative program. Here is an example of this. We are given an odd natural integer x. In base 2, its representation begins and ends with the bit 1. We form the sequence of bits obtained by reversing the representation of x. This too begins and ends with 1 and represents in binary an odd number y. The problem is, given x, to compute y: another integer problem passing for a problem with character strings. As above, it must have a direct solution. We go back to the method which was used for character strings. One bit of x is detached, for example, the rightmost bit $x = 2*x' + r$. The required number is obtained by writing r to the left of the mirror image of x'. For that we must know the order of magnitude of x, that is to say the power of 2, say h(x), such that

$$h(x) \leq x < 2*h(x)$$

If $x = 1$, h(x) = 1. We thus obtain a pair of recursive definitions:

$$h(x) \simeq \text{IF } x = 1 \text{ THEN } 1 \text{ ELSE } 2*h(x:2) \text{ FI}$$
$$m(x) \simeq \text{IF } x = 1 \text{ THEN } 1$$
$$\qquad \text{ELSE } r*h(x) + m(x')$$
$$\text{FI}$$
$$\text{WHERE } (x', r = \text{div}(x, 2))$$

The generalisation of this definition is very difficult. We would have to write

$$\text{result} = u*h(v) + m(w)$$

If m(w) is replaced by its value, we have

$$\text{result} = u*h(v) + r*h(w) + m(w')$$

and we can go no further, because the two functions h cannot be combined. A relation between v and w is thus needed. We shall therefore change the recursive definition to make this relation show itself. By the definition of h,

$$h(x) = 2*h(x:2) = h(x')$$

This gives for m(x)

$$2*r*h(x') + m(x')$$

To eliminate the leading factor 2, we could also change the definition of h, taking for this function the smallest power of 2 greater than x; thus,

$$h(x)/2 \leq x < h(x)$$

We also modify the terminating values

$$h(0) = 1 \qquad m(0) = 0$$

We obtain

$$h(x) \simeq \text{IF } x = 0 \text{ THEN } 1 \text{ ELSE } 2 * h(x:2) \text{ FI}$$
$$m(x) \simeq \text{IF } x = 0 \text{ THEN } 0$$
$$\text{ELSE } r * h(x') + m(x')$$
$$\text{FI}$$
$$\text{WHERE } (x', r = \text{div}(x, 2))$$

From here on the generalisation is easy:

$$\text{result} = u * h(v) + m(v)$$

It is finished if $v = 0$, for then $h(v) = 1$, $m(v) = 0$ giving result $= u$. If it is not finished, replacing $m(v)$ by its value

$$\text{result} = u * h(v) + r * h(v') + m(v')$$

But

$$h(v) = 2 * h(v:2) = 2 * h(v')$$

$$\text{result} = 2 * u * h(v') + r * h(v') + m(v')$$
$$= (2 * u + r) * h(v') + m(v')$$

Leaving for a moment the question of initialisation:

$$\text{WHILE } v \neq 0 \text{ DO}$$
$$v, r := \text{div}(v, 2);$$
$$u := 2 * u + r$$
$$\text{OD};$$
$$\text{result} := u$$

To start, we must express $m(x)$ in the form $u * h(v) + m(v)$ and then take $u = 0$ and $v = x$. We obtain finally,

$$u := 0; v := x;$$
$$\text{WHILE } v \neq 0 \text{ DO}$$
$$v, r := \text{div}(v, 2);$$
$$u := 2 * u + r$$
$$\text{OD};$$
$$\text{result} := u$$

This program was expected. The iterative strategy for the reversal of a string has been explained. The rightmost character of the given string is detached and placed at the right of the reverse string. The division by 2 removes the rightmost bit r of the given number, and the following instruction concatenates this bit r to the right of the reverse string. Knowing what we do, we might have written the program directly.

But what is surprising is first, the great complexity of the recursive definition—it needed the associated function $h(x)$. Next, the simplification which appeared in the course of the transformation. The function h occurs in the invariant for the loop but has disappeared from the final program. It is quite certain that the computation of $m(x)$ by two recursive procedures h and m is rather worse than direct iterative computation.

Nevertheless, such an example is relatively isolated. We do not know how to infer any general "law" about the relative complexities of a recursive definition and the associated iterative form. We shall see cases where a recursive definition leads to more rapid computation than any associated iterative form.

Finally, we note how easy it was to proceed from the second given recursive form. The reader will probably not have imagined the first form and will not have considered its transformation into the iterative form. We have said that the transformation is very sensitive to the recursive form from which it begins. We have deliberately shown here how to operate when a recursive form has been chosen which could not have been foreseen as not lending itself to the transformation. There again, the transformation mechanism itself gives some indications as to possible corrections.

5.6   Happy Numbers

We shall consider a problem on the fringes of brainteasers and recreational informatics to illustrate the power of the methods presented here.

Happy numbers are defined, as given below, by a variant of the Sieve of Eratosthenes. We know that this allows the generation of the sequence of prime numbers, when at each stage all the multiples of a prime n are deleted; the numbers remaining are the primes. Here is this variant.

We write down the natural integers starting with 2:

$$2 \quad 3 \quad \cancel{4} \quad 5 \quad \cancel{6} \quad 7 \quad \cancel{8} \quad 9 \quad \cancel{10} \quad 11 \quad \cancel{12} \quad 13 \quad \cancel{14} \quad 15 \quad \cancel{16} \quad \ldots$$

The first number in the sequence is "happy": $h[1] = 2$. We delete every second number from the sequence and so obtain the new sequence:

$$3 \quad 5 \quad 7 \quad \cancel{9} \quad 11 \quad 13 \quad \cancel{15} \quad 17 \quad 19 \quad \cancel{21} \quad 23 \quad 25 \quad \cancel{27} \quad 29 \quad 31 \quad \ldots$$

The first number in this sequence is happy: $h[2] = 3$. We delete every third number and obtain

$$5 \quad 7 \quad 11 \quad 13 \quad 17 \quad 19 \quad 23 \quad 25 \quad 29 \quad 31 \quad 35 \quad 37 \quad 41 \quad 43 \quad \ldots$$

Each time, the first number x in the sequence is happy, and every xth number is deleted to give the next sequence.

If we know the happy numbers from 1 to $i - 1$, can $h[i]$ be computed? For that, the different sequences must be defined correctly. We are not (yet) writing the program; we are looking for a recurrence rule to enable the happy numbers to be generated. Let $g(j, i)$ be the jth sequence, its terms being numbered from $i = 0$:

$$g(1, 0) = 2 \qquad g(1, 1) = 3 \qquad g(1, 2) = 4 \qquad \ldots \qquad g(1, i) = i + 2 \qquad \ldots$$
$$g(2, 0) = 3 \qquad g(2, 1) = 5 \qquad g(2, 2) = 7 \qquad \ldots \qquad g(2, i) = 2 * i + 3 \qquad \ldots$$
$$g(3, 0) = 5 \qquad g(3, 1) = 7 \qquad g(2, 2) = 11 \qquad \ldots$$

It is already difficult to give a rule for the sequence. It may be better to look for a way of passing from the sequence $g(j - 1,)$ to the sequence $g(j,)$.

By the definition of happy numbers, the first term in each sequence is happy, and so $h[j] = g(j, 0)$.

In passing from the sequence $g(j - 1,)$ to the sequence $g(j,)$, the numbers whose ranks are multiples of x in $g(j - 1,)$ are deleted, where

$$x = h[j - i] = g(j - 1, 0)$$

The elements

$$g(j - 1, x) \qquad g(j - 1, 2x) \qquad \ldots \qquad g(j - 1, kx) \ldots$$

are thus not copied into $g(j)$:

$$g(j, 0 : x - 2) = g(j - 1, 1 : x - 1)$$

(the elements of $g(j,)$ from 0 to $x - 2$ are those of $g(j - 1,)$ from 1 to $x - 1$).

The next group of elements of $g(j,)$ comes from $x - 1$ elements of $g(j - 1,)$, x itself being skipped:

$$g(j, x - 1 : 2x - 3) = g(j - 1, x + 1 : 2x - 1)$$

and more generally,

$$g(j, q * (x - 1) : x - 2 + q * (x - 1)) = g(j - 1, 1 + q * x : (x - 1) + q * x)$$

We can now look at each term of g:

$$g(j, q * (x - 1) + r) = g(j - 1, q * x + r + 1) \qquad 0 \le r < x - 1$$

We thus have a rule permitting the construction of the sequence $g(j, i)$ starting from $g(j - 1, i)$. Since the first sequence $g(1, i)$ is given by an explicit rule, $g(1, i) = i + 2$, we can compute all of the g sequence. It remains for $g(j, i)$ to be expressed in the form above, that is, to express i in the form

$$i = q * (x - 1) + r \qquad 0 \le r < x - 1$$

This shows that

$$q = i:(x - 1) \quad \text{and} \quad r = \text{mod}(i, x - 1)$$

Then,

$$q * x + r + 1 = q * (x - 1) + r + 1 + q = i + 1 + i:(x - 1)$$

We thus have the recursive definition of the function g:

$$g(j, i) \simeq \text{IF } j = 1 \text{ THEN } i + 2$$
$$\text{ELSE } g(j - 1, i + 1 + (i:(h[j - 1] - 1)))$$
$$\text{FI}$$
$$h[j] = g(j, 0)$$

Knowing the previous values of h, we can now begin the computation of $h[k]$. By the definition above,

$$h[k] = g(k, 0)$$

We have been brought back to the computation of a recursively defined function. We generalise the recursive definition. The required result is a function g of two arguments. We take as recurrence hypothesis

$$h[k] = g(j, i)$$

It is finished if the first argument has the value 1:

$$\text{IF } j = 1 \text{ THEN } [[h[k] = g(1, i) = i + 2]]$$

If not, the recursive definition gives the new values of i and j:

$$i := i + 1 + (i:(h[j - 1] - 1));$$
$$j := j - 1$$

At the start, $j = k$ and $i = 0$, from the definition of h.

We thus have a first form of the program which computes $h[k]$ (eventually this piece of program will have to be placed in a loop over k, but this is not urgent):

$$j := k; i := 0;$$
$$\text{WHILE } j \neq 1 \text{ DO}$$
$$i := i + 1 + (i:(h[j - 1] - 1));$$
$$j := j - 1$$
$$\text{OD};$$
$$h[k] := i + 2$$

When such a program has been obtained, before anything else its functioning must be examined to see whether any simplification is possible. As we have already indicated, we have not developed a computing strategy;

rather, we have deduced it from the recursive definition, and we do not yet know altogether what it is.

The loop above operates in the sense of decreasing j, thus of decreasing $h[j]$. In contrast, i increases. For the first values, i is less than $h[j-1]-1$, the integer division giving a zero quotient, and the loop can be simplified. We shall therefore cut the loop into two:

–in a first loop, all the values for which there is no need to carry out the division will be dealt with.

–the second loop will deal with those remaining to be computed. This will be based upon the following equivalence (which will be demonstrated later, but which will be assumed for the moment):

$$\text{WHILE } t \text{ DO } a \text{ OD} \simeq$$
$$\text{WHILE } t \text{ AND } u \text{ DO } a \text{ OD};$$
$$\text{WHILE } t \text{ DO } a \text{ OD}$$

(The first loop of the second form computes a while t and u are both true; it stops

–either because t has become false, when every case has been dealt with, u being true for all—here the second loop does nothing because at its entry t is false;

–or because although t is still true, u has become false; not all cases having been dealt with, the second loop completes the work.)

Applying this here, a new program is obtained:

$$j := k; i := 0;$$
$$\text{WHILE } j \neq 1 \text{ AND } i < h[j-1]-1 \text{ DO}$$
$$\qquad i := i + 1 + (i : (h[j-1]-1));$$
$$\qquad j := j - 1$$
$$\text{OD};$$
$$\text{WHILE } j \neq 1 \text{ DO}$$
$$\qquad i := i + 1 + (i : (h[j-1]-1));$$
$$\qquad j := j - 1$$
$$\text{OD};$$

The first loop simplifies because the quotient in it is zero:

$$j := k; i := 0;$$
$$\text{WHILE } j \neq 1 \text{ AND } i < h[j-1]-1 \text{ DO}$$
$$\qquad i := i + 1;$$
$$\qquad j := j - 1$$
$$\text{OD};$$
$$\dots$$

The sum $i + j$ is invariant through this loop. By the initialisation, its value is k. Thus the computation of i in the loop can be avoided by changing i into $k - j$ in the test and assigning the value of this expression to i at the exit from the loop:

$$j := k;$$
$$\text{WHILE } j \neq 1 \text{ AND } k - j < h[j - 1] - 1 \text{ DO}$$
$$j := j - 1$$
$$\text{OD};$$
$$i := k - j;$$

The test of the loop can be rearranged:

$$j := k;$$
$$\text{WHILE } j \neq 1 \text{ AND } k < h[j - 1] + j - 1 \text{ DO}$$
$$j := j - 1$$
$$\text{OD};$$
$$i := k - j;$$

$h[j]$ increases with j, and so also does $h[j] + j$; the effect of this loop is thus to find j such that

$$h[j - 1] + j - 1 \leq k < h[j] + j$$

Suppose we initialise the program by setting $h[1] = 2$ and $h[2] = 3$; k is then greater than or equal to 3. For $j = 2$,

$$h[j - 1] + j - 1 = h[1] + 1 = 3 \leq k$$

We are thus certain that the loop will stop before reaching $j = 1$, and the corresponding test can be omitted. In this way, we have a new piece of program, much more efficient than the previous version (it saves a good number of divisions):

$$j := k;$$
$$\text{WHILE } k < h[j - 1] + j - 1 \text{ DO } j := j - 1 \text{ OD};$$
$$i := j - k;$$
$$\text{WHILE } j \neq 1 \text{ DO}$$
$$i := i + 1 + (i : (h[j - 1] - 1));$$
$$j := j - 1$$
$$\text{OD};$$
$$h[k] := i + 2$$

If we now take the complete program for computing the sequence of happy numbers, we shall find a new type of simplification. We replace the first loop by a phrase describing its effect:

$$h[1] := 2 \,; h[2] := 3 \,; k := 3 \,;$$
$$\text{WHILE } k \leq m \text{ DO}$$
$$\quad \text{find the smallest } j \text{ such that } h[j] + j > k \,;$$
$$\quad i := j - k \,;$$
$$\quad \text{WHILE } j \neq 1 \text{ DO}$$
$$\qquad i := i + 1 + (i : (h[j-1] - 1)) \,;$$
$$\qquad j := j - 1$$
$$\quad \text{OD} \,;$$
$$\quad h[k] := i + 2$$
$$\quad k := k + 1$$
$$\text{OD}$$

Let us give a name p to the smallest j computed at the beginning of the loop. At the entry to the loop, its value is 2:

$$h[1] := 2 \,; h[2] := 3 \,; k := 3 \,; p := 2 \,;$$
$$\text{WHILE } k \leq m \text{ DO}$$
$$\quad [[p \text{ is the smallest } j \text{ such that } h[j] + j > k]]$$
$$\quad j := p \,; i := j - k \,;$$
$$\quad \ldots \ldots$$
$$\quad h[k] := i + 2 \,;$$
$$\quad [[p \text{ is the smallest } j \text{ such that } h[j] + j > k]]$$
$$\quad k := k + 1$$

We are no longer certain that p is the correct j, for k has been increased. If in fact k reaches the value $h[p] + p$ (it increases in steps of 1, so it cannot pass this value), then $p + 1$ and not p is the required smallest value. Thus we obtain the final program:

$$h[1] := 2 \,; h[2] := 3 \,; k := 3 \,; p := 2 \,;$$
$$\text{WHILE } k \leq m \text{ DO}$$
$$\quad j := p \,; i := k - p \,;$$
$$\quad \text{WHILE } j \neq 1 \text{ DO}$$
$$\qquad i := i + 1 + (i : (h[j-1] - 1)) \,;$$
$$\qquad j := j - 1$$
$$\quad \text{OD} \,;$$
$$\quad h[k] := i + 2$$
$$\quad k := k + 1$$
$$\quad \text{IF } k = h[p] + p \text{ THEN } p := p + 1 \text{ FI}$$
$$\text{OD}$$

In several courses for varied groups, I have asked the participants to solve this problem. I have never been offered this solution, which seems unobtainable by any other method. In contrast, I have obtained a different solution, given below without justification (remember that EXIT(2) means exit from two nested loops):

$$h[1] := 2; h[2] := 3; k := 3; n := 3;$$
```
WHILE k ≤ m DO
    DO
        n := n + 2; j := 2; z := (n − 1):2;
        DO
            IF z < h[j] THEN EXIT(2) FI;
            q, r := div(z − 1, h[j]);
            IF r = 0 THEN EXIT FI;
            z := z − q − 1; j := j + 1
        OD
    OD;
    h[k] := n
OD
```

This program, incidentally, generates the function g. We leave it as an exercise for the reader to show that $n = g(j, z − 1)$; but note that here j increases and so the recurrence between the g must be slightly modified.

This program is a lot more complex, requires an EXIT(2), and takes more computing time than the other one. Instead of operating directly in computing the next happy number, it sees whether the next odd number can be a happy one. We have compared the execution times of these two programs under the same conditions on the same microcomputer. The computation of the first 500 happy numbers took 78 seconds with the first program and 195 seconds with the second. Here again the problem of the inventor is shown up clearly. The first program cannot be devised directly; it can only be deduced from a good recursive definition.

The importance of the work of simplification of the raw form obtained by the transformation from recursive to iterative must be emphasised. We did not show this raw form in the k-loop; here it is:

$$h[1] := 2; h[2] := 3; k := 3;$$
```
WHILE k ≤ m DO
    j := k; i := 0;
    WHILE j ≠ 1 DO
        i := i + 1 + (i:(h[j − 1] − 1));
        j := j − 1
    OD;
    h[k] := i + 2;
    k := k + 1
OD
```

It differs from the better program only in the initialisation of *j* and *i* in the loop and in the manipulation of *p*. But on the same microcomputer, to compute the first 500 happy numbers, instead of 78 seconds it takes 475.

5.7   The Haming Sequence

From all of the foregoing there emerges a good method of working: given a problem to solve, first look for a recursive solution; then transform this into an iterative solution. The question is to know whether there is not a risk of a fruitless digression and whether it might not have been better to have gone immediately to the iterative solution. There is no simple answer to such a question. Some people are suspicious of recursion; perhaps because they have for too long used a language which makes it hardly practicable, their first thought is for iteration. Such was my own case, having begun programming in Fortran. If good results come from this, perhaps there is no need to look further. But there are, all the same, cases which, it seems to me, are much more quickly solved by means of recursion. The example of the happy numbers is one of those where I can hardly see how the solution can be achieved without the use of recursion. The following example is on the borderline; it has an easily obtained iterative solution [DI3] [GRI], and its recursive form is particularly unfavourable. Nevertheless, this form is instructive, and the work done in deriving it is about the same as that which gives the iterative form. There is no question of wasted time or useless work....

The sequence attributed to Haming is that of those numbers which have no prime factors other than 2, 3, and 5, arranged in increasing order. The sequence might also be defined as follows:

$h[1] = 1$ and for all   *i*:
$h[i] < h[i + 1]$
$2 * h[i]$ $3 * h[i]$ $5 * h[i]$ are elements of *h*

It is required to place the first *n* elements of *h* into an array $h[1:n]$.

If we suppose the array filled up to $i - 1$, we are left with the problem of computing the next element of *h*. We give an outline of the program. First we form the beginning of the sequence:

$h[1] = 1$ $h[2] = 2$ $h[3] = 3$ ... $h[6] = 6$ $h[7] = 8$

```
i := 1;
WHILE i ≤ 6 DO h[i] := i; i := i + 1 OD;
WHILE i ≤ n DO
    x := s(h[i − 1]);
    h[i] := x;
    i := i + 1
OD
```

The function $s(x)$ is that which gives the number immediately following x in the sequence:

$$x < s(x)$$
$$s(x) \text{ belongs to } h$$
$$\text{there is no element of } h \text{ between } x \text{ and } s(x)$$

The function $s(x)$ has been defined in Section 2.7:

$$s(x) \simeq \text{IF } x < 6 \text{ THEN } x + 1$$
$$\text{ELSE } \min(2 * s(x:2), 3 * s(x:3), 5 * s(x:5))$$
$$\text{FI}$$

To take this into the program above would lead to excessive computing times, the same operations being repeated over and over again. In fact, we replace s in the second loop of the program by its value:

WHILE $i \leq n$ DO
    $x := \min(2 * s(h[i - 1] : 2), 3 * s(h[i - 1] : 3), 5 * s(h[i - 1] : 5))$;
    $h[i] := x$;
    $i := i + 1$
OD

As before, we pretend to know the quantities that are difficult or tiresome to compute; these are $s(h[i - 1] : 2)$ and the two other $s(\ldots)$. We define then three indices $i2, i3, i5$ such that

$$s(h[i - 1] : 2) = h[i2] \quad \text{and similarly for 3 and 5:}$$

WHILE $i \leq n$ DO
    $[[h[ip] = s(h[i - 1] : p) \quad \text{for} \quad p = 2, 3, 5]]$
    $x := \min(2 * h[i2], 3 * h[i3], 5 * h[i5])$;
    $h[i] := x$;
    $i := i + 1$
OD

Having reached this point, we do not meet the invariant for the loop again; i has been modified, and the ip give the successors of $h[i - 2] : p$. We note that by the definition of x itself, using the function min,

$$x \leq p * h[ip]$$

If $x < h[ip] * p$, then $x : p < h[ip]$ and so ip still denotes the successor of $x : p$. Conversely, if $x = p * h[ip]$, then

$$h[ip] = x : p$$

and the successor of $x : p$ is now the next term in the sequence, $ip + 1$.

At the start, we need to give the ip for $i = 7$, which is simple. Thus we have a first program:

$$i := 1;$$
WHILE $i \leq 6$ DO $h[i] := i; i := i + 1$ OD;
$$i2 := 4; i3 := 3; i5 := 2;$$
WHILE $i \leq n$ DO
    $x := \min(2 * h[i2], 3 * h[i3], 5 * h[i5]);$
    $h[i] := x;$
    IF $x = 2 * h[i2]$ THEN $i2 := i2 + 1$ FI;
    IF $x = 3 * h[i3]$ THEN $i3 := i3 + 1$ FI;
    IF $x = 5 * h[i5]$ THEN $i5 := i5 + 1$ FI;
    $i := i + 1$
OD

There are too many expressions of the form $p * h[ip]$. Here again, we suppose them to be known, and we place their computation at an opportune point in the program (at initialisation and at each modification of ip). We thus obtain the final program, which differs from others already published only in the method by which it was obtained:

$$i := 1;$$
WHILE $i \leq 6$ DO $h[i] := i; i := i + 1$ OD;
$$i2 := 4; c2 := 8;$$
$$i3 := 3; c3 := 9;$$
$$i5 := 2; c5 := 10;$$
WHILE $i \leq n$ DO
    $x := \min(c2, c3, c5); h[i] := - x;$
    IF $x = c2$ THEN $i2 := i2 + 1; c2 := 2 * h[i2]$ FI;
    IF $x = c3$ THEN $i3 := i3 + 1; c3 := 3 * h[i3]$ FI;
    IF $x = c5$ THEN $i5 := i5 + 1; c5 := 5 * h[i5]$ FI;
    $i := i + 1$
OD

The examples presented here offer considerable variety of situations while by no means exhausting all possibilities. As we have already remarked, the important thing is not to have a list of program schemes which we know how to handle but to have a general method which can be adapted to each particular case. The examples given have no other purpose than to stimulate the imagination.

Exercises

E.5.1 By the method developed in this chapter, construct the iterative algorithm associated with the following recursive definitions (Section 2.2.2):

$-\exp1(x, n),$
$-\exp2(x, n),$
$-\exp3(x, n).$

E.5.2 Permutations by exchange of adjacent elements: Given a vector of n elements, of which no two are the same, it is required to construct the sequence of permutations of this vector in such a way that in passing from one permutation to the next only one pair of adjacent elements is interchanged.

Give a recursive definition of the function $s(i)$, which gives the rank of the element which is interchanged with its successor in order to pass from the permutation of rank i to that of rank $i + 1$. Hence, deduce an iterative program which prints all the permutations of a by exchange of adjacent elements.

E.5.3 Write the iterative program computing an approximation to the logarithm of x to the base b, starting from the recursive definition of Exercise E.2.2.

E.5.4 The same exercise for the division of reals, Exercise E.2.1.

E.5.5 Write three procedures for the comparison of character strings according to lexicographic order, for the operators $=, <, \le$. They are to call a single procedure for examining the strings (see Exercise E.2.9).

E.5.6 Write an iterative procedure which decides whether one word is an anagram of another, following Exercise E.2.10.

E.5.7 Write directly an iterative procedure to print the character string which represents an integer n in base b. Note that the number zero is printed 0, and this is the only case where the representation begins with the figure 0.

Work out the iterative procedure which follows from the recursive definition in Section 2.2.4.

Chapter 6

Regular Actions

6.1 Intuitive Presentation of the Idea of an Action

It was said in Chapter 1 that a program describes the sequence of transformations needed to pass from the given initial situation to the final situation through a series of intermediate situations. Situations have been described in terms of predicates connecting the variables of the program.

The program may be broken down into elementary actions each of which serves to take it from one given situation to the next, or, more generally, to each of its immediate successors. Then we can isolate those situations to be considered as the "pivots" of the program and say how the program passes from one of these to another. It is more usual to speak of "states" than of situations, but that is only a matter of terminology. We use either word indifferently.

Consider an example. Given two character strings a and b each terminating with the character $. It is required to determine whether they are equal "apart from blanks" (the "space" character being regarded as non-significant). This problem is not at all as innocent as it appears at first sight; I have set it as an exercise to many different groups. I have been given many complicated answers and as many false solutions; only the school teachers to whom I was presenting programming methods have given me the elegant solution which appears below. It is understood that no intermediate strings are to be generated (otherwise, one solution would be to copy a to a', suppressing the blanks, and then do the same for b, copied to b', and finally to see whether $a' = b'$).

Suppose part of the work has been done and that

$$sbs(a, 1, i) \simeq sbs(b, 1, j)$$

129

(the symbol $\simeq$ here denotes equality apart from blanks). Let us call this state G. We now look at the next character of a. If it is a space, there is still equality apart from blanks, and we are still in state G. Otherwise, if it is the symbol $, we have reached the end of the string a and are in a state which we call FA. Finally, if it is some other symbol, we have a significant character of a. We call this state CA. We have thus,

$$[[\text{sbs}(a, 1, i) \simeq \text{sbs}(b, 1, j)]]$$

G $=\doteq$ $i := i + 1$;
      IF sbs$(a, i, 1) = $ " " THEN G
               ELSE IF sbs$(a, i, 1) = $ "$" THEN FA
                                    ELSE CA
                              FI
    FI

In the state CA (there is a significant character in position i of the string a), we look at the next character of b. If this is a blank, we stay in the same state; if it is a $, a is not exhausted, but b is exhausted, the strings are not equal, and so the result is FALSE, state F. If, finally, there is a significant character in b, then either this is different from that of a, and we have reached state F, or we are again in state G:

$$[[\text{sbs}(a, 1, i - 1) \simeq \text{sbs}(b, 1, j) \text{ and sbs}(a, 1, i) \text{ is significant}]]$$

CA $==$ $j := j + 1$;
      IF sbs$(b, j, 1) = $ " " THEN CA
               ELSE IF sbs$(b, j, 1) = $ "$" THEN F
                                    ELSE
          IF sbs$(a, i, 1) \neq$ sbs$(b, j, 1)$ THEN F ELSE G FI
                              FI
    FI

Consider now the state FA. The string a has been examined completely. We must look at the next character of b. If it is a blank we are in the same state; $ gives equality of the two complete strings, apart from blanks—result TRUE, state T; any other character gives the result FALSE, state F:

$$[[a \simeq \text{sbs}(b, 1, j)]]$$

FA $==$ $j := j + 1$;
      IF sbs$(b, j, 1) = $ " " THEN FA
               ELSE IF sbs$(b, j, 1) = $ "$" THEN T ELSE F FI
    FI

It remains to initiate the process. At the beginning of the program, nothing is known of the two strings, so we can take $i = 0$ and $j = 0$. We call the program P:

$$F == i := 0; j := 0; G$$
$$F == \text{result} := \text{FALSE}; Z$$
$$T == \text{result} := \text{TRUE}; Z \qquad (Z \text{ is the action stopping the program})$$

The system comprising the six actions P, G, CA, FA, F, T completely defines the program.

6.2   Systems of Regular Actions

An action is a named sequence of instructions. The name of the sequence is itself an instruction. Thus the action named P is defined by a sequence of three instructions:

$$P == i := 0; j := 0; G$$

the third of which is represented by G, the name of an action.

With each action name is associated a state, denoted by the same name; this is the preassertion of its sequence of instructions. The preassertion must be true before any call of the corresponding action.

An action is called *regular* if the two following conditions are satisfied:

–Every execution of the action ends with a call of an action; thus for example an execution of FA ends with a call of FA or of T or of F, and there is no other possibility. (This is why the action Z has been introduced to terminate the program. An action name has to occupy the last position of the program.)

–Every call of an action in the body of the definition is in a terminal position; that is to say that it is not followed by any instruction in the body of the action.

We denote

by   a, a′, a″,...   a sequence of instructions not containing any calls of actions;
by   f, f′, f″,...   the bodies of regular actions
by   X, X′, X″,...   names of actions
by $t, t′, t″,...$ predicates

There is no other possible form for the body of an action than

$$f = a; X$$
$$f = a; \text{IF } t \text{ THEN } f' \text{ ELSE } f'' \text{ FI}$$

Later, this framework will be enlarged to admit the introduction of iterations. By this definition, it appears that the terminal position of a sequence of instructions is that of the last instruction of the sequence and that the terminal positions of a selection are those of each of its alternatives.

It should be noted also that this definition does not allow the use of a selection whose second alternative is empty. We cannot have

$$\text{IF } t \text{ THEN f FI}$$

This is because the body of an action cannot be empty; it contains at least a call of an action. In practice, particular attention must be paid to this point. In an earlier book [AR2], the second alternative was carefully and systematically written in every case; the effect on the programs was somewhat fattening, and what had been gained in security (there was no risk of forgetting the second alternative) was lost in legibility...

Let us consider an action which involves only one action name A. We show that such an action can always be expressed in the form

$$a; A$$

If A occurs only once, it is true by the definition given above, because there is no other possible form than

$$a; A$$

Otherwise, we proceed by recurrence on the number of selections. If the definition depends only on A and includes at least one selection, then it is of the form

$$f(A) = a; \text{IF } t \text{ THEN f}'(A) \text{ ELSE f}''(A) \text{ FI}$$

f' and f'' having one less selection than f. If f'(A) and f''(A) can be expressed in the form

$$f'(A) = a'; A \qquad \text{and} \qquad f''(A) = a''; A$$

then

$$f(A) = a; \text{IF } t \text{ THEN a}'; A \text{ ELSE a}''; A \text{ FI}$$

We can extract from the selection the common termination of the two alternatives

$$f(A) = a; \text{IF } t \text{ THEN a}' \text{ ELSE a}'' \text{ FI}; A$$

which establishes the proposition.

It is interesting to see how this last form is obtained. The call of A is suppressed in f(A), and A is concatenated to the end of the resultant form. We denote the empty instruction by EXIT(0). This is justified by the following considerations:

EXIT(p) means: exit from p loops and continue in sequence
(see EXIT(2) in Chapter 1).
EXIT(0) means, therefore, exit from no loops and continue in sequence,

thus do nothing and continue in sequence—it is the empty, or null, instruction.

To suppress A in f(A) is to replace A by the empty instruction, that is, by EXIT(0):

$$f(A) = f(EXIT(0)); A$$

The significance of this result must be understood. Because every action X in the body of a regular action is in a terminal position, the replacement of X by EXIT(0) has the effect of making the program leave the body of the action and continue in sequence.

This cannot be used when the body of the action contains calls of several different actions. Suppose for example we have an action body

$$f(A, B)$$

If A is replaced by the empty instruction EXIT(0), an execution of f terminating with a call of A will give rise to an exit from f before the continuation in sequence. To retrieve the call of A, it will be necessary to concatenate A to the end of f, as was done above. But as calls of B remain in f, B will no longer be in a terminal position.

The converse of the above relation (which is a particular case of simple expansion—see below) must be handled very carefully. At the present state of the discussion, a sequence

$$a; A$$

can be replaced by an expression of the form f(A) only if it contains no iteration. All the terminal positions of the sequence a must be filled with A. In particular,

$$IF\ t\ THEN\ a\ FI; A$$

has two terminal positions—that following a in the TRUE alternative of the selection and the empty instruction in the implicit FALSE alternative:

$$IF\ t\ THEN\ a\ FI; A = IF\ t\ THEN\ a; A\ ELSE\ A\ FI$$

6.3   Interpretation of a System of Regular Actions

6.3.1   Interpretation as Label

The definition of an action may be considered as a sequence of instructions marked by a label, the name of the action. An action name used as an instruction in the body of an action is interpreted as a branch to the corresponding label. Thus the action FA will be interpreted as

FA: $j := j + 1$;
    IF sbs$(b, j, 1)$ = " " THEN GOTO FA
          ELSE IF sbs$(b, j, 1)$ = "\$" THEN GOTO T
                        ELSE GOTO F
                FI
    FI

One of these actions is designated as the program, and its name is then the entry point of the program. The transcription of the system of actions of Section 6.1 into programs is then easy. The starting point is indicated by a suitable ordering of the sequence of actions. Thus for example we begin with P, which is the name of the program. As P calls only G, we write G after P:

P : $i := 0$; $j := 0$; GOTO G
G: $i := i + 1$;
    IF sbs$(a, i, 1)$ = " " THEN GOTO G
          ELSE IF sbs$(a, i, 1)$ = "\$" THEN GOTO FA
                        ELSE GOTO CA
                FI
    FI

The writing can clearly be simplified. If the action G is written immediately after P, then GOTO G is an empty instruction and can be omitted. Moreover, the conditional instructions can be unpacked since

              IF t THEN a; GOTO X
                  ELSE b
              FI

is equivalent to

              IF t THEN a; GOTO X FI;
              b

Using these two simplifications we obtain the following program:

          P: $i := 0$; $j := 0$;
          G: $i := i + 1$;
             IF sbs$(a, i, 1)$ = " " THEN GOTO G FI;
             IF sbs$(a, i, 1)$ = "\$" THEN GOTO FA FI;
        CA: $j := j + 1$;
             IF sbs$(b, j, 1)$ = " " THEN GOTO CA FI;
             IF sbs$(b, j, 1)$ = "\$" THEN GOTO F FI;
             IF sbs$(a, i, 1)$ $\neq$ sbs$(b, j, 1)$ THEN GOTO F FI;
             GOTO G;

FA : $j := j + 1$;
    IF sbs$(b, j, 1) =$ " " THEN GOTO FA FI ;
    IF sbs$(b, j, 1) =$ "\$" THEN GOTO T FI ;
    F : result := FALSE ; GOTO Z ;
    T : result := TRUE ;
    Z : continuation of program

We may well doubt the qualities of style evident in this program with all its GOTO statements, but it is only a first attempt. The interest of actions lies precisely in the possibilities for manipulation which they provide; this program will be tidied up in due course. For the moment, we have sought only to give a more concrete sense to the idea of an action.

We have said that attached to each action there is a preassertion or a state which characterises it. We come across these preassertions again here; each of them is true at the entry to the corresponding labelled sequence of instructions.

6.3.2 Decomposition of a Program into Actions

We now consider, conversely, a program with branching instructions. We suppose all the loops to have been broken down and replaced by sequences of instructions with tests and branches. If necessary, the first line will have been supplied with a label.

An action is associated with each label of the program. If a and b are sequences of instructions, and L a label, the sequence

$$a ; L : b$$

is replaced by

$$a ; GOTO L ; L : b$$

The program can then be cut up into labelled sequences of instructions, each such sequence having only one label declaration (at its beginning). In the body of each sequence, the instruction GOTO L is replaced more simply by L. A sequence

$$IF\ t\ THEN\ GOTO\ L\ FI ; b$$

where b represents the end of the action is replaced by

$$IF\ t\ THEN\ L\ ELSE\ b\ FI$$

These are the inverse transformations of those which were implemented in Section 6.3.1.

From this it follows that any program can be decomposed into a set of regular actions. Note that by the last transformation, L comes into a terminal position whatever the sequence b. Because a GOTO L is eventually added into the end of the action, the last instruction of every action is a GOTO, so that every terminal position becomes occupied by a a call of an action.

This also shows how every program can be reduced to an automaton whose states are the situations associated with the labels of the program.

This reduction might be seen as having a "de-structuring" effect. The loops are broken down, and the program turns into a quite intricate system of elementary actions. But this is too hasty a judgment. The same operation also "structures" the program by bringing out the important situations and the way these are interconnected. As, moreover, the actions are easy to handle, we have here an absolutely essential tool for the creation and transformation of programs.

6.3.3 Actions as Procedures without Parameters

An action may also be considered as a subroutine without either formal parameters or local variables. Each action works on the set of variables which are global to the system. To execute the program, the procedure whose name is the name of the program is called.

We take as self-evident the semantic equivalence of the two interpretations. An attempt to justify this might be made as follows. Consider an action as

$$P == i := 0; j := 0; G$$

The execution of P is as follows:

–initialisation of P by executing the instructions $i := 0; j := 0;$
–call of G
  –initialisation of G
  –execution of G
  –termination of G
–termination of P

If, then, G is executed correctly in this interpretation, the same will be true for P. By induction, the required equivalence can be deduced. It will be noted that this interpretation differs from the preceding one only in the existence of the termination of actions at the end of their execution. This is so because all the actions are in terminal positions.

It may appear strange, from the point of view of style, to base a method of programming on the use of procedures without either parameters or local variables, and so working systematically with side-effects. But first note that this is not entirely true. The side effects are inherent in the functions, for the reason that they introduce an order of computation into expressions which normally have none. They are not otherwise troublesome, as regards sub-programs, unless they are unforeseen. There is no question of that here, everything taking place precisely by action on the global variables. This is no more troublesome than the type of modification effected by assignment instructions.

We have associated a preassertion, or state, with each action. This preassertion is that of the parameterless procedure; how to associate a preassertion with a procedure is well known. There is no need to be concerned here with postassertions; every action terminating with a call of another action, its postassertion is the preassertion of this new action.

6.4   The Graph of a System of Actions

Consider a program defined by a system of regular actions. One of these actions is designated as the program. There is one particular action (which we usually denote by Z) which is the exit from the program and does not have to be defined in the system. Apart from this exit (or stopping) action, every action is defined once and once only in the system.

There is no ordering in the writing of the actions within the system; this is interpreted easily in the double framework presented in Section 6.3.3.

−as regards labelled sequences, each sequence nominates its successor explicitly, wherever it is written;

−as regards parameterless procedures, these are all defined at the same level (as in Algol 60, and not hierarchically as in Pascal) and without ordering among themselves.

We define a precedence relation between actions. Let X and Y be two actions. We say that X precedes Y if the execution of X calls Y or if Y has an occurrence in X. The graph of this relation has a unique entry point, which is the action whose name is that of the program, and a unique exit point, which is the exit action Z. The graph may contain circuits which correspond to the loops of the program.

We give in the figure on the next page the graph of the program of Section 6.1. The vertices G, CA, and FA are looped, corresponding to three loops in the program. There is also a loop from G to CA to G. Such a structure is apparent in the form of Section 6.2.2.

This graph is also the flowchart of the program with boxes and lozenges replaced by points, and so shows no more than the links between the labels.

We shall use this graph occasionally as a guide to the structuring of a program given as a system of regular actions.

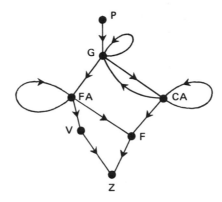

6.5   Substitution

6.5.1   The Copy Rule

Actions being parameterless procedures, we can apply the copy rule to them. There is no need of special precautions—because they have no formal parameters, the problem of parameters defined by name, reference, or value does not arise; and because there are no local variables, no conflict of names is possible. The copy rule for them can be stated thus:

The call of an action can always be replaced in a sequence of instructions by the body of that action.

This is quite simply the replacement of the name of an action by the definition of that action, which is known in mathematics as substitution—the name is replaced by the value.

As an example of this, in the action FA of Section 6.1, we replace V and F by their values

FA $==$ $j:=j+1$;
       IF sbs$(b, j, 1) =$ " " THEN FA
              ELSE
              IF sbs$(b, j, 1) =$ "\$" THEN result$:=$ TRUE; Z
                       ELSE   result$:=$ FALSE; Z
              FI
    FI

This can be rearranged. In anticipation of a semantic point which will be considered later,

        IF sbs$(b, j, 1) =$ "\$" THEN result$:=$ TRUE; Z
                     ELSE   result$:=$ FALSE; Z
    FI

is equivalent to

$$\text{IF sbs}(b, j, 1) = \text{``\$'' THEN result} := \text{TRUE}$$
$$\text{ELSE result} := \text{FALSE}$$
$$\text{FI}; Z$$

(Z, the common end of each alternative, has been removed from the selection). As each alternative is an assignment to result, this is

$$\text{result} := \text{IF sbs}(b, j, 1) = \text{``\$'' THEN TRUE ELSE FALSE FI}; Z$$

or, finally,

$$\text{result} := \text{sbs}(b, j, 1) = \text{``\$''}; Z$$

Substituting this in FA, we obtain a new form

$$\text{FA} == j := j + 1;$$
$$\text{IF sbs}(b, j, 1) = \text{`` '' THEN FA}$$
$$\text{ELSE result} := \text{sbs}(b, j, 1) = \text{``\$''}; Z$$
$$\text{FI}$$

Substitution will be used principally for two forms of simplification:

–Substitution allows two actions to be brought together, their common features and interdependence considered, and thus any possible simplification realised. We shall see several examples of this.

–A vertex of a graph with only one predecessor and only one successor is called a "transmitter". If a transmitter is copied into its predecessor, there is no longer a call on it, and it can be removed from the system. Moreover, as the transmitter has only one successor, this does not change the complexity of the system; one action name has been replaced by a sequence of instructions comprising one single name.

6.5.2   The Inverse Transformation

The inverse transformation is to remove a sequence of instructions from an action, give this sequence a name, and replace it in the sequence from which it has been taken by its new name. A new action has been created by the association of the sequence with the name given to it.

It is always necessary for the name which replaces the sequence to be in a terminal position. It comes to the same thing to say that the removed sequence must have been terminal or in a terminal position.

For example, in the action FA we can call the second alternative of the selection X

$$\text{FA} == j := j + 1; \text{IF sbs}(b, j, 1) = \text{`` '' THEN FA ELSE X FI}$$
$$\text{X} == \text{IF sbs}(b, j, 1) = \text{``\$'' THEN T ELSE F FI}$$

Similarly for CA:

$$CA == j := j + 1; \text{IF sbs}(b, j, 1) = \text{" " THEN CA ELSE Y FI}$$
$$Y == \text{IF sbs}(b, j, 1) = \text{"\$" THEN F ELSE U FI}$$
$$U == \text{IF sbs}(a, i, 1) \neq \text{sbs}(b, j, 1) \text{ THEN F ELSE G FI}$$

The interest of this transformation lies in the simplification because the same sequence of instructions occurring at several places afterwards occurs at only one place in the system; in a more fragmented form other comparisons are possible.

6.6 Transformation from Terminal Recursion to Iteration

6.6.1 A Particular Case

First, let us consider a regular recursive action, in the body of which only one other action is involved. This can be expressed simply by

$$A == f(A, B)$$

The action is recursive because A occurs in the body of the action, and the only other action whose name appears in the body of A is B. The recursion is called terminal because, the action being regular, all the occurrences of A are in terminal positions. Since there are two occurrences of actions in the body of A, there must be at least two terminal positions, and so at least one selection.

We shall explain this action in terms of branch instructions:

```
A: . . . . . .
        IF . . . THEN
        . . . . . .
              GOTO A
        . . . . . .
              GOTO B
        . . . . . .
        ELSE
        . . . . . .
              GOTO A
        . . . . . .
              GOTO B
   FI
```

The instructions GOTO A make this sequence of instructions into a program loop (indicated by the loop on A in the associated graph). The instructions

GOTO B cause exit from the loop in order to proceed with B. We could say that they effect the EXIT instruction from the loop which is followed by a branch to B.

We write the sequence of instructions in a (formal) loop:

$$\text{DO } f(\ldots) \text{ OD}; \text{GOTO B}$$

The instruction GOTO A must be replaced by an instruction causing the looping, an instruction leading to OD. Now we have seen that the replacement of an action name by the empty instruction EXIT(0) causes execution to continue in sequence after f, in this case therefore to pass to OD. We have thus the following equivalence (for greater clarity, f where A is replaced by EXIT(0) and B by EXIT is denoted by f[A → EXIT(0); B → EXIT]):

$$A == f(A, B) =$$
$$A == \text{DO}$$
$$\qquad f[A \to \text{EXIT}(0), B \to \text{EXIT}]$$
$$\text{OD};$$
$$B$$

Thus a recursive action on A has been replaced by an iterative action. This is an absolutely fundamental operation, at the heart of the problem of the elimination of branch instructions, which can always be replaced by calls of recursive procedures [FLK]. By way of example, we apply this result to the definition of CA (Section 6.1). This action contains a terminal recursive call of CA, and calls of F and G. Thus, apparently we have not the desired conditions. But all these latter calls are in one and the same alternative. Let us call this X; by the inverse of substitution,

$$CA == j := j + 1;$$
$$\qquad \text{IF sbs}(b, j, 1) = \text{“ ” THEN CA ELSE X FI}$$
$$X == \text{IF sbs}(b, j, 1) = \text{“\$” THEN F}$$
$$\qquad\qquad \text{ELSE   IF sbs}(a, i, 1) \neq \text{sbs}(b, j, 1) \text{ THEN F}$$
$$\qquad\qquad\qquad\qquad\qquad\qquad\qquad\qquad \text{ELSE G}$$
$$\qquad\qquad\qquad\qquad \text{FI}$$
$$\qquad \text{FI}$$

Now CA satisfies the hypotheses considered here. We replace CA by EXIT(0) and X by EXIT, obtaining

$$CA == \text{DO}$$
$$\qquad j := j + 1;$$
$$\qquad \text{IF sbs}(b, j, 1) = \text{“ ” THEN EXIT}(0) \text{ ELSE EXIT FI}$$
$$\text{OD};$$
$$X$$

We can now reverse the selection by negating the test condition interchanging the alternatives, and then replacing EXIT(0), the empty instruction, by nothing:

$$DO$$
$$j := j + 1;$$
$$\text{IF } sbs(b, j, 1) \neq \text{“”} \text{ THEN EXIT ELSE FI}$$
$$OD$$

We suppress the ELSE with its empty clause:

$$CA == DO$$
$$j := j + 1;$$
$$\text{IF } sbs(b, j, 1) \neq \text{“”} \text{ THEN EXIT FI}$$
$$OD;$$
$$X$$

We shall often use this transformation.

6.6.2   The General Case

Suppose now that the definition of A contains calls of several actions with different names. The recursive call is again an iteration because it is in a terminal position. If in

$$A == f(A, B, \ldots, X)$$

A is replaced by EXIT(0), there will be continuation in sequence after f and iteration if f is enclosed in the parentheses DO...OD.

But it is no longer possible to replace any of B,...,X by EXIT, for all will continue in sequence after the loop and not go to B,...,X. We shall make use of a conventional notation. In the loop we shall denote by B + 1 a call of B modified to represent: exit from one loop and go to B. More generally,

$$B + p \text{ signifies: exit from } p \text{ loops and go to B}$$

(or call B, according to the interpretation).
With this notation,

$$A == f(A, B, \ldots, X) =$$
$$A == DO$$
$$f[A \to \text{EXIT}(0), B \to B + 1, \ldots, X \to X + 1]$$
$$OD$$

This requires the definition of regular actions to be generalised. Thus we say that if

$$A == f(A, B, \ldots, X)$$

is a regular action, then

$$A == DO\ f(EXIT(0), B + 1, \ldots, X + 1)\ OD$$

is also a regular action.

Substitution must be generalised. Consider the replacement of X by its value

$$X == g(A, B, \ldots)$$

in an occurrence X + p.

The notation X + p can be interpreted either as "exit from p loops and execute X" or as "execute X and exit from p loops". In this second interpretation, X is executed at the level at which it is placed, and each of its exits must be associated with the leaving of p loops. In other words, each of the exits must be incremented by p:

$$g(A, B, \ldots) + p = g(A + p, B + p, \ldots)$$

In a regular action, any iteration is at a terminal position. This is a consequence of the mechanism for the introduction of iterations. When a recursive action is made iterative, the body is formed of a single iteration in terminal position since there is no instruction after the iteration. (This result is apparently contradicted by the form of Section 6.6.1; it is a matter of absorption, a point to which we shall return.) To introduce an iteration into an action, we might also operate by substitution, replacing an action name by the action body. But the substitution takes place at a terminal position, thus confirming the result.

Let us take an example. Suppose the system has two regular actions A and B, where A is the name of the program and Z the exit action, and that A, B, Z occur in both f and g:

$$A == f(A, B, Z)$$
$$B == g(A, B, Z)$$

We make B iterative:

$$B == DO\ g(A + 1, EXIT(0), Z + 1)\ OD$$

Replacing B in A,

$$A == f(A, DO\ g(A + 1, EXIT(0), Z + 1)\ OD, Z)$$

To make A iterative, A must be replaced by EXIT(0). But A has an occurrence A + 1. Thus some meaning must be given to EXIT(0) + 1. We have seen that to make A iterative, the calls of A have to be changed into instructions continuing in sequence after f. For A in terminal position, the replacement by the empty instruction EXIT(0) is enough. But A + 1 is in an iteration and in terminal position. To leave f, it is sufficient to leave the iteration and continue in sequence. Thus A + 1 must be replaced by EXIT. More generally, A + p is in p loops of which the outermost is in terminal position. It is sufficient to exit from the p loops. Thus A + p is replaced by EXIT(p). We can express this by the rule

$$\text{EXIT}(0) + p = \text{EXIT}(p)$$

With this, the iterative form of A is

$$A == \text{DO } f(\text{EXIT}(0), \text{DO } g(\text{EXIT}, \text{EXIT}(0), Z + 2) \text{ OD}, Z + 1) \text{ OD}$$

This action depends only on Z. We can replace Z by EXIT(0), giving EXIT for Z + 1 and EXIT(2) for Z + 2, and then copy Z in sequence at the end (Section 6.2):

$$A == \text{DO } f(\text{EXIT}(0), \text{DO } g(\text{EXIT}, \text{EXIT}(0), \text{EXIT}(2)) \text{ OD}, \text{EXIT}) \text{ OD}; Z$$

We now have an action comprising one iteration, which no longer has calls of actions, followed by the call of the final action Z. We can suppress Z and call this the "resolved form" of the program, a form which no longer has calls of actions.

6.7   The Structure of a System of Regular Actions

6.7.1   The General Case

Consider a program X1 given by a system of regular actions $X1, X2, \ldots, Xn$, which we represent symbolically in the most general form:

$$Xi == f_i(X1, X2, \ldots, Xn, Z)$$

It may be that one of the actions Xj other than X1 (which is the program itself and so cannot be eliminated from the system) contains no call of Xj, or, in other words, is not recursive. In this case, f_j can be copied in the place of Xj in the bodies of the other actions, and so Xj will be eliminated as no calls of it remain. This will reduce the depth of the system.

If now all the actions are recursive, then any one of them, say Xi, can be chosen arbitrarily and made iterative:

$$Xi == DO \, f_i[Xi \to EXIT(0), Xj \to Xj + 1] \, OD$$

Now Xi no longer contains calls of Xi. Thus, Xi can be substituted in the other actions and its definition suppressed. In this way and in every case, the depth of the system is reduced, and after a finite number of steps it will be reduced to a single action

$$X1 == f'(Z)$$

By the expansion of Section 6.2, this becomes

$$X1 == f'(EXIT(0)); Z$$

Z being the action which stops the program. In f' there are no calls of actions but only instructions of the language. We have a structured form of the program equivalent to the system of regular actions. Thus, the required program is

$$f'(EXIT(0))$$

Here is a very powerful tool. Given a program with branch instructions, we can transform it into a system of regular actions (Section 6.3.2) and then resolve this system into a program comprising only selections, iterations, and loop exits, but no GOTO instructions. The form of the program depends on the order of the transformations effected, but the history of the computation (sequence of assignments and tests) is not in any way affected by that order. This structural process has been amply studied in the literature [LE2][KOS]. Programs written only with these instructions are called RE*n*, the index *p* of the EXIT(*p*) instructions being limited to *n*. The reader is referred to the cited articles and to the present author's previous work [AR2] for the study of these questions. Here we have no need of anything more than RE2.

6.7.2   *Example: Finding a Substring of a String*

We are given the function pos(*a*, 1, *b*) whose value is 0 if the string *b* does not occur as a substring in *a*, and *i* if

$$sbs(a, i, length(b)) = b \qquad 1 \le i \le length(a) - length(b) + 1$$

We shall write the piece of program which computes pos(*a*, 1, *b*).

We begin with the following general state. The first j characters of b have been found in a substring of a beginning at i:

$[[\text{sbs}(a, i, j) = \text{sbs}(b, 1, j)]]$
$G \ == \ \text{IF } j = \text{length}(b) \text{ THEN } Z$
$\qquad\qquad\qquad \text{ELSE} \quad j := j + 1;$
$\qquad\qquad\qquad\qquad \text{IF } \text{sbs}(a, i + j - 1, 1) = \text{sbs}(b, j, 1) \text{ THEN } G$
$\qquad\qquad\qquad\qquad\qquad\qquad\qquad\qquad\qquad\qquad\qquad\qquad \text{ELSE} \quad F$
$\qquad\qquad\qquad\qquad \text{FI}$
$\qquad \text{FI}$
$F \ == \ i := i + 1;$
$\qquad \text{IF } i > \text{length}(a) - \text{length}(b) + 1 \text{ THEN } i := 0; Z$
$\qquad\qquad\qquad\qquad\qquad\qquad\qquad\qquad\qquad\qquad \text{ELSE} \quad j := 0; G$
$\qquad \text{FI}$
$P \ == \ i := 0; F$

F corresponds to the state: there is no occurrence of b beginning in $\text{sbs}(a, 1, i)$.

The graph of this program shows that there is one loop on G, included in a loop on F.

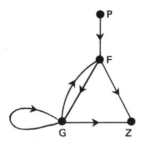

We begin by making G iterative. Z and F are incremented by 1; G is replaced by EXIT(0). The first alternative of the second selection becomes empty; some simplification is gained by inverting the selection by negating the test condition.

$\qquad G \ == \ \text{DO}$
$\qquad\qquad\qquad \text{IF } j = \text{length}(b) \text{ THEN } Z + 1$
$\qquad\qquad\qquad\qquad\qquad\qquad \text{ELSE} \quad j := j + 1;$
$\qquad\qquad\qquad\qquad\qquad\qquad\qquad \text{IF } \text{sbs}(a, i + j - 1, 1) \neq \text{sbs}(b, j, 1)$
$\qquad\qquad\qquad\qquad\qquad\qquad\qquad\qquad \text{THEN } F + 1$
$\qquad\qquad\qquad\qquad\qquad\qquad\qquad \text{FI}$
$\qquad\qquad\qquad \text{FI}$
$\qquad\qquad \text{OD}$

We can now take G into F:

F == i:= i + 1;
  IF i > length(a) − length(b) + 1
    THEN i:= 0; Z
    ELSE j:= 0;
      DO
        IF j = length(b)
          THEN Z + 1
          ELSE j:= j + 1;
            IF sbs(a, i + j − 1, 1) ≠ sbs(b, j, 1)
              THEN F + 1
            FI
        FI
      OD
  FI

Only F and Z occur in F. The replacement of F by EXIT(0) causes the appearance of EXIT(1) = EXIT; Z + 1 becomes Z + 2. Now we can take the iterative F into P:

P == i:= 0;
  DO
    i:= i + 1;
    IF i > length(a) − length(b) + 1
      THEN i:= 0; Z + 1
      ELSE j:= 0;
        DO
          IF j = length(b)
            THEN Z + 2
            ELSE j:= j + 1;
              IF sbs(a, i + j − 1, 1) ≠ sbs(b, j, 1)
                THEN EXIT
              FI
          FI
        OD
    FI
  OD

Now we have an action P = = f(Z). We replace Z by EXIT(0); this causes EXIT to appear in the place of Z + 1 and EXIT(2) in the place of Z + 2. The instruction

$$\text{IF } t \text{ THEN a; EXIT}(p) \text{ ELSE b FI}$$

can be rewritten as

$$\text{IF } t \text{ THEN } a; \text{EXIT}(p) \text{ FI}; b$$

to reduce nesting of the selection instructions. We thus obtain a first form of the program:

```
i := 0;
DO
  i := i + 1;
  IF i > length(a) − length(b) + 1 THEN i := 0; EXIT FI;
  j := 0;
  DO
    IF j = length(b) THEN EXIT(2) FI;
    j := j + 1;
    IF sbs(a, i + j − 1, 1) ≠ sbs(b, j, 1) THEN EXIT FI
  OD
OD
```

We have here a program with no surprises; in the outer loop, i runs from 1 to $\text{length}(a) - \text{length}(b) + 1$, and for each i the inner loop determines whether the successive characters of a and b coincide.

But we can resolve the system in another way. The action F is not recursive. Thus it can be eliminated by writing it out in P and in G. First see what happens to P:

```
P == i := 0;
     i := i + 1;
     IF i > length(a) − length(b) + 1 THEN i := 0; Z
                                       ELSE j := 0; G
     FI
```

The sequence $i := 0; i := i + 1$ can be simplified to $i := 1$. With this value of i $(i = 1)$,

$$\text{IF } i > \text{length}(a) - \text{length}(b) + 1$$

becomes

$$\text{IF } 1 > \text{length}(a) - \text{length}(b) + 1 \qquad \text{or} \qquad \text{IF length}(b) > \text{length}(a)$$

To simplify things, we suppose that b is not longer than a. Then this condition is false, and the selection is not needed, only the second of its alternatives being accessible. (For these semantic transformations, see below.)

There remains only

$$P == i := 1; j := 0; G$$

We shall now see what becomes of G after substitution of F. As above, we invert the test on the comparison of characters:

G == IF $j = \text{length}(b)$ THEN Z
                ELSE $j := j + 1$;
                            IF $\text{sbs}(a, i + j - 1, 1) \neq \text{sbs}(b, j, 1)$
                                    THEN $i := i + 1$;
                                            IF $i > \text{length}(a) - \text{length}(b) + 1$
                                                    THEN $i := 0$; Z
                                                    ELSE $j := 0$; G
                                            FI
                                    ELSE G
                            FI
        FI

We make G iterative, replacing G by EXIT(0), the empty instruction, and Z by Z + 1. We then copy G into P:

P == $i := 1$; $j := 0$;
    DO
            IF $j = \text{length}(b)$ THEN Z + 1
                            ELSE $j := j + 1$:
                                    IF $\text{sbs}(a, i + j - 1, 1) \neq \text{sbs}(b, j, 1)$
                                            THEN $i := i + 1$;
                                                    IF $i > \text{length}(a) - \text{length}(b) + 1$
                                                            THEN $i := 0$; Z + 1
                                                            ELSE $j := 0$;
                                                    FI
                                            ELSE EXIT(0)
                                    FI
            FI
    OD

Now, P depends only on Z. We can replace Z by EXIT(0) and then Z + 1 by EXIT. We can unpack the selections by the transformation already mentioned:

$i := 1$; $j := 0$;
DO
    IF $j = \text{length}(b)$ THEN EXIT FI;
    $j := j + 1$;
    IF $\text{sbs}(a, i + j - 1, 1) \neq \text{sbs}(b, j, 1)$
            THEN $i := i + 1$;
                    IF $i > \text{length}(a) - \text{length}(b) + 1$ THEN $i := 0$; EXIT FI;
                    $j := 0$
    FI
OD

We have a new program equivalent to the preceding one (when the string *a* is at least as long as the string *b*), but unlike the preceding program it contains only a single loop. This difference of structure is remarkable, and it should be considered carefully by the reader. It does not correspond with a change of strategy. The two programs give rise to the same sequence of operations (apart from the initial test on *i*). It is simply that they are not organised in the same way. This means that the structure of a program (number of loops and nesting of loops) is not an essential characteristic. We have strongly insisted on this in the previous book [AR2], because at that time it was a new phenomenon which deserved comment. We believe that today the question does not arise. There is hardly any reason to prefer one form to the other. If the complexity of a program is measured by the number of its loops, the second program is preferable to the first. But its strategy is less clear, and the first is easier to present in terms of simple actions (as has been done above).

The most important conclusion is that the best form is that which does not raise problems, that is to say the form of the system of actions. This is the most primitive of these forms, and the others can be deduced from it. It is the clearest, for it shows up the automaton underlying the program, with its three associated states as preassertions to the actions P, G, F.

6.8   Identification

Consider two regular actions:

$$X1 == f1(X1, X2, \ldots, Xn, Z)$$
$$X2 == f2(X1, X2, \ldots, Xn, Z)$$

which differ only in the occurrences of the actions X1 and X2. They contain the same instructions and the same tests; they have the same calls of actions other than X1 and X2. Their executions are the same except that some calls of X1 in one are calls of X2 in the other and vice versa.

More precisely, the two actions are the same if X2 is changed to X1 throughout:

$$f1[X2 \rightarrow X1] = f2[X2 \rightarrow X1]$$

The effects of the two actions cannot be distinguished. Any call of either X1 or X2 causes the execution of the same sequence of instructions and tests, with the same exits to the outside or the same call of their common sequence. We regard these two actions as identical.

We replace X2 by X1 in every call in the system (and not only in X1), then we suppress the action X2. We thus obtain a new system which is equivalent to the preceding one. This can modify the preassertion of X1:

$$[[P1]] X1 == f1(X1, X2, \ldots)$$
$$[[P2]] X2 == f2(X1, X2, \ldots)$$

After changing X2 into X1 and identifying X2 with X1, we have

$$[[P1 \text{ or } P2]] X1 == f1(X1, X1, \ldots)$$

This transformation is very important for the simplification of programs, but it can in general be used only after semantic transformations (see Chapter 7).

We shall apply it to the problem dealt with at the beginning of the present chapter, the comparison of strings apart from blanks. The actions CA and FA look somewhat alike. We shall enhance their resemblance and then make them identical. First we shall rewrite CA, dividing it into two actions as was done in Section 6.6.1:

CA == $j := j + 1$;
     IF sbs$(b, j, 1) = $ " " THEN CA ELSE X FI
  X == IF sbs$(b, j, 1) = $ "\$" THEN F
                ELSE   IF sbs$(a, i, 1) \neq$ sbs$(b, j, 1)$ THEN F
                                     ELSE G
                    FI
     FI

Similarly for FA:

FA == $j := j + 1$;
        IF sbs$(b, j, 1) = $ " " THEN FA ELSE Y FI
   Y == IF sbs$(b, j, 1) = $ "\$" THEN T ELSE F FI

A preassertion of CA is

$$sbs(a, i, 1) \neq \text{"\$"}$$

For FA

$$sbs(a, i, 1) = \text{"\$"}$$

We define a new action:

W == IF sbs$(a, i, 1) = $ "\$" THEN Y ELSE X FI

As the leading instructions of CA and FA act only on j and do not modify i, we can write

[[sbs$(a, i, 1) \neq$ "\$"]]
CA == $j := j + 1$;
      IF sbs$(b, j, 1) = $ " " THEN CA
            ELSE [[sbs$(a, i, 1) \neq$ "\$"]] X FI

With this assertion, X can be replaced by W:

[[sbs($a, i, 1$) ≠ "\$"]] W == IF sbs($a, i, 1$) = "\$" THEN Y ELSE X FI

This in fact reduces to X. Similarly, Y can be replaced by W. We obtain thus

$$CA == j := j + 1;$$
$$\quad\quad IF\ sbs(b, j, 1) = "\ "\ THEN\ CA\ ELSE\ W\ FI$$
$$FA == j := j + 1;$$
$$\quad\quad IF\ sbs(b, j, 1) = "\ "\ THEN\ FA\ ELSE\ W\ FI$$
$$W == IF\ sbs(a, i, 1) = "\$"\ THEN\ Y\ ELSE\ X\ FI$$

If in FA we change FA into CA, the bodies of the two actions become identical. We can thus identify both actions with CA and suppress FA. The new preassertion of CA is

$$sbs(a, i, 1) = "\$" \quad\quad or \quad\quad sbs(a, i, 1) \neq "\$"$$

which is always true. We replace FA by CA in G:

G == $i := i + 1$;
    IF sbs($a, i, 1$) = " " THEN G
                  ELSE IF sbs($a, i, 1$) = "\$" THEN CA ELSE CA FI
    FI

After simplification we obtain the new program

$$G == i := i + 1;$$
$$\quad\quad IF\ sbs(a, i, 1) = "\ "\ THEN\ G\ ELSE\ CA\ FI$$
$$CA == j := j + 1;$$
$$\quad\quad IF\ sbs(b, j, 1) = "\ "\ THEN\ CA\ ELSE\ W\ FI$$
$$W == IF\ sbs(a, i, 1) = "\$"\ THEN\ Y\ ELSE\ X\ FI$$
$$X == IF\ sbs(b, j, 1) = "\$"\ THEN\ F$$
$$\quad\quad\quad\quad\quad ELSE\quad IF\ sbs(a, i, 1) \neq sbs(b, j, 1)\ THEN\ F$$
$$\quad\quad\quad\quad\quad\quad\quad\quad\quad\quad\quad\quad\quad\quad ELSE\ G$$
$$\quad\quad\quad\quad\quad\quad\quad\quad FI$$
$$\quad\quad FI$$
$$Y == IF\ sbs(b, j, 1) = "\$"\ THEN\ T\ ELSE\ F\ FI$$
$$P == i := 0;\ j := 0;\ G$$
$$F == result := FALSE;\ Z$$
$$T == result := TRUE;\ Z$$

We make G iterative:

$$G == DO$$
$$\quad\quad\quad\quad i := i + 1;$$
$$\quad\quad\quad\quad IF\ sbs(a, i, 1) \neq "\ "\ THEN\ EXIT\ FI$$
$$\quad\quad\quad OD;$$
$$\quad\quad\quad CA$$

That is,

$$G == \text{REPEAT } i := i + 1 \text{ UNTIL } \text{sbs}(a, i, 1) \neq \text{“ ”}; \text{CA}$$

Similarly,

$$CA == \text{REPEAT } j := j + 1 \text{ UNTIL } \text{sbs}(b, j, 1) \neq \text{“ ”}; W$$

We take CA into G and suppress its definition:

$$\begin{aligned} G == \ &\text{REPEAT } i := i + 1 \text{ UNTIL } \text{sbs}(a, i, 1) \neq \text{“ ”}; \\ &\text{REPEAT } j := j + 1 \text{ UNTIL } \text{sbs}(b, j, 1) \neq \text{“ ”}; \\ &W \end{aligned}$$

Thus G has a symmetrical form of two similar actions, one acting on a, the other on b. This is not surprising; the problem as set gave identical roles to the two strings. We shall have to maintain this symmetry in W. We take X and Y into W:

$$\begin{aligned} W == \ &\text{IF } \text{sbs}(a, i, 1) = \text{“\$” THEN IF } \text{sbs}(b, j, 1) = \text{“\$” THEN T ELSE F FI} \\ &\quad\quad \text{ELSE   IF } \text{sbs}(b, j, 1) = \text{“\$” THEN F} \\ &\quad\quad\quad\quad\quad\quad\quad\quad\quad\quad \text{ELSE} \\ &\quad \text{IF } \text{sbs}(a, i, 1) \neq \text{sbs}(b, j, 1) \text{ THEN F ELSE G FI} \\ &\quad\quad\quad\quad\quad \text{FI} \\ &\text{FI} \end{aligned}$$

We shall regroup the tests, after listing the possible cases:

$\text{sbs}(a, i, 1) = \text{“\$”}$	$\text{sbs}(b, j, 1) = \text{“\$”}$	T
$\text{sbs}(a, i, 1) = \text{“\$”}$	$\text{sbs}(b, j, 1) \neq \text{“\$”}$	F
$\text{sbs}(a, i, 1) \neq \text{“\$”}$	$\text{sbs}(b, j, 1) = \text{“\$”}$	F
$\text{sbs}(a, i, 1) \neq \text{“\$”}$	$\text{sbs}(b, j, 1) \neq \text{“\$”}$	comparison

Thus we can rewrite W:

$$\begin{aligned} W == \ &\text{IF } \text{sbs}(a, i, 1) = \text{“\$” AND } \text{sbs}(b, j, 1) = \text{“\$”} \\ &\text{THEN T} \\ &\text{ELSE   IF } \text{sbs}(a, i, 1) = \text{“\$” OR } \text{sbs}(b, j, 1) = \text{“\$”} \\ &\quad\quad\quad \text{THEN F} \\ &\quad\quad \text{ELSE IF } \text{sbs}(a, i, 1) \neq \text{sbs}(b, j, 1) \\ &\quad\quad\quad\quad\quad\quad\quad\quad \text{THEN F ELSE G FI} \\ &\quad\quad\quad\quad \text{FI} \\ &\text{FI} \end{aligned}$$

It is now easy to proceed. We replace F and T by their values, which brings in Z as the only variable other than G in W. We take W into G and eliminate this action, which is no longer called. The action G is recursive; it is made iterative:

G == DO
          REPEAT $i := i + 1$ UNTIL sbs$(a, i, 1) \neq$ " ";
          REPEAT $j := j + 1$ UNTIL sbs$(b, j, 1) \neq$ " ";
          IF sbs$(a, i, 1) =$ "\$" AND sbs$(b, j, 1) =$ "\$"
             THEN result := TRUE; $Z + 1$
             ELSE IF sbs$(a, i, 1) =$ "\$" OR sbs$(b, j, 1) =$ "\$"
                  THEN result := FALSE; $Z + 1$
                  ELSE IF sbs$(a, i, 1) \neq$ sbs$(b, j, 1)$
                       THEN result := FALSE; $Z + 1$
                     FI
             FI
       FI
  OD

We copy G into P, replace Z by EXIT(0), and then $Z + 1$ by EXIT; we unpack the selections. We obtain the final program:

          $i := 0; j := 0;$
          DO
             REPEAT $i := i + 1$ UNTIL sbs$(a, i, 1) \neq$ " ";
             REPEAT $j := j + 1$ UNTIL sbs$(b, j, 1) \neq$ " ";
             IF sbs$(a, i, 1) =$ "\$" AND sbs$(b, j, 1) =$ "\$"
                THEN result := TRUE; EXIT FI;
             IF sbs$(a, i, 1) =$ "\$" OR sbs$(b, j, 1) =$ "\$"
                THEN result := FALSE; EXIT FI;
             IF sbs$(a, i, 1) \neq$ sbs$(b, j, 1)$
                THEN result := FALSE; EXIT FI
          OD

This form is the most symmetrical possible, it being understood that within the framework considered here we have no means of placing the two passes through a and b of the REPEAT loops in parallel.

In most cases, those who are asked to write this program begin effectively enough by searching for the next non-space in a (the first REPEAT loop). But then they test the character so found immediately (as we have done in the system of actions). If it is the symbol \$, the string a has been exhausted, but not perhaps b. They leave the loop to execute a complementary pass through b.

The following form, which I obtained while recycling the work of professional programmers, is subtly false:

```
    i:= 0; j:= 0;
  G: search for the next non-blank in a;
       IF this is "$" THEN GOTO FA;
       search for the next non-blank in b;
       IF this is "$" THEN GOTO FB;
       IF the characters are equal THEN GOTO G ELSE GOTO F FI;
 FA: search for the next non-blank in b;
       IF this is "$" THEN GOTO T ELSE GOTO F FI;
 FB: search for the next non-blank in a;
       IF this is "$" THEN GOTO T ELSE GOTO F FI;
  T: result:= TRUE; GOTO Z;
  F: result:= FALSE;
  Z:
```

This program is at least symmetrical in its form. The general idea is that if one string is exhausted, but not the other, then the result has the value FALSE.

But suppose that the program has stopped in a at the last non-blank character before the \$. It does not go into FA, but it looks for the next non-blank in b; suppose this is none other but the symbol \$. The string b is exhausted, but not a, and so the result is FALSE. As the symbol \$ in b has been reached, the program goes into FB, where it looks for the next non-blank in a. So the last character of a is not examined, and as the non-blank which follows is \$, the result TRUE is given.

What has happened here is that the concern of the authors to preserve symmetry, or perhaps their instinct as to what is symmetry, has led them towards a false form. If it is true that when a is exhausted, b must be run through by FB, conversely, if FB is entered it is because a is not exhausted (otherwise FA would have been entered) and b is exhausted. Thus FB is to be replaced by F.

This shows the danger of not starting with the assertions of a program. The use of the result of the pass of a before the pass through b destroys the symmetry, which then becomes a trap into which these professional programmers have fallen. It goes without saying that this program had passed its tests (the very particular case discussed here had not been tested) and had been presented to me as correct. I must say that it was not until after the end of this stage that I discovered the error.

The other matter for reflection, or, to be more precise, for perplexity, is the fact that only rarely are programmers capable of imagining the correct, perfectly symmetrical, form given here. I have not found it myself, even by using program transformations. It was the school teachers who gave it to me.

This poses brutally and cruelly the problem of creative invention in programming. Correct programs can be obtained by sound methods of reasoning. The "good" program which solves the problem not only correctly but even elegantly can be passed by if one has not the imagination to see the end to be reached. The example given here is not the only case of discomfiture. One suggestion, even a wrong one, is enough to light the spark which will show the right direction and lead to the desired result. Once the teachers had told me that the two strings should be operated on symmetrically—two passes, tests grouped with AND and OR, program transformations, these soon gave the result from the starting point of the actions which I had previously written down, following the method set out in detail here.

For a teacher as I am, the crucial question remains—how do I get good ideas, and how do I teach students how to get good ideas?

Exercises

E.6.1   It is required to remove the redundant blanks from a text, that is to say:

–those at the beginning, preceding the first non-blank,
–those at the end, following the last non-blank,
–those beyond the first, between consecutive words.

Construct an automaton to do this; give the corresponding system of actions; and derive the iterative programs.

E.6.2   Here is a program in the style of Fortan:

```
1   i = root
4   IF (son(i) ≠ 0) GO TO 5
2   write i
    IF (brother(i) ≠ 0) GO TO 3
    IF (i = root) GO TO 9
    i = father(i)
    GO TO 2
3   i = brother(i)
    GO TO 4
5   i = son(i)
    GO TO 4
9   continuation of program
```

Write the system of regular actions associated with this program. Resolve this into a structured program.

E.6.3   Using the operations on actions, how can the instruction

REPEAT a UNTIL *t*

be written with the aid of the WHILE loop?

E.6.4   Make an automaton for the so-called "plateau" problem [GRI]. Given a vector of *n* integer elements, in non-decreasing order, it is required to find the length of the longest constant sub-sequence of the vector.

E.6.5   Given the instruction

WHILE *t* DO a;
  WHILE *u* DO b OD
OD

where a and b are sequences of instructions not containing EXIT, (for example sequences of assignments and tests) and *t* and *u* are tests, find an equivalent system of regular actions and then resolve this into a program with one single DO loop containing a single non-indexed EXIT.

E.6.6   The same exercise for the loop

REPEAT a;
  REPEAT b
  UNTIL *u*
UNTIL *t*

Chapter 7

Program Transformations

7.1 Definitions and Notations

We shall give here a number of definitions without which it would be impossible to describe the principal syntactic transformations. This will be done without demonstration or proof, as that would require the use of a weighty formal apparatus with which we would not wish to burden the reader. For those who are interested in rigour, the proofs can be found in the work of Guy Cousineau [C01][C02]. In our earlier work [AR2], an attempt was made at justifying the results, but this has lost all interest now that there are better means of demonstration.

Terminal Instruction of a Sequence. Let f be a sequence of instructions and s an instruction of this sequence. We say that s is terminal for f if the successor of s is not in f. This is denoted by s = ti(f).

Terminal Value. We say that the terminal value of s = ti(f) in f is null, or empty, if the instruction s means "leave f and continue in sequence after f". We say that it is $p > 0$ if it means "exit from p loops enclosing f and continue in sequence". We denote the terminal value of s in f by $\tau(s, f)$.

Depth of s in f. This is the number of iterations enclosing s and contained in f. It is denoted by $\delta(s, f)$.

Terminal Position. This concept has already been defined in connection with regular actions.

Reducible Sequence. A terminal instruction of value 0 makes the program continue in sequence and leave f; thus it is necessarily in terminal position if its depth is 0. If its depth is δ, it makes the program leave δ loops before

159

continuing in sequence after f, and so the outermost of the iterations which contain it is in terminal position.

A terminal instruction of non-empty value is not necessarily in terminal position. We say that the sequence of instructions is reducible if all its terminal instructions are in terminal positions. Thus,

$$f = \text{IF } t \text{ THEN EXIT FI}; b; \text{EXIT}(0)$$

has two terminal instructions, both at depth 0. EXIT(0), of empty value, is in terminal position. EXIT, of value 1, is not. This sequence is not reducible. By contrast, the sequence

$$f' = \text{IF } t \text{ THEN EXIT ELSE } b; \text{EXIT}(0) \text{ FI}$$

is reducible, as EXIT, as well as EXIT(0), is in terminal position.

Proper Sequence.   The sequence f of instructions is said to be proper if all its terminal instructions are of empty value.

Notation.   By the preceding definitions any instruction can be terminal. In the sequence

$$i := 0; j := 0$$

the terminal instruction is $j := 0$. To avoid the need to consider such possibilities and to simplify the notation, it is understood that there is inserted an (additional) empty instruction EXIT(0) immediately after every basic instruction in terminal position so that every terminal instruction is now of the form EXIT(p), where $p \geq 0$.

In this way, the terminal selection

$$\text{IF } t \text{ THEN a FI}$$

will be changed into

$$\text{IF } t \text{ THEN a ELSE EXIT}(0) \text{ FI}$$

showing explicitly its empty second alternative, so that its terminal instructions are those of a and the EXIT(0) of the second alternative.

Incrementation.   Let p be a natural integer. We define $f + p$

$$f + p = f[s \rightarrow s + p]$$

which is to be read as "$f + p$ is obtained by incrementing each of the terminal instructions of f by p".

These are all of the form EXIT(q) with $q \geq 0$. The incrementation of an EXIT instruction has already been defined:

$$\text{EXIT}(q) + p = \text{EXIT}(q + p)$$

The principal syntactic transformations will now be described. These are transformations which do not change the computational process—that is, the sequence of tests and assignments—and therefore are always valid, even in the presence of side-effects.

7.2 Simple Absorption and Simple Expansion

Let f and g be two sequences of instructions. Simple absorption is defined by the following equivalence, where $\simeq$ denotes the fact that two sequences of instructions describe the same computational sequence:

$$f; g \simeq f[s : \tau(s, f) = 0 \to g + \delta(s, f)]$$

Intuitively, this can be expressed as follows. A terminal instruction of f with value 0 leads in sequence to what is after f, that is, to g. In the equivalent form, instead of the program leaving f to go to g, g is executed inside f. If the terminal instruction is contained within δ iterations, the execution of g must include the leaving of these δ iterations before it can leave g; this ensures the incrementation of δ.

Let us examine some particular cases.

Let $f = \text{EXIT}(0)$. The only terminal instruction of f is the EXIT(0) itself at depth 0. As δ is null, EXIT(0) is replaced by g:

$$\text{EXIT}(0); g \simeq g$$

EXIT(0) is the neutral element for concatenation; this is consistent with the definition of EXIT(0) as the empty instruction.

Similarly,

$$f; \text{EXIT}(0) \simeq f[s : \tau(s, f) = 0 \to \text{EXIT}(0) + \delta(s, f)]$$
$$= f[s : \tau(s, f) = 0 \to \text{EXIT}(\delta(s, f))]$$

Now a terminal instruction of value 0 at depth δ can only be EXIT(δ). Its effect is to leave δ loops and continue in sequence. This, then, leaves s unchanged:

$$f; \text{EXIT}(0) \simeq f$$

Let $f = \text{EXIT}(p)$ with $p \neq 0$. The only terminal instruction of f is EXIT(p), at depth 0, of non-empty value p. There is no terminal instruction of empty value, and so the simple absorption requires no modification to f. As for g:

$$\text{EXIT}(p); g \simeq \text{EXIT}(p) \qquad p \neq 0$$

Let us now take

$$f = \text{IF } t \text{ THEN } f' \text{ ELSE } f'' \text{ FI}$$

From what we have just seen, this is

$$f = IF\ t\ THEN\ f';\ EXIT(0)\ ELSE\ f'';\ EXIT(0)\ FI$$

Note that in this form f″ can be empty, corresponding to

$$IF\ t\ THEN\ f'\ FI$$

The only terminal instructions of value 0 are the two EXIT(0) instructions terminating the two alternatives. (It should be noted that this form of f is not reducible; there may be terminal instructions of non-empty value in non-terminal positions in f′ and f″.) These instructions are at depth 0. They are replaced by g:

$$IF\ t\ THEN\ f'\ ELSE\ f''\ FI;\ g$$
$$\simeq\quad IF\ t\ THEN\ f';\ g\ ELSE\ f'';\ g\ FI$$

This is a fundamental transformation and one that we have already used. It takes a special form when

$$f' = a;\ EXIT\qquad and\qquad f''\ is\ empty$$

f′ = a; EXIT cannot have terminal instructions of value 0 (those of a are not in terminal positions and so are not terminal for f′). Thus,

$$f';\ g = a;\ EXIT;\ g \simeq a;\ EXIT$$

$$IF\ t\ THEN\ a;\ EXIT\ FI;\ g$$
$$\simeq\quad IF\ t\ THEN\ a;\ EXIT\ ELSE\ g\ FI$$

This is the transformation which was frequently used in Chapter 6 to unpack the selections in a loop.

Simple Expansion.   Simple expansion is the inverse of simple absorption. Let f be a sequence of instructions. If there are two sequences f′ and g such that f is the result of the simple absorption of g in f′, then

$$f \simeq f';\ g$$
$$if\quad f = f'[s: \tau(s, f') = 0 \to g + \delta(s, f')]$$

A direct characterisation of f′ can be given in terms of f [AR2] but that would require the introduction of complex notations and needlessly obscure the exposition. In simple terms, we replace in f the terminal occurrences of g by EXIT(0) and so obtain a possible f′. In the latter, if the application of simple absorption leads back to the original f, then the expansion has been realised; if it does not, then the expansion is not possible.

In Section 6.2.1, a particular equivalence was given—if f(A) is a regular action in which only the action name A occurs,

$$f(A) \simeq f(EXIT(0));\ A$$

All the terminal positions of f(A) are occupied by an action name. As there is no other name than A, they are all occupied by A. By the construction of regular actions, A appears in the form A + p if it is inside exactly p loops and as A if it is inside no loop. The replacement of A by EXIT(0) thus gives rise to a terminal instruction, in terminal position and of value 0, and besides these there is no other terminal instruction so generated. This means above all that f(EXIT(0)) is a proper sequence. The replacement in f(EXIT(0)) of the terminal instructions of value 0 by A incremented by the depth yields A for an instruction at depth 0 and A + p for an instruction inside p loops, and thus reconstructs f(A). This equivalence is thus an immediate application of simple expansion.

7.3   Double Iteration and Loop Absorption

Let f be a reducible sequence and

$$DO\ DO\ f\ OD\ OD$$

be a double iteration.

A terminal instruction of f of value 0 makes the program go in sequence to what is after f, the inner OD, and hence again to the beginning of f.

A terminal instruction of value 1 makes the program leave the inner loop, go in sequence to the outer OD, and then begin f again. It has the same effect as a terminal instruction of value 0. The computation is not changed if a terminal instruction of value 1 of f is replaced by a terminal instruction of value 0, or, in other words, if this terminal instruction is decremented by 1. This instruction must always remain terminal after the transformation and be in terminal position; this is assured if f is reducible (f has all its terminal instructions in terminal positions). A terminal instruction of value $p > 1$ makes the program leave p loops enclosing f, including the two in which it is immediately enclosed. An equivalent sequence having no more than one iteration is obtained by replacing the instructions of value 1 by instructions of value 0, and reducing by 1 the instructions originally of value greater than 1. This amounts to reducing by 1 all the instructions originally of non-null value:

$$\begin{aligned}&DO\ DO\ f\ OD\ OD\\ \simeq\ &DO\ f[s:\tau(s,f)>0\to s-1]\ OD\\ &\textit{if and only if}\ f\ \textit{is reducible}\end{aligned}$$

This transformation can be used in two cases. In resolving a system of actions it is possible inadvertently to generate a double iteration. Rather than starting again, one can eliminate it by this transformation. The loop absorption follows from the combination of the simple absorption and the double iteration.

Suppose the sequence of instructions is

$$
\begin{array}{l}
\text{DO} \\
\quad \text{DO f OD}; \\
\qquad \text{g} \\
\text{OD}
\end{array}
$$

Here g can be absorbed in its preceding instruction. In

$$
\text{DO f OD}
$$

the terminal instructions of value 0 must be replaced by $g + \delta$. But these instructions, which lead to g, are those of f which cause the inner loop to be left and followed in sequence; that is, they are those of value 1 in f. Their depth in DO f OD is their depth in f increased by 1. Absorption in

$$
\text{DO f OD}
$$

thus replaces $s : \tau(s,f) = 1$ by $g + \delta(s,f) + 1$

$$
\begin{array}{ll}
& \text{DO DO f OD}; \text{g OD} \\
\simeq & \text{DO DO f}[s : \tau(s,f) = 1 \rightarrow g + \delta(s,f) + 1] \text{ OD OD}
\end{array}
$$

This has caused a double iteration to appear, which we shall eliminate. All the terminal instructions of non-null value must be decremented by 1, and those of value 1 must remain terminal. (This is enough, for those of value greater than 1 may not be in terminal position.) Now these terminal instructions are either those of f of value greater than 1, or those of $g + \delta + 1$. Those of value 1 come from those of g of value 0 and in terminal position. So we obtain

$$
\begin{array}{ll}
& \text{DO DO f OD}; \text{g OD} \\
\simeq & \text{DO} \\
& \quad \text{f}[s : \tau(s,f) = 1 \rightarrow g + \delta(s,f), s : \tau(s,f) > 1 \rightarrow s - 1] \\
& \text{OD}
\end{array}
$$

if and only if f *is reducible*

Remark. The equivalences just derived are valid only for reducible sequences; this is a constraint, not a restriction. If a sequence is not reducible, that is because there is in it a terminal instruction of non-null value in a non-terminal position. Let this sequence be f. The terminal instruction s in non-terminal position belongs to a sub-sequence f′ of f in which it is in terminal position, and f′ is followed by a certain g, so that

$$
f = f'; g
$$

s being terminal for f and f′ and in terminal position in f′.

By simple absorption, g can be put into f', giving an equivalent sequence in which s is in terminal position (for s, being of non-null value in f', is not modified by the absorption).

It follows from this that absorption can always be applied to a loop or to a double iteration, provided that first simple absorptions are applied to bring the terminal instructions of value 1 into terminal positions.

The Importance of Loop Absorption. It must be noted that, at the cost of some simple absorptions, any system of nested loops with adjacent entries can be replaced by a single loop.

The expansion of the loop is the inverse transformation. As with simple expansion, no direct characterisation will be given. But we shall make use of the transformation as it is the only way that we have of generating loops with adjacent entries. It has been pointed out already that the manipulation of regular actions can make one loop appear inside another, though always in terminal position. The interest in loop expansion is that it can clarify the operation of a complex loop.

Example. As an example, we shall consider again the problem of finding a substring within a string, as in Section 6.7.2. With the same notation, the action G

$$G == \text{IF } j = \text{length}(b) \text{ THEN } Z$$
$$\text{ELSE} \quad j:= j + 1;$$
$$\text{IF } sbs(a, i + j - 1, 1) = sbs(b, j, 1) \text{ THEN } G$$
$$\text{ELSE} \quad F$$
$$\text{FI}$$
$$\text{FI}$$

is cut into two by naming H all that follows $j := j + 1$:

$$G == \text{IF } j = \text{length}(b) \text{ THEN } Z \text{ ELSE } j:= j + 1; H \text{ FI}$$
$$H == \text{IF } sbs(a, i + j - 1, 1) = sbs(b, j, 1) \text{ THEN } G \text{ ELSE } F \text{ FI}$$

For the rest, we use the form of P valid for length $(a) \geq \text{length}(b)$:

$$P == i:= 1; j:= 0; G$$
$$F == i:= i + 1;$$
$$\text{IF } i > \text{length}(a) - \text{length}(b) + 1 \text{ THEN } i:= 0; Z$$
$$\text{ELSE} \quad j:= 0; G$$
$$\text{FI}$$

Substituting for G in P,

$$P === i:= 1; j:= 0; \text{IF } j = \text{length}(b) \text{ THEN } Z \text{ ELSE } j:= j + 1; H \text{ FI}$$

Suppose further that b is non-empty; that is, $\text{length}(b) \neq 0$. Then in P the test has the value "FALSE", and it can be suppressed:

$$P == i:= 0; j:= 0; j:= j + 1; H$$

which simplifies to

$$P == i:= 0; j:= 1; H$$

The same can be done in F:

F == $i:= i + 1$;
        IF $i >$ length(a) − length(b) + 1 THEN $i:= 0; Z$
                                 ELSE $j:= 1; H$

      FI

Substituting this in H, and so making H iterative,

H == DO
        IF sbs($a, i + j − 1, 1$) = sbs($b, j, 1$)
            THEN IF $j =$ length(b) THEN EXIT
                              ELSE $j:= j + 1$ FI
            ELSE $i:= i + 1$;
                IF $i >$ length(a) − length(b) + 1
                    THEN $i:= 0$; EXIT
                    ELSE $j:= 1$
              FI
      FI
  OD

(Z has been replaced by EXIT(0) as if H had been copied into P.)

It can be verified, by applying the loop absorption to the final form of the program, that the loop expansion takes effect after both the sequence of instructions contained in the innermost loop and the sequence between the two OD instructions have been made reducible by simple absorption:

$i:= i + 1; j:= 1$;
DO
    DO
        IF sbs($a, i + j − 1$) = sbs($b, j, 1$) THEN EXIT FI;
        $i:= i + 1$;
        IF $i >$ length(a) − length(b) + 1 THEN $i:= 0$; EXIT(2) FI;
        $j:= 1$
    OD;
    IF $j =$ length(b) THEN EXIT FI;
    $j:= j + 1$
  OD

This program is usable only if *b* is non-empty and if *a* is at least as long as *b*. But in this case, we have three equally valid programs:

–the first (Section 6.7.2, first form) consists of two loops; the inner loop increments *j* and the outer loop increments *i*;

–the second (Section 6.7.2) has only a single loop;

–the third (given here) again consists of two loops, but the inner loop increments *i*, while *j* is incremented in the outer loop.

Not only can we change the number of loops, but here we can even transfer an operation from the inner loop to the outer loop. This points to the need for extreme caution with regard to *a priori* statements as to the structure of a program. The structure of a program is quite flexible...

7.4 Proper Inversion

We shall establish this equivalence formula for a particular case. The generalisation has been established elsewhere [AR2].

Consider the regular action

$$A == a; f(A, B)$$

where a is a sequence of instructions containing no calls of actions and such that a has only one successor, which is f(A, B). This is a proper sequence in the sense of Section 7.1.

If we make A iterative, we obtain

$$A == DO\ a; f(EXIT(0), EXIT)\ OD; B$$

We introduce a new action C:

$$A == a; C$$
$$C == f(A, B)$$

We substitute for A in C:

$$C == f(a; C, B)$$

We make C iterative:

$$C == DO\ f(a; EXIT(0), EXIT)\ OD; B$$

which simplifies, since $a; EXIT(0) \simeq a$, to

$$C == DO\ f(a, EXIT)\ OD; B$$

Now we try to get a out of f by simple expansion. We replace a by EXIT(0).

Consider

$$f(EXIT(0), EXIT); a$$

The only terminal instructions of value 0 in f(EXIT(0), EXIT) are those which arise from the replacement of A by EXIT(0); it was said in Section 6.6.1 that A is changed into EXIT(0) to make the program continue in sequence after f at the OD instruction, and this is indeed the effect of a terminal instruction of value 0. If then a is absorbed into f, every EXIT(0) coming from the replacement of A is changed into a, giving f(a, EXIT).

Thus,

$$C == DO\ f(EXIT(0),\ EXIT);\ a\ OD;\ B$$

Substituting for C in A,

$$A == a;\ DO\ f(EXIT(0), EXIT);\ a\ OD;\ B$$

Compare this with the initial form:

$$A == DO\ a;\ f(EXIT(0), EXIT)\ OD;\ B$$

The order of the two sequences a and f in the loop has been inverted, a having been pushed out in front of the loop. It has been shown [AR2] that this result can be generalised for any sequence

$$DO\ a;\ f\ OD$$
$$\simeq\quad a;\ DO\ f;\ a\ OD$$
if and only if a is proper

In most cases, this transformation will not have been used in this way, recourse to it having been avoided by the processing of a system of actions (although it is, by the way, through such a system that it has been introduced here). However, it is very important to be aware of it as it can be very useful.

Here is a well-known example. We have a sequential file, which must be processed record by record, until it is exhausted. The manipulation of the file is achieved by means of the two instructions:

–OPEN, which prepares the file for access to its first record;
–NEXT RECORD, which accesses the next record. This instruction acts upon a boolean variable END OF FILE, global to the system, and having the value TRUE when access is attempted to a record beyond the last. The program has the following form:

```
P == OPEN file; T
T == NEXT RECORD;
     IF END OF FILE THEN Z
                     ELSE process the record; T
     FI
```

The resolution of this system is simple—T is made iterative and copied into P; then Z is replaced by EXIT(0). We obtain

```
OPEN file;
DO
     NEXT RECORD;
     IF END OF FILE THEN EXIT FI;
     process the record
OD
```

By proper inversion or by some other manipulation of the system (the selection in T is named U; T is replaced throughout by its value; this action is eliminated; and the system is resolved), we find

```
OPEN file;
NEXT RECORD;
DO
     IF END OF FILE THEN EXIT FI;
     process the record;
     NEXT RECORD
OD
```

This program is of interest because it can be rewritten more simply with a WHILE loop:

```
OPEN file;
NEXT RECORD;
WHILE NOT END OF FILE DO
                          process the record;
                          NEXT RECORD
          OD
```

This is often used in a language such as Pascal, whose principal loop structure is the WHILE loop. From my point of view, what we have here is a programming trick which allows one to get around the constraint introduced by the WHILE (a single exit test at the head of the loop). Now teachers of information processing are not fond of the use of tricks. In fact, several experiences with different audiences have convinced me that systematic recourse to the WHILE loop does not help the construction of correct loops by the students. They begin by writing WHILE and then try to find the exit condition. Following the method presented at the beginning of this book (and in my earlier works [AR1][AR2]) and which is also to be found in *The Science of Programming* [GR1] by David Gries, the work begins with the invariant for the loop, then with conditions implying that the computation has been finished and the loop can be left. It may be that a simple test is enough, in which case a WHILE instruction will do it. Equally, it may be that a certain evaluation, or a succession of evaluations and tests, is needed before the exit condition can be determined. That is not to say that the WHILE loop is unusable. We think that it is better first to construct the program with convenient control structures (essentially EXIT, or systems of actions), and then by appropriate transformations put it into the required form. That is what program transformations are there for.

7.5 Repetition

Suppose we have a regular action

$$A == f(A, B)$$

We make it iterative:

$$A == DO\ f(EXIT(0), EXIT)\ OD\ ;\ B$$

By substitution, we first substitute for A in f,

$$A == f(f(A, B), B)$$

and make that iterative:

$$A == DO\ f(f(EXIT(0), EXIT), EXIT)\ OD\ ;\ B$$

Going back to what has been done for proper inversion, we can make use of the simple expansion:

$$f(f(\ EXIT(0), EXIT), EXIT) \simeq f(EXIT(0), EXIT)\ ;\ f(EXIT(0), EXIT)$$

We can show that this can be generalised to any sequence of instructions:

$$DO\ f\ OD \simeq DO\ f\ ;\ f\ OD$$

This form can be generalised further, but we have no need of any more powerful result.

7.6 Local Semantic Transformations

7.6.1 Assignments

By *semantic* we mean a transformation which changes the course of a computation. In general, such a transformation is possible only after the demonstration or verification of a condition of validity. In particular, careful attention must be paid to side-effects. We shall assume that no side-effect due to the presence of a function modifying a variable of the program will occur.

A semantic transformation will be called *local* if its validity can be decided solely on the basis of those instructions which are executed (except, perhaps, as far as side-effects are concerned—it is certain that there are no side-effects if there are no functions calls, but that is too strong a condition).

Permutation of Two Assignments

Consider the sequence of two assignments

$$x1 := f1(x1, x2); x2 := f2(x1, x2)$$

In general these instructions cannot be permuted. Let us suppose that the initial values of $x1$ and $x2$ are $a1$ and $a2$:

$$[[x1 = a1 \qquad x2 = a2]] \, x1 := f1(x1, x2);$$
$$[[x1 = f1(a1, a2) \qquad x2 = a2]] \, x2 := f2(x1, x2)$$
$$[[x1 = f1(a1, a2) \qquad x2 = f2(f1(a1, a2), a2)]]]$$

If the assignments are permuted, the postassertion becomes

$$[[x1 = f1(a1, f2(a1, a2)) \qquad x2 = f2(a1, a2)]]]$$

It can be said, schematically, that as the first instruction destroys $x1$ it cannot be displaced without care; but its effect could first be copied in f2. However, in its turn f2 modifies $x2$, and f1 cannot be computed after $x2$. If, on the other hand, f1 does not depend on $x2$, the permutation is possible:

$$x1 := f1(x1); x2 := f2(x1, x2)$$
is semantically equivalent to
$$x2 := f2(x1 \to f1(x1), x2); x1 := f1(x1)$$

Let us be clear: the course of the computation has been changed (f1 is now computed twice). The condition for validity is (apart from side-effects) given by the non-occurrence of $x2$ in f1. But we must be more careful. We have implicitly assumed that the variables $x1$ and $x2$ are different. Suppose that $x1$ does not occur in f2:

$$x1 := f1(x1); x2 := f2(x2)$$
is semantically equivalent to
$$x2 := f2(x2); x1 := f1(x1)$$

In particular, this is the case if f1 and f2 are constants. Suppose then

$$a[i] := 1; a[j] := 2$$

We make the permutation

$$a[j] := 2; a[i] := 1$$

The two sequences are equivalent only if $i \neq j$; for if $i = j$, the first sequence gives the common variable the value 2, the second the value 1. Therefore we must add a supplementary condition for validity: the variables $x1$ and $x2$ have to be distinct. This condition may perhaps not be decidable locally; in the foregoing example it has to be shown that $i \neq j$, a result dependent on the rest of the program. Nevertheless, only the variables i and j matter. We shall keep the name "local semantic transformation", it being understood that it might happen in certain locally recognisable cases that the verification of the validity of application cannot be local:

$$x1 := f1(x1); x2 := f2(x1, x2)$$
is semantically equivalent to
$$x2 := f2(x1 \to f1(x1), x2); x1 := f1(x1)$$
if and only if $x1$ and $x2$ are distinct

The Merging of Two Assignments

Suppose there are two successive assignments to the same variable:

$$x := f1(x); x := f2(x)$$

Assuming the initial value of x, we can write the assertions for this sequence:

$$[[x = a]] \, x := f1(x); [[x = f1(a)]] \, x := f2(x) [[x = f2(f1(a))]]$$

This can be written

$$x := f1(x); x := f2(x)$$
is semantically equivalent to
$$x := f2(f1(x))$$
if and only if there is no side-effect on the name x

The restriction can be explained by means of an example. Let $i = 3$, $a[3] = 3$, and suppose the sequence is

$$a[a[i]] := 1; a[a[i]] := 2$$

With the values given above, the first assignment gives $a[3]$ the value 1; the second gives $a[1]$ the value 2. But the result of the merging of the two is

$$a[a[i]] := 2$$

and this gives $a[3]$ the value 2. The validity of the transformation can usually be decided locally.

It must be noted how the use of subscripted variables can introduce side-effects which may be very difficult to fathom. Extreme care is needed when there are assignments to subscripted variables.

7.6.2   Selection Instructions

Ineffective Selections

Consider the selection

$$\text{IF } t \text{ THEN f ELSE g FI}$$

Suppose it can be affirmed that t is true (or false). This implies that we have an assertion concerning t, which is not local. The selection can thus be suppressed and only one of the alternatives, true (or false), retained. Certainly this is not valid unless there are no side effects in t; if there are, to suppress the computation of t might change the context of f or g:

$$[[t]] \text{ IF } t \text{ THEN f ELSE g FI}$$
is semantically equivalent to
$$f$$
$$[[\text{NOT } t]] \text{ IF } t \text{ THEN f ELSE g FI}$$
is semantically equivalent to
$$g$$

Redundant Selections

In the previous example, suppose that f began with a test on t. As f is in the "true" alternative of the selection, t is known to be true and simplification is possible:

$$\text{IF } t \text{ THEN IF } t \text{ THEN f' ELSE f'' FI ELSE g FI}$$
is semantically equivalent to
$$\text{IF } t \text{ THEN f' ELSE g FI}$$

Similar simplification occurs if the selection is in the "false" alternative, t then being known to have the value FALSE. The result is still valid if the selection on t is more deeply embedded in the considered alternative; it is necessary and sufficient that there be no computation after the first evaluation of t which can modify the value of this predicate.

This is an extremely common transformation in the processing of programs.

Tautology

We shall call a selection whose two alternatives are identical a tautology:

IF *t* THEN f ELSE f FI
is semantically equivalent to
f

Appearances to the contrary, this transformation is useful. Tautologies are rarely found written in programs, but a succession of transformations can make a tautology appear, and the usual way of introducing a test is by the creation of a tautology.

As an example, consider the inversion of the order of two tests:

IF *t* THEN IF *u* THEN f' ELSE g' FI
ELSE IF *u* THEN f'' ELSE g'' FI
FI

We wish to begin with the test on *u*. One way is to use a decision table. We want a test on *u* on the outside; we introduce it by tautology:

IF *u* THEN IF *t* THEN IF *u* THEN f' ELSE g' FI
ELSE IF *u* THEN f'' ELSE g'' FI
FI
ELSE IF *t* THEN IF *u* THEN f' ELSE g' FI
ELSE IF *u* THEN f'' ELSE g'' FI
FI
FI

All the interior tests on *u* are redundant and can be suppressed. In the first alternative, *u* is true, and only f' and f'' remain; in the second, *u* is false and only g' and g'' remain.

IF *u* THEN IF *t* THEN f' ELSE f'' FI
ELSE IF *t* THEN g' ELSE g'' FI
FI

Left Absorption

Consider the sequence

$x := f(x)$; IF $t(x)$ THEN g ELSE h FI

We can move the assignment instruction into the selection if we make consequential changes to the test:

$$x := f(x); \text{ IF } t(x) \text{ THEN g ELSE h FI}$$
is semantically equivalent to
$$\text{IF } t(f(x)) \text{ THEN } x := f(x); \text{ g ELSE } x := f(x); \text{ h FI}$$

It is perhaps not a good idea to generalise this transformation further. It requires considerable care in use. A better plan is to reconstruct it each time on the basis of assertions.

The primitive transformations just described are sufficient for a great variety of applications, of which only a hint can be given here through the examples which follow.

7.7 The Development of More Complex Transformations

7.7.1 WHILE Loops

In Section 5.6, the following sequence was considered:

$$\text{WHILE } t \text{ AND } u \text{ DO a OD};$$
$$\text{WHILE } t \text{ DO a OD}$$

We shall try to simplify it. For this, we first replace the iterations by terminal recursive actions. The program is named, and the program is made to terminate with the terminal action Z. The WHILE instructions are replaced by loops with EXIT instructions:

$$A == \text{DO}$$
$$\quad\quad \text{IF } t \text{ AND } u \text{ THEN a ELSE EXIT FI}$$
$$\quad \text{OD};$$
$$\quad \text{DO}$$
$$\quad\quad \text{IF } t \text{ THEN a ELSE EXIT FI}$$
$$\quad \text{OD};$$
$$\quad \text{Z}$$

Calling the second loop B, a system of two regular actions is obtained:

$$A == \text{DO}$$
$$\quad\quad \text{IF } t \text{ AND } u \text{ THEN a ELSE EXIT FI}$$
$$\quad \text{OD}; \text{B}$$
$$B == \text{DO}$$
$$\quad\quad \text{IF } t \text{ THEN a ELSE EXIT FI}$$
$$\quad \text{OD}; \text{Z}$$

B is absorbed into the first loop. The only terminal instruction of null value belonging to this loop is EXIT, at depth 1. EXIT is replaced by B incremented by 1. The same is done for Z in B:

$$A == DO$$
$$\qquad IF\ t\ AND\ u\ THEN\ a\ ELSE\ B + 1\ FI$$
$$\qquad OD$$
$$B == DO$$
$$\qquad IF\ t\ THEN\ a\ ELSE\ Z + 1\ FI$$
$$\qquad OD$$

By the inverse operation to that of Section 6.6, these actions are made terminal and recursive. The loop parentheses DO...OD are removed. The terminal instructions of null value in the iterating part are replaced by the name of the loop, and the others are decremented by 1:

$$A == IF\ t\ AND\ u\ THEN\ a;\ A\ ELSE\ B\ FI$$
$$B == IF\ t\ THEN\ a;\ B\ ELSE\ Z\ FI$$

To replace the conjunction AND in A by a nest of tests, we enclose the selection in a tautology on t:

$$A == IF\ t\ THEN\ IF\ t\ AND\ u\ THEN\ a;\ A\ ELSE\ B\ FI$$
$$\qquad\quad ELSE\ IF\ t\ AND\ u\ THEN\ a;\ A\ ELSE\ B\ FI$$
$$\quad FI$$

In the first alternative, t being true, t AND u is equivalent to u. In the second, t being false, t AND u is false:

$$A == IF\ t\ THEN\ IF\ u\ THEN\ a;\ A\ ELSE\ B\ FI$$
$$\qquad\quad ELSE\ B$$
$$\quad FI$$

We take B into A:

$$A == IF\ t\ THEN\ IF\ u\ THEN\ a;\ A$$
$$\qquad\qquad\qquad\quad ELSE\ IF\ t\ THEN\ a;\ B\ ELSE\ Z\ FI$$
$$\qquad\qquad\quad FI$$
$$\qquad\quad ELSE\ IF\ t\ THEN\ a;\ B\ ELSE\ Z\ FI$$
$$\quad FI$$

The internal tests are redundant (they are separated from the test on t only by the computation of u, assumed not to have side effects):

$$A == IF\ t\ THEN\ IF\ u\ THEN\ a;\ A\ ELSE\ a;\ B\ FI$$
$$\qquad\quad ELSE\ Z$$
$$\quad FI$$
$$B == IF\ t\ THEN\ a;\ B\ ELSE\ Z\ FI$$

We try to make B more like A. For this, we enclose the first alternative of B in a tautology on u, thus obtaining two actions which have the same test structure:

$$\text{B} == \text{IF } t \text{ THEN IF } u \text{ THEN a}; \text{B ELSE a}; \text{B FI}$$
$$\qquad\qquad \text{ELSE Z}$$
$$\quad \text{FI}$$

If throughout B is changed into A, B becomes identical to A. The two actions can then be identified, and the system reduces to

$$\text{A} == \text{IF } t \text{ THEN IF } u \text{ THEN a}; \text{A ELSE a}; \text{A FI}$$
$$\qquad\qquad \text{ELSE Z}$$
$$\quad \text{FI}$$

The selection on u is a tautology and can be suppressed:

$$\text{A} == \text{IF } t \text{ THEN a}; \text{A ELSE Z FI}$$

This action is made iterative:

$$\text{A} == \text{DO IF } t \text{ THEN a ELSE EXIT FI OD}; \text{Z}$$

which reduces to

$$\text{WHILE } t \text{ DO a OD}$$

We have thus established the semantic equivalence

$$\text{WHILE } t \text{ AND } u \text{ DO a OD};$$
$$\text{WHILE } t \text{ DO a OD}$$
$$\text{is equivalent to}$$
$$\text{WHILE } t \text{ DO a OD}$$

7.7.2   A Transformation due to Suzan Gerhardt [GER]

Consider the following loop:

$$\text{WHILE } t \text{ DO}$$
$$\qquad \text{WHILE } t \text{ AND } u \text{ DO a OD};$$
$$\qquad \text{WHILE } t \text{ AND NOT } u \text{ DO b OD}$$
$$\quad \text{OD}$$

We try to simplify this. As before, we make it a regular action and call it S after the name of its author and concatenate with it the terminal action Z:

$$\text{S} == \text{WHILE } t \text{ DO}$$
$$\qquad\qquad \text{WHILE } t \text{ AND } u \text{ DO a OD};$$
$$\qquad\qquad \text{WHILE } t \text{ AND NOT } u \text{ DO b OD}$$
$$\qquad \text{OD}; \text{Z}$$

We replace the WHILE instructions by loops with EXIT:

S == DO
            IF *t* THEN DO IF *t* AND *u* THEN a ELSE EXIT FI OD;
                        DO IF *t* AND NOT *u* THEN b ELSE EXIT FI OD
                  ELSE   EXIT
            FI
      OD; Z

Z is absorbed into the loop, where, incremented by 1, it replaces the last EXIT:

S == DO
            IF *t* THEN DO IF *t* AND *u* THEN a ELSE EXIT FI OD;
                        DO IF *t* AND NOT *u* THEN b ELSE EXIT FI OD
                  ELSE   Z + 1
            IF
      OD

To make S recursive, S is added to the end of the first alternative, and Z + 1
becomes Z again:

S == IF *t* THEN DO IF *t* AND *u* THEN a ELSE EXIT FI OD;
                  DO IF *t* AND NOT *u* THEN b ELSE EXIT FI OD;
                  S
            ELSE Z
      FI

To be able to replace the loops by recursions, they must first be named. We call
them X and Y:

        S == IF *t* THEN X ELSE Z FI
        X == DO IF *t* AND *u* THEN a ELSE EXIT FI OD; Y
        Y == DO IF *t* AND NOT *u* THEN b ELSE EXIT FI OD; S

Y is absorbed into the X loop, S into the Y loop:

        S == IF *t* THEN X ELSE Z FI
        X == DO IF *t* AND *u* THEN a ELSE Y + 1 FI OD
        Y == DO IF *t* AND NOT *u* THEN b ELSE S + 1 FI OD

These actions are made recursive:

        S == IF *t* THEN X ELSE Z FI
        X == IF *t* AND *u* THEN a; X ELSE Y FI
        Y == IF *t* AND NOT *u* THEN b; Y ELSE S FI

We now have a regular system on which we can set to work.

We decompose the tests with AND into nested tests, as in the foregoing Section. The details will not be repeated:

$$S == \text{IF } t \text{ THEN X ELSE Z FI}$$
$$X == \text{IF } t \text{ THEN IF } u \text{ THEN a; X ELSE Y FI}$$
$$\text{ELSE Y FI}$$
$$Y == \text{IF } t \text{ THEN IF NOT } u \text{ THEN b; Y ELSE S FI}$$
$$\text{ELSE S FI}$$

We take S into Y, having inverted the selection on NOT u:

$$Y == \text{ IF } t \text{ THEN IF } u \text{ THEN IF } t \text{ THEN X ELSE Z FI}$$
$$\text{ELSE b; Y}$$
$$\text{FI}$$
$$\text{ELSE IF } t \text{ THEN X ELSE Z FI}$$
$$\text{FI}$$

The internal selections on t are redundant. Simplifying,

$$Y == \text{ IF } t \text{ THEN IF } u \text{ THEN X}$$
$$\text{ELSE b; Y}$$
$$\text{FI}$$
$$\text{ELSE Z}$$
$$\text{FI}$$

Notice that by suppressing the tests which were required in the first form we have changed the order of the computation and reduced the computing time.
   We take X into Y:

$$Y == \text{ IF } t \text{ THEN IF } u \text{ THEN IF } t \text{ THEN IF } u \text{ THEN a; X ELSE Y FI}$$
$$\text{ELSE Y}$$
$$\text{FI}$$
$$\text{ELSE b; Y}$$
$$\text{FI}$$
$$\text{ELSE Z}$$
$$\text{FI}$$

In the first line, the second test on u is redundant, and the selection reduces to a; X. Similarly, the second test on t is redundant, and the selection reduces again to a; X. Once more we have suppression of tests and reduction of computing time:

$$Y == \text{ IF } t \text{ THEN IF } u \text{ THEN a; X}$$
$$\text{ELSE b; Y}$$
$$\text{FI}$$
$$\text{ELSE Z}$$
$$\text{FI}$$

We take Y into X:

X == IF *t* THEN IF *u* THEN a; X
                         ELSE IF *t* THEN IF *u* THEN a; X ELSE b; Y FI
                                       ELSE Z
                               FI
                  FI
       ELSE IF *t* THEN IF *u* THEN a; X ELSE b; Y FI
                  ELSE Z
            FI
       FI

We suppress all the redundant tests:

X == IF *t* THEN IF *u* THEN a; X ELSE b; Y FI
            ELSE Z
       FI

From this it follows that X and Y are identical. We suppress Y by replacing it throughout by X:

S == IF *t* THEN X ELSE Z FI
X == IF *t* THEN IF *u* THEN a; X ELSE b; X FI
            ELSE Z
       FI

Taking X into S,

S == IF *t* THEN IF *t* THEN IF *u* THEN a; X ELSE b; X FI
                         ELSE Z
                  FI
            ELSE Z
       FI

Simplifying, to remove the redundant second test on *t*,

S == IF *t* THEN IF *u* THEN a; X ELSE b; X FI
            ELSE Z
       FI

X and S are identical apart from their names. Replacing X by S, we obtain two identical actions. So X is identified with S, and there remains

S == IF *t* THEN IF *u* THEN a; S ELSE b; S FI
            ELSE Z
       FI

This is rcsolved into

```
DO
      IF t THEN IF u THEN a ELSE b FI
            ELSE EXIT
      FI
OD
```

and finally,

```
WHILE t DO
                  IF u THEN a ELSE b FI
            OD
```

We have thus obtained the following equivalence:

```
WHILE t DO
            WHILE t AND u DO a OD;
            WHILE t AND NOT u DO b OD
      OD
is equivalent to
WHILE t DO
            IF u THEN a ELSE b FI
      OD
```

7.7.3   Remark on the AND Operator

The two transformations which have just been described work through the replacement of a selection

```
IF t AND u THEN f ELSE g FI
```

by nested selections:

```
IF t THEN IF u THEN f ELSE g FI
      ELSE  g
FI
```

This is always possible. The inverse transformation is a delicate one; we must be certain that the test on u is defined when t has the value FALSE. A typical example is provided by the linear table look-up:

```
DO
      IF i ≤ n THEN IF a[i] ≠ x THEN i := i + 1 ELSE EXIT FI
            ELSE EXIT
      FI
OD
```

The tests cannot be rearranged with AND because $a[i] = x$ can only be computed if $i \leq n$. This is a condition for the validity of the foregoing transformations, in the direction which introduces AND.

7.8   Application to a Problem of Termination

Consider the following program:

```
READ n;
WHILE n ≠ 1 DO
              IF even(n) THEN n := n : 2
                        ELSE  n := n + 1
         FI
    OD
```

For a given natural integer n, the problem is to determine whether the execution of this program terminates. We can in general decide whether a program stops if we can find a function of natural integer value, zero for the solution, and decreasing at each step of the loop. If we can, we are certain to reach the solution in a finite number of steps. Here there is a single variable n. The solution is characterised by $n = 1$, so perhaps $n - 1$ can be taken as the distance function. But $n - 1$ will be decreased only when n is even. There is no obvious way of finding a function $f(n)$ which will always decrease. Another approach is to modify the program so that we can show that it will always stop for any natural integer n.

As a start, we rewrite it in the form of regular actions. The program is named D (after Dijkstra, who set this problem during a meeting of the IFIP Working Group 2.3 on Programming Methodology at St. Pierre de Chartreuse in 1976). The loop is named E and the exit Z:

```
D = = READ n; E
E = = WHILE n ≠ 1 DO
                 IF even(n) THEN n := n : 2
                           ELSE  n := n + 1
            FI
         OD;
    Z
```

We replace the WHILE loop by a loop with EXIT:

```
E == DO
         IF n ≠ 1 THEN IF even(n) THEN n := n : 2 ELSE n := n + 1 FI
                  ELSE EXIT
         FI
    OD;
    Z
```

Then Z is absorbed into the loop:

E == DO
        IF $n \neq 1$ THEN IF even(n) THEN $n := n:2$ ELSE $n := n + 1$ FI
            ELSE Z + 1
    FI
  OD

The action can now be made recursive:

E == IF $n \neq 1$ THEN IF even(n) THEN $n := n:2$
                             ELSE $n := n + 1$
                FI; E
           ELSE Z
    FI

The difficulty arises because, in certain cases, n increases. Let us try to see what happens on the next step of the loop. We must examine the sequence $n := n + 1$; E. We shall make it appear explicitly. Absorbing E in the selection which precedes it,

E == IF $n \neq 1$ THEN IF even(n) THEN $n := n:2$; E
                            ELSE $n := n + 1$; E
                FI
           ELSE Z
    FI

We replace E by its value after $n := n + 1$ and write a few assertions drawn directly from the tests:

E == IF $n \neq 1$ THEN [[$n > 1$]]
                IF even(n)
                    THEN $n := n:2$; E
                    ELSE [[n odd > 1]]
                        $n := n + 1$;
                        [[n even > 2]]
                        IF $n \neq 1$ THEN IF even(n)
                                THEN $n := n:2$; E
                              ELSE $n := n + 1$; E
                                    FI
                            ELSE Z
                      FI
              FI
           ELSE Z
    FI

Immediately under the assertion $n > 2$, and therefore $n \neq 1$, the selection is unnecessary and can be suppressed. At the same point n is even, and so the inner selection, on even(n) is unnecessary and can be suppressed. There remains

E == IF $n \neq 1$ THEN IF even(n) THEN $n := n : 2$; E
                                     ELSE $n := n + 1$; $n := n : 2$; E
                      FI
            ELSE Z
    FI

The two successive assignments to n are merged:

$$n := n + 1 ; n := n : 2 \quad \text{becomes} \quad n := (n + 1) : 2$$

It is very easy to resolve this system of actions. We obtain thus the new program, semantically equivalent to its predecessor:

            READ n;
            WHILE $n \neq 1$ DO
                            IF even(n) THEN $n := n : 2$
                                         ELSE $n := (n + 1) : 2$
                            FI
                OD

In this form, n decreases at each step of the loop, and so the program must stop.
    But suppose that instead of $n := n + 1$, we had been given $n := 3 * n + 1$. In that case we should have found

$$n := (3 * n + 1) : 2$$

which is greater than n, and so nothing would have been proved about the termination of that program. In fact, the termination of the program

            READ n;
            WHILE $n \neq 1$ DO
                            IF even(n) THEN $n := n : 2$
                                         ELSE $n := (3 * n + 1) : 2$
                            FI
                OD

has still not been demonstrated...

7.9   Change of Strategy

We shall now apply transformations to a very well-known program. This is Euclid's algorithm for computing the greatest common divisor of two non-zero natural integers a and b. Here is Euclid's algorithm:

```
READ a, b;
DO
    r := mod(a, b);
    IF r = 0 THEN EXIT FI;
    a := b; b := r
OD;
write(b)
```

We call this program E, the final action Z, and the loop F. We introduce an action Y for the exit from the loop:

```
E == READ a, b; F
F == DO
        r := mod(a, b);
        IF r = 0 THEN EXIT FI;
        a := b; b := r
    OD;
    Y
Y == write(b); Z
```

The action E is made recursive:

```
E == READ a, b; F
F == r := mod(a, b);
     IF r = 0 THEN Y ELSE a := b; b := r; F FI
Y == write(b); Z
```

We shall develop the computation of the remainder of the division of a by b by using the method of successive subtraction:

$$r := mod(a, b)$$

is computed as

```
r := a;
WHILE r ≥ b DO r := r − b OD
```

We call the WHILE loop G and rewrite it with an EXIT:

```
F == r := a; G
G == DO
        IF r < b THEN EXIT FI;
        r := r − b
    OD;
    H
H == IF r = 0 THEN Y ELSE a := b; b := r; F FI
```

We make G recursive:

$$F == r := a; G$$
$$G == \text{IF } r < b \text{ THEN H ELSE } r := r - b; G \text{ FI}$$
$$H == \text{IF } r = 0 \text{ THEN Y ELSE } a := b; b := r; F \text{ FI}$$

So far we have taken only one initiative—that of computing mod(a, b) by successive subtraction of b. The rest is only computing, and always in the same direction, which is to make the actions recursive. We have used several actions in order to keep their bodies simple.

We must now do something new. We have one idea in mind. There exists an algorithm, which we should like to find, which subtracts the smaller number from the larger until they have become equal. But, for the moment, there is no sign of it. Some writers say that the transformations should be directed towards an objective [WEG]. This is a point of view which we dispute strongly, with our practical experience of transformations. Quite often, as here, the objective pursued is of no help at all in choosing the next transformation. We have to trust our senses and not be afraid of taking a step which turns out to be fruitless. We try something, and if this does not help, we leave that and try something else. This costs writing paper, but no great mental effort.

The action F has a body reduced to one instruction and an action call. Let us see if eliminating can help:

$$E == \text{READ } a, b; r := a; G$$
$$G == \text{IF } r < b \text{ THEN H ELSE } r := r - b; G \text{ FI}$$
$$H == \text{IF } r = 0 \text{ THEN Y}$$
$$\qquad \text{ELSE } a := b; b := r; r := a; G$$
$$\qquad \text{FI}$$
$$Y == \text{write}(b); Z$$

It has produced something altogether surprising—the appearance in H of a sequence

$$a := b; b := r; r := a$$

which can be identified with swap(b, r) as a serves only as a temporary store. But this is possible only if a is otherwise unused. Now a occurs only in E. We can therefore make this modification:

$$H == \text{IF } r = 0 \text{ THEN Y ELSE swap}(b, r); G \text{ FI}$$
$$G == \text{IF } r < b \text{ THEN H ELSE } r := r - b; G \text{ FI}$$

Let us be clear: Euclid's algorithm defines new values for a and b. Here, a has disappeared, and what was a definition of a and b has become a swap between *b* and *r*. We have not intended this. We have simply tried a transformation and obtained this effect. Now let us see where this leads us. Even without having the algorithm of subtractions at the beginning, we have here a system which has increased the symmetry between the roles of *b* and *r*. Also, the termination by comparison of *r* with 0 is undesirable. We need termination by comparison of *b* with *r*.

At the beginning, in E, we have $a \neq 0$, $b \neq 0$ (by hypothesis), and then $b \neq 0$ AND $r \neq 0$ is a preassertion of G.

In G, the subtraction $r := r - b$ does not affect *b* but can make *r* zero. This is not the case unless, before this subtraction, $r = b$. It is a symmetrical test on *b* and *r*. We shall try to bring this out. To find the effect of this modification on the program as a whole, we first take H into G:

$$G == \text{IF } r < b \text{ THEN IF } r = 0 \text{ THEN Y}$$
$$\text{ELSE swap}(b, r); G$$
$$\text{FI}$$
$$\text{ELSE } r := r - b; G$$
$$\text{FI}$$

We enclose all this in a tautology on $r = b$:

$$G == \text{IF } r = b \text{ THEN IF } r < b \text{ THEN IF } r = 0 \text{ THEN Y}$$
$$\text{ELSE swap}(b, r); G$$
$$\text{FI}$$
$$\text{ELSE } r := r - b; G$$
$$\text{FI}$$
$$\text{ELSE IF } r < b \text{ THEN IF } r = 0 \text{ THEN Y}$$
$$\text{ELSE swap}(b, r); G$$
$$\text{FI}$$
$$\text{ELSE } r := r - b; G$$
$$\text{FI}$$
$$\text{FI}$$

In the first alternative, $r < b$ is false. Simplifying,

$$G == \text{IF } r = b \text{ THEN } r := r - b; G$$
$$\text{ELSE IF } r < b \text{ THEN IF } r = 0 \text{ THEN Y}$$
$$\text{ELSE swap}(b, r); G$$
$$\text{FI}$$
$$\text{ELSE } r := r - b; G$$
$$\text{FI}$$
$$\text{FI}$$

In the first line, $[[r = b]] r := r - b; [[r = 0]] G$. By the hypothesis $r = 0$, G reduces to Y, for b is non-zero and thus r cannot be equal to b:

$$G = = \text{IF } r = b \text{ THEN } r := r - b; \text{Y}$$
$$\text{ELSE} \ldots$$

Y uses only b. We can thus omit the modification to r and simplify to

$$G = = \text{IF } r = b \text{ THEN Y}$$
$$\text{ELSE IF } r < b \text{ THEN IF } r = 0 \text{ THEN Y}$$
$$\text{ELSE swap}(b, r); \text{G}$$
$$\text{FI}$$
$$\text{ELSE } r := r - b; \text{G}$$
$$\text{FI}$$
$$\text{FI}$$

We have said that at the entry to the program $b \neq 0$ AND $r \neq 0$ is a preassertion of G. If we suppose this to be true before G, it will remain true through the above action. We cannot in fact leave it through G unless $r \neq b$, either by swap of b and r, which preserves this assertion, or by the subtraction of b from r (greater than b), which also preserves it. Thus, $r \neq 0$ AND $b \neq 0$ is the preassertion of G, and $r = 0$ cannot be true in G, which now simplifies:

$$G = = \text{IF } r = b \text{ THEN Y}$$
$$\text{ELSE IF } r < b \text{ THEN swap}(b, r); \text{G}$$
$$\text{ELSE } r := r - b; \text{G}$$
$$\text{FI}$$
$$\text{FI}$$
$$E = = \text{READ } a, b; r := a; \text{G}$$
$$Y = = \text{write}(b); \text{Z}$$

We have a new program which is worth spending a little more time on. Its resolution is very simple and is left as an exercise for the reader:

```
READ a, b; r := a;
WHILE r ≠ b DO
                IF r < b THEN swap(b, r) ELSE r := r − b FI
         OD;
write(b)
```

We can use the transformation of Section 7.7.2 on the WHILE loop. It becomes

```
WHILE r ≠ b DO
                WHILE r ≠ b AND r < b DO swap(b, r) OD;
                WHILE r ≠ b AND r ≥ b DO r := r − b OD
         OD
```

The first inner loop can be simplified:

$$r < b \qquad \text{implies} \qquad r \neq b$$

Thus, it reduces to

WHILE $r < b$ DO swap(b, r) OD

Call this loop U, its exit V, and rewrite it with an EXIT:

U == DO IF $r < b$ THEN swap(b, r)
                     ELSE EXIT
            FI
        OD; V

Make U recursive:

U == IF $r < b$ THEN swap(b, r); U ELSE V FI

We rewrite U in U, adding some assertions taken from the tests and from the semantics of the swap:

U == IF $r < b$ THEN $[[r < b]]$ swap(b, r); $[[r > b]]$
                     IF $r < b$ THEN swap(b, r) ELSE V FI
             ELSE V
     FI

In the first alternative, we can suppress the test on $r < b$, whose value is FALSE:

U == IF $r < b$ THEN swap(b, r); V ELSE V FI

or finally, by simple expansion,

U == IF $r < b$ THEN swap(b, r) FI; V

This selection replaces the WHILE loop. The new program is

WHILE $r \neq b$ DO
               IF $r < b$ THEN swap(b, r) FI;
               WHILE $r \geq b$ AND $r \neq b$ DO $r := r - b$ OD
        OD

The expression $r \geq b$ AND $r \neq b$ simplifies to $r > b$:

READ a, b; $r := a$;
WHILE $r \neq b$ DO
               IF $r < b$ THEN swap(b, r) FI;
               WHILE $r > b$ DO $r := r - b$ OD
            OD;
     write(b)

The strategy of this program is remarkably different:

−we begin with a and b;
−if the first number in this pair is not greater than or equal to the second, they are swapped;
−if possible, the second is subtracted from the first; if this results in the equality of the two numbers, the program has finished; if not, the numbers are permuted and we begin again.

We are already a long way from Euclid's strategy. But we could perhaps expect more of symmetry in the parts played by b and r.

We return to the system of actions. We replace G by its value after the swap of b and r, because some possibility of simplification must appear, all the tests on b, r having known values:

$$G == \text{IF } r = b \text{ THEN Y}$$
$$\text{ELSE IF } r < b$$
$$\text{THEN swap}(b, r);$$
$$\text{IF } r = b \text{ THEN Y}$$
$$\text{ELSE IF } r < b \text{ THEN swap}(b, r); \text{ G}$$
$$\text{ELSE } r := r - b; \text{ G}$$
$$\text{FI}$$
$$\text{FI}$$
$$\text{ELSE } r := r - b; \text{ G}$$
$$\text{FI}$$
$$\text{FI}$$

After $r < b$ and swap(b, r), $b < r$ is true. Thus there remains

$$G == \text{IF } r = b \text{ THEN Y}$$
$$\text{ELSE IF } r < b \text{ THEN swap}(b, r); r := r - b; \text{ G}$$
$$\text{ELSE } r := r - b; \text{ G}$$
$$\text{FI}$$
$$\text{FI}$$

By a local semantic transformation, we can replace

$$\text{swap}(b, r); r := r - b$$

by

$$b := b - r; \text{swap}(b, r)$$

We introduce a new action L:

$$L \ == \ \mathrm{swap}(b,r); \ G$$
$$G \ == \ \mathrm{IF} \ r = b \ \mathrm{THEN} \ Y$$
$$\mathrm{ELSE \ IF} \ r < b \ \mathrm{THEN} \ b := b - r; \ L$$
$$\mathrm{ELSE} \ \ r := r - b; G$$
$$\mathrm{FI}$$
$$\mathrm{FI}$$

To make the symmetry complete, we must have L = = G. Let us try to verify this. We take G into L:

$$L \ == \ \mathrm{swap}(b,r);$$
$$\mathrm{IF} \ r = b \ \mathrm{THEN} \ Y$$
$$\mathrm{ELSE \ IF} \ r < b \ \mathrm{THEN} \ b := b - r; \ L$$
$$\mathrm{ELSE} \ \ r := r - b; G$$
$$\mathrm{FI}$$
$$\mathrm{FI}$$

We advance the instruction $\mathrm{swap}(b, r)$ into the selections which follow it. This has no effect on the test $b = r$.

After this test, if it has the value TRUE, we find

$$\mathrm{swap}(b,r); \ Y$$

But if $b = r$, the swap produces nothing and the instruction can be suppressed. The test $r < b$ is changed into $b < r$:

$$\mathrm{swap}(b,r); \ b := b - r; \ L$$

becomes

$$r := r - b; \ \mathrm{swap}(b,r); \ L$$

We replace L by its value:

$$r := r - b; \ \mathrm{swap}(b,r); \ \mathrm{swap}(b,r); \ G$$

The sequence of two swap instructions has no effect. There remains

$$r := r - b; \ G$$

Then

$$\mathrm{swap}(b,r); \ r := r - b; \ G$$

becomes

$$b := b - r; \ \mathrm{swap}(b,r); \ G \qquad \text{or} \qquad b := b - r; \ L$$

Finally,

$$L == \text{IF } r = b \text{ THEN Y}$$
$$\text{ELSE IF } b < r \text{ THEN } r := r - b; G$$
$$\text{ELSE } b := b - r; L$$
$$\text{FI}$$
$$\text{FI}$$

This form is identical to that of G, except that the test on $r < b$ has been turned around and the alternatives permuted. It follows that $L == G$, and we obtain a new program:

$$E == \text{READ } a, b; r := a; G$$
$$G == \text{IF } r = b \text{ THEN Y}$$
$$\text{ELSE IF } r < b \text{ THEN } b := b - r; G$$
$$\text{ELSE } r := r - b; G$$
$$\text{FI}$$
$$\text{FI}$$
$$Y == \text{write}(b); Z$$

The solution of this is quite clear, and so we obtain the required program:

```
READ a, b; r := a;
WHILE r ≠ b DO
            IF r < b THEN b := b − r ELSE r := r − b FI
      OD;
write(b)
```

Its strategy is plain; as long as the two numbers are distinct, the smaller is subtracted from the larger. We have done enough manipulation of this program and will not find yet another form for it. But we must emphasise the result obtained here.

It is fashionable to say that a program is constructed on the basis of the properties of the entities manipulated and of the desired objective. The axioms of theorems concerning the function to be computed are used. Along these lines, it is said that Euclid's algorithm is founded on the following theorem:

Let a and b be two non-zero natural integers and q and r the quotient and remainder of the division of a by b. Then,

$$a = b * q + r \qquad 0 \le r < b$$

and *either* r is zero, and b is the required greatest common divisor, *or* r is non-zero, and any number which divides a and b also divides r, so that the required number is also the greatest common divisor of b and r.

This is seen clearly in the first version of the program. The last algorithm is based on another property:

Any number which divides a and b also divides *either* $a - b$ (if $a > b$) *or* $b - a$ (if $b > a$).

This is what is seen in the last algorithm. What is rather surprising for us is that we have passed from one program to the other without any axiomatic change and without any appeal to any property of the greatest common divisor. This is by no means an isolated phenomenon; we have several examples of the same kind.

What should we conclude from this? I do not know how to reply, if not to say that programming offers new paths of research and new ways to construct algorithms of which we should both take account and give account. I ignore completely how they relate to the ways of mathematics.

Exercises

E.7.1   Apply the transformation due to S. Gerhardt (Section 7.7.2) to the program of Section 7.8; then simplify it and comment on it.

E.7.2   Here is a program, n being an odd natural integer:

WHILE $n \neq 1$ DO
$n := n + 1$;
WHILE even(n) DO $n := 3 * n : 2$ OD;
$n := n - 1$;
WHILE even(n) DO $n := n : 2$ OD
OD

How is it related to

WHILE $n \neq 1$ DO
IF even(n) THEN $n := n : 2$ ELSE $n := 3 * n + 1$ FI
OD

E.7.3   The plateau problem was presented in Exercise E.6.4. It can be given in three iterative forms, based on the following recurrence hypotheses:

—we have gone through the vector as far as a certain point, which is the end of a plateau, and we know the length of the longest plateau so far;

—we have gone through the vector as far as a certain point, whose position in a plateau is arbitrary, and we know the length of the longest plateau so far; we know in addition the position of the beginning of the plateau in which that certain point is;

—we have gone through the vector as far as a certain point, whose position in a plateau is arbitrary; we know the length of the longest plateau so far, but the positions of the beginnings of the plateaus have not been recorded.

Write these three forms. Relate them to the automaton of Exercise E.6.4. How can one pass from one form to another?

E.7.4 Write a sorting program for the following method:

—the vector a is supposed sorted from 1 to i. If the sorting is not finished, we take the element $i + 1$ to its place in the sorted part, exchanging it step by step with its predecessors as long as it is smaller than each one.

This will give rise to a loop containing an operation which swaps neighbouring elements

$$\text{swap}(a[j + 1], a[j])$$

Making this operation explicit can be done in two ways:

$$x := a[j]; a[j] := a[j + 1]; a[j + 1] := x$$

and

$$x := a[j + 1]; a[j + 1] := a[j]; a[j] := x$$

In one of these forms, it happens that x has a value constant over the loop, which allows some simplification and leads to a change of strategy. Show evidence for this, and set out the new strategy.

E.7.5 Consider again the sorting program of Section 1.7. Find a transformation which allows it to be changed into the program of Exercise E.7.4. This requires a careful treatment of assertions.

Chapter 8

The Transformation of Sub-Programs from Recursive to Iterative

8.1 Generalised Actions

8.1.1 Intuitive Presentation

Let a be a non-empty, correctly parenthesised, string of characters and i a pointer directed at a character of the string which is either an opening parenthesis or a character of a substring of i enclosed within a pair of parentheses. We wish to find an action AACP which will advance i to point at the associated closing parenthesis (associated, that is, either with the opening parenthesis at i or with the sub-string containing the character at i).

Advance to the next character. If this is a closing parenthesis, we have reached the goal. If it is not a parenthesis, we are still with the conditions of the problem as they were, the character i being between the same pair of parentheses, and we are again faced with the same problem. If, finally, it is an opening parenthesis, we have to jump to its associated closing parenthesis (by the action AACP itself) and then continue to advance towards the parenthesis sought for, having returned to the original parenthetic level:

$$\text{AACP} == i := i + 1;$$
$$\text{IF } sbs(a, i, 1) = \text{``)'' THEN finished}$$
$$\text{ELSE IF } sbs(a, i, 1) \neq \text{``(''}$$
$$\text{THEN AACP}$$
$$\text{ELSE AACP; AACP}$$
$$\text{FI}$$
$$\text{FI}$$

The action AACP is not regular; it has a non-terminal call. Experience has shown that many readers are put off by such a procedure. In the sequence

AACP; AACP, the first call makes the pointer jump to the closing parenthesis associated with the opening parenthesis which has just been found, and the second causes resumption of the scanning:

$$\ldots\ldots \quad (\quad \ldots(\ldots\ldots)\ldots \quad) \quad \ldots\ldots)$$
$$i \quad \text{AACP} \underline{\hspace{2cm}} \text{AACP}$$

We shall discuss later what is most suitable to put in place of the word "finished", whose significance here is clear—we have satisfied the postassertion assigned to the action, and so the action is complete. This implies nothing about what is to happen afterwards; that will be discussed now.

8.1.2   Definition

By defining new actions as they are needed, a system of actions containing a generalised action can be put into such a form that it contains

−regular actions;
−a generalised action X having $n + 1$ non-terminal occurrences in the noted actions

$$\text{U}i == \text{X}; \text{Y}i \qquad i = 0, 1, \ldots, n$$

This implies that the system for concatenating actions should be generalised. A regular action designates its successors explicitly. Every terminal position being occupied by an action name, every execution terminates by calling an explicitly named action.

Here, two mechanisms for concatenation are put to work:

−X may, in some executions, terminate with the explicit designation of a successor; this is the case for every terminal position occupied by an action name. For example, in AACP, the fact of reaching some character other than a parenthesis causes AACP, the explicitly designated successor, to be called.

−X, in every other execution, does not designate its successor, but the execution continues in sequence after X. The successor is therefore the action which follows X in a non-terminal call.

If, for example, the execution of X in

$$\text{U}i == \text{X}; \text{Y}i$$

is followed in sequence, then the successor of X is Yi. It is defined by the context, not in the body of X.

This means that not all the terminal positions of X are occupied by action names, but certain of them lead in sequence to what is after X. An instruction leading in sequence to what is after a sequence of instructions has been called "a terminal instruction of empty value". In other words, a terminal position of a generalised action is occupied

–either by an action name,
–or by a terminal instruction of value 0.

In AACP, the word "finished" designates, therefore, a terminal instruction of value 0. As it is not enclosed in any iteration, it must be the the instruction EXIT(0) (the empty instruction). For simplicity, we shall attach to every generalised action X an empty action, denoted by $-X$, to represent this terminal instruction of value 0 and so to maintain in a conventional way the fact that every terminal position is occupied by an action name. But one of these names is empty, is not defined in the system, and only marks the route of continuation in sequence. With this convention, AACP becomes

$$\text{AACP} == i := i + 1;$$
$$\text{IF } sbs(a, i, 1) = \text{")" THEN } -\text{AACP}$$
$$\text{ELSE } \text{IF } sbs(a, i, 1) \neq \text{"("}$$
$$\text{THEN AACP}$$
$$\text{ELSE AACP; AACP}$$
$$\text{FI}$$
$$\text{FI}$$

8.1.3 Interpretation

From what we have just seen, the action $-X$ represents exit in sequence from X, and it leads to one of the Yi, depending on the context. So $-X$ stands for one of the Yi, and it has no defined syntactic value.

We cannot, then, replace the action calls syntactically by branchings. The only possible interpretation is to consider the actions as procedures without parameters.

We shall expand the precedence relation defined over a regular system (Section 6.4) in the following way:

$-\alpha$ being an action distinct from the Ui and β an action having one terminal occurrence in α, α precedes β,
$-Ui$ precedes X (for all i),
$--X$ precedes each of the Yi.

If there is only one non-terminal call,

$$U0 == X; Y0$$

the only possible value for $-X$ is Y0. We can then directly replace U0 by X and $-X$ by Y0, so obtaining a regular system. This is a degenerate case which we do not need to consider further.

The power of expression of generalised actions is considerable [HEN]. We shall not consider all the possible situations. We shall confine ourselves to the case where X represents a "procedure" in the usual sense of the term; it is entered by X, and it is left by $-X$. We translate this by saying that, in the graph of actions, there exists a sub-graph having as unique entry point X and as unique exit point $-X$.

To be precise, all the successors of X belong to the sub-graph; all the predecessors of $-X$ are in the sub-graph; no arc penetrates into the sub-graph other than through X, and no arc leaves the sub-graph other than by $-X$.

There are two extreme cases. First there is the case where none of the Ui belongs to the sub-graph. Here the sub-graph is that of a regular system of actions, having X as entry point and $-X$ for exit point. This system can be resolved into

$$X == a; -X$$

where a is a proper sequence.

We can substitute this resolved form into each of the calls

$$Ui == X; Yi$$

which then becomes

$$Ui == a; -X; Yi$$

Here the value of $-X$ is defined explicitly, and this sequence is equivalent, more simply, to

$$Ui == a; Yi$$

The system is now regular. In fact, we have resolved the procedure X into a body a, and then, by the copy rule, we have replaced each call of X by a copy of the body of the procedure. This case is simple, and no more will be said of it.

The other extreme case is that where all the Ui except one, U0 say, belong to the sub-graph X. There is then one single arc entering the sub-graph, the arc from U0 to X, and one arc leaving it, that from $-X$ to Y0. We shall term the call of X in U0 the initial call, or the first activated call. The other calls of X in the Ui are recursive calls of X in the body of the procedure. This is the case we shall consider below. If there are several U at the outside of the graph, we are again dealing with a recursive procedure, several non-recursive calls of which exist outside the procedure. We shall not examine this case; in practice X will first be transformed into an iterative procedure, of the form

$$X == a; -X$$

by techniques which will be set out; after this a is substituted for X in the different calls.

The procedure AACP given above does not have the canonical form which we are considering. Its initial call has not been marked. It should be

$$
\begin{array}{ll}
P == AACP; Z & \text{the initial call}\\
U == AACP; AACP & \text{is the recursive call}\\
AACP == i := i + 1; \\
\quad\text{IF sbs}(a, i, 1) = \text{``)''}\\
\quad\quad\text{THEN } -AACP\\
\quad\quad\text{ELSE IF sbs}(a, i, 1) \neq \text{``(''} \text{ THEN AACP ELSE U FI}\\
\quad\text{FI}
\end{array}
$$

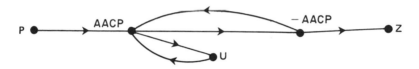

In the accompanying associated graph, U belongs to the sub-graph AACP, and this procedure is thus truly recursive. It has been used in this form on a microprocessor in assembly language. A description is given here in plain language, each line corresponding to one machine instruction. The microprocessor has two ordinary registers and an index register. The subroutine calls can be recursive, the computer stacking the return addresses at the moment of call and unstacking them at exit:

P	assign to register 1	")"
	assign to register 2	"("
	assign to the index register	i
AACP	increment the index register	
	compare register 1 to	a, index
	branch if equal to	−AACP
	compare register 2 to	a, index
	branch if not equal to	AACP
U	call subroutine	AACP
	branch to	AACP
−AACP	return	

The terminal calls have been translated into branchings. The non-terminal call has been translated into a recursive call of the procedure. This is a particularly effective form to which we shall return.

8.2 Regularisation

8.2.1 The General Case

Non-terminal calls have to be eliminated, and this is only possible if we use the one mechanism of explicit concatenation by terminal calls. This is a matter of replacing $-X$ by its value, which is one of the Yi:

$$-X == f(Y0, Y1, \ldots, Yn)$$

If we can find explicitly this sequence f, then each call

$$Ui == X; Yi \qquad \text{will be replaceable by} \quad Ui == X$$

The whole problem is to construct f, an operation which is semantic in nature.

8.2.2 The Use of Predicates

Let us suppose that $n + 1$ mutually exclusive predicates $t0$, $t1, \ldots, tn$, preassertions for the Yi, can be determined. They can be used to define $-X$:

$$
\begin{aligned}
-X == \text{IF } t0 \text{ THEN Y0} \\
\text{ELSE IF } t1 \text{ THEN Y1} \\
\text{ELSE} \ldots \ldots \\
\text{FI} \\
\text{FI}
\end{aligned}
$$

These predicates will be obtained usually as the result of a careful study of the assertions of the program. We shall give some examples because, when it is possible, it is the best solution. When such predicates are not available, they have to be created by means of a global variable.

8.2.3 The Property of Invariance

We shall go on with the same recursive procedure X, with an initial call

$$U0 == X; Y0$$

and the recursive calls, all in the body of X:

$$Ui == X; Yi \quad 1 \leq i \leq n$$

We shall add to the system a global variable k (necessarily global, for all the variables of the system are global), distinct from all other variables. Because of this, k is not affected by any of the actions of the system.

We wish to have k invariant over X. If then $k0$ is the value of k before the call of X, we require

$$[[k = k0]] \, X \, [[k = k0]]$$

To ensure the invariance of k over X, we operate by recurrence. We suppose that k is modified only in the Ui, $i \neq 0$. Since k is a variable added to the system and modified only in the Ui, its value is invariant if X is left through $-X$ without any intervening recursive call.

We set out the modifications of k in Ui:

$$Ui == k := f_i(k); X; k := g_i(k); Yi$$

By recurrence, we suppose k invariant over the inner call:

$$[[k = k0]] \, Ui == [[k = k0]] \, k := f_i(k) \, [[k = f_i(k0)]];$$
$$X; [[k = f_i(k0)]]$$
$$k := g_i(k) \, [[k = g_i(f_i(k0))]]; Yi$$

We can keep k invariant only if this last assertion guarantees $k = k0$; and if this is so, then k is invariant over each sequence Ui. As it is not modified anywhere else, it is invariant over X.

This result is obtained if f_i has an inverse and $g_i = f_i^{-1}$:

$$Ui == k := f_i(k); X; k := f_i^{-1}(k); Yi$$

We can then initialise k in $U0$.

$$U0 == k := k0; X; [[k = k0]] \, Y0$$

8.2.4 The Activation Counter

We consider first the case where there is only one recursive call: $n = 1$. There are two non-terminal calls:

-the initial call $U0 == X; Y0$
-the recursive call $U1 == X; Y1$

An activation counter, giving the depth of recursion attained, is sufficient to distinguish them. The counter is initialised in $U0$, for example, to the value 0, and then incremented before the recursive call of X:

$$U0 == k := 0; X; [[k = 0]] Y0$$

In U1, $f_1(x)$ is $x + 1$ and $f_1^{-1}(x)$ is $x - 1$:

$$U1 == k := k + 1; X; [[k \neq 0]] k := k - 1; Y1$$

To make things clearer, we can introduce here a new action Y1P:

$$U1 == k := k + 1; X; [[k \neq 0]] Y1P$$
$$Y1P == k := k - 1; Y1$$

It is then easy to define $-X$ because we have a predicate $k = 0$ characterising the first activation. We obtain the regular system

$$U0 == k := 0; X$$
$$U1 == k := k + 1; X$$
$$-X == \text{IF } k = 0 \text{ THEN Y0 ELSE Y1P FI}$$

The action Y1P can now be eliminated:

$$U0 == k := 0; X$$
$$U1 == k := k + 1; X$$
$$-X == \text{IF } k = 0 \text{ THEN Y0 ELSE } k := k - 1; \text{Y1 FI}$$

8.2.5   The n-ary Counter

We can now consider the general case $n > 1$. The initial call has to be distinguished from the recursive calls, and each recursive call from the others. One way would be to stack before each recursive call an integral value proper to that call, for example, its serial number:

$$Ui == \text{push}(i); X; \text{pop}(i); Yi$$

This ensures the global invariance of the stack, initialised to the empty state in U0. In $-X$, an empty stack characterises the initial call, a non-empty stack a recursive call. By removing the integer from the top of the stack, one obtains the serial number of the call.

But this stack contains only integers in the range $1:n$. It can thus be considered as the representation of an integer in some convenient base.

The base $n + 1$ could be used, but the number 0 is not used. It would appear more economical then to stack not i but $i - 1$, an integer in the range $0:n - 1$. The stack then represents an integer in base n. The difficulty will be in distinguishing between the empty stack and a stack containing only zeros, and so read as the integer 0. We might overcome this by, for example, starting at the number 1 for the n-ary counter. We would then have

$$U0 == k := 1; X; [[k = 1]] \; Y0$$
$$Ui == k := n * k + i - 1; X;$$
$$[[k > 1 \text{ AND } \text{mod}(k, n) = i - 1]]$$
$$k, r := \text{div}(k, n); Yi$$

The assignment $k, r := \text{div}(k, n)$ placed between X and Yi effects the inverse of the modification made before the call of X. The variable r is another supplementary variable introduced here for convenience, but which is needed only in the tests distinguishing the values of $-X$.

There is no point in having supplementary actions representing what follows X in the Ui. All the assignments $k, r := \text{div}(k, n)$ are regrouped in $-X$.

Thus the system

$$U0 == X; Y0$$
$$Ui == X; Yi \qquad 1 \le i \le n$$

is regularised to

$$U0 == k := 1; X$$
$$Ui == k := n * k + i - 1; X \qquad 1 \le i \le n$$
$$-X == \text{IF } k = 1 \text{ THEN } Y0$$
$$\qquad \text{ELSE} \quad k, r := \text{div}(k, n);$$
$$\qquad\qquad \text{IF } r = 0 \text{ THEN } Y1$$
$$\qquad\qquad \text{ELSE} \quad \text{IF } r = 1 \text{ THEN } Y2$$
$$\qquad\qquad\qquad\qquad \cdots\cdots$$
$$\qquad\qquad\qquad\qquad \text{FI}$$
$$\qquad\qquad \text{FI}$$
$$\qquad \text{FI}$$

This does not of course prejudice any simplifications which may be possible in each particular case.

This solution is by no means unique. Any way of marking the calls Ui so that their exits Yi will be distinguished, thus ensuring a definition of $-X$, is acceptable. We shall see other examples of this.

8.3   Example

Let us apply this to AACP. We can symbolise the program calling AACP by

$$P == f; AACP; Y$$

We isolate the non-terminal call

$$Q == AACP; AACP$$

We have then the system

$$P == f; AACP; Y$$
$$Q == AACP; AACP$$
$$AACP == i := i + 1;$$

　　　IF sbs$(a, i, 1) =$ ")" THEN $-$AACP

　　　　　　ELSE IF sbs$(a, i, 1) \neq$ "(" THEN AACP

　　　　　　　　　　ELSE Q

　　　　　　　FI

　　FI

We have no information which would enable us to distinguish between the initial call and the recursive calls. There are only two non-terminal calls. An activation counter is enough:

$$P == f; k := 0; AACP$$
$$Q == k := k + 1; AACP$$
$$-AACP == \text{IF } k = 0 \text{ THEN Y}$$

　　　　　　　ELSE $k := k - 1; AACP$

　　FI

　$AACP == i := i + 1;$

　　　IF sbs$(a, i, 1) =$ ")" THEN $-$AACP

　　　　　　ELSE IF sbs$(a, i, 1) \neq$ "(" THEN AACP

　　　　　　　　　　ELSE Q

　　　　　　　FI

　　FI

We leave the resolution of this regular system to the reader, giving only the resolved form:

$f; k := 0;$

DO

　$i := i + 1;$

　IF sbs$(a, i, 1) =$ ")" THEN IF $k = 0$ THEN EXIT

　　　　　　　　　　　　　ELSE $k := k - 1$

　　　　　　　　　　FI

　　　　　　　ELSE IF sbs$(a, i, 1) =$ "(" THEN $k := k + 1$ FI

　　FI

OD;

Y

This is the traditional form of a procedure for finding the associated closing parenthesis. A counter k is incremented by 1 at each opening parenthesis and decremented at each closing parenthesis, the process terminating with the closing parenthesis associated with level 0. A "physical" interpretation might be given of k—it is the number of opening parentheses which have not yet been balanced by their corresponding closing parentheses.

This form is not very efficient on a microprocessor because it requires the manipulation of a supplementary variable. We could ask ourselves how the first procedure was found. In fact, the call of procedure involves the stacking of the return address (that of the preceding line, $-$AACP in the program of Section 8.1.3). At each recursive call, the height of the stack increases by 1. When a closing parenthesis is detected, the procedure is left, and so the height of the stack reduces by 1. It is thus the height which plays the part of the counter.

I find it remarkable that I had never found the efficient form of Section 8.1.3 before I did this work on actions and recursion. However, this form does not depend on any special knowledge; it is no more than an application of recursive thinking. On the contrary, once this procedure has been found and well understood, a new style of programming becomes apparent, which uses systematically the recursion of sub-programs without formal parameters or local variables. In this way I have written a system LSE for a microprocessor. It achieves very interesting performance figures with regard to computing time and storage requirements.

8.4   The Schemes of Irlik

Jacek Irlik has put forward [IRL] a number of models of recursive procedures and has given for each one an equivalent iterative scheme on the basis of a semantic interpretation. We shall study the most complex of these schemes to show how the method proposed here takes account of it and to compare our result with that of Irlik.

The procedure considered by Irlik is

$$X == \text{IF } p \text{ THEN a}; -X$$
$$\text{ELSE } f_0; X; f_1; \ldots; X; f_n; -X$$
$$\text{FI}$$

By the creation of new actions, we put it into the canonical form, and we add the action Q which calls X and represents the initial call and whose exit is Z (Q is written for U0).

$$Q == X; Z$$
$$X == \text{IF } p \text{ THEN a}; -X$$
$$\text{ELSE } f_0; U1$$
$$\text{FI}$$
$$Ui == X; Yi \qquad \text{for} \quad i = 1 \text{ to } n-1$$
$$Yi == f_i; Uj \qquad \text{with} \quad j = i+1$$
$$Yn == f_n; -X$$

We can apply the results of Section 8.3 directly:

$$Q == k := 1; X$$
$$X == \text{IF } p \text{ THEN } a; -X \text{ ELSE } f_0; U1 \text{ FI}$$
$$U1 == k := n * k; X$$

$$\ldots$$

$$Ui == k := n * k + i - 1; X$$

$$\ldots$$

$$Un == k := n * k + n - 1; X$$
$$Y1 == f_1; U2$$

$$\ldots$$

$$Yi == f_i; Uj \qquad \text{with} \quad j = i + 1$$

$$\ldots$$

$$Yn == f_n; -X$$

Finally,

$$-X == \text{IF } k = 1 \text{ THEN Z}$$
$$\text{ELSE} \quad k, r := \text{div}(k, n);$$
$$\text{IF } r = 0 \text{ THEN Y1}$$
$$\text{ELSE} \quad \text{IF } r = 1$$
$$\text{THEN Y2}$$
$$\ldots\ldots$$
$$\text{ELSE IF } r = n - 2$$
$$\text{THEN Y}n - 1$$
$$\text{ELSE} \quad Yn$$
$$\ldots\ldots$$
$$\text{FI}$$
$$\text{FI}$$
$$\text{FI}$$
$$\text{FI}$$

If we replace Yi by its value

$$Yi == f_i; Uj$$

and then Uj by its value

$$Yi == f_i; k := n * k + j - 1; X$$

we see that all the exits from the alternatives are through X except the first, which is through Z, and the last, by way of Yn:

$$Yn == f_n; -X$$

through $-X$.

We shall modify the numbering of the exits so that Yn comes with the case $r = 0$, and in such a way that the first exit is through Z, the second through $-X$, and all the others through X.

We thus change Ui to

$$Ui == k := n * k + n - i; X$$

giving for U1

$$U1 == k := n * k + n - 1; X$$

We thus obtain, with the Yi replaced by their values,

$$X == \text{IF } p \text{ THEN } a; -X \text{ ELSE } f_0; k := n * k + n - 1; X \text{ FI}$$
$$-X == \text{IF } k = 1 \text{ THEN } Z$$
$$\text{ELSE} \quad k, r := \text{div}(k, n);$$
$$\text{IF } r = 0 \text{ THEN } f_n; -X$$
$$\text{ELSE IF } r = 1 \text{ THEN } f_{n-1}; k := n * k; X$$
$$\text{ELSE} \quad \ldots\ldots$$
$$\ldots\ldots$$
$$\text{ELSE IF } r = n - 2 \text{ THEN } f_2; k := n * k + n - 3; X$$
$$\text{ELSE} \quad f_1; k := n * k + n - 2; X$$
$$\text{FI}$$
$$\ldots\ldots$$
$$\text{FI}$$
$$\text{FI}$$
$$\text{FI}$$

We can now reorganise the tests on k. We note that $k = 1$ gives $\text{mod}(k, n) \neq 0$:

$$-X == \text{IF } \text{mod}(k, n) = 0 \text{ THEN } k := k : n; f_n; -X \text{ ELSE } R \text{ FI}$$
$$R == \text{IF } k = 1 \text{ THEN } Z \text{ ELSE } S \text{ FI}$$
$$S == k, r := \text{div}(k, n);$$
$$\text{IF } r = 1 \text{ THEN } f_{n-1}; k := n * k; X$$
$$\text{ELSE} \ldots.$$
$$\text{FI}$$

Let $k_0 = n * k' + i$ be the value of k at the entry to S. The values of k and r are obtained from $k, r := \text{div}(k, n)$; they are $k = k'$ and $r = i$.

Next,

$$f_{i-1}; k := n * k + i - 1; X$$

is executed. The final value of k is

$$n * k' + i - 1 = k_0 - 1$$

independent of the value of i. Over the sequence S, k decreases by 1 whichever branch is followed. We can "factorise" this operation out, and the computation of k' is now unnecessary:

$$S == r := \mod(k, n);$$
$$\text{IF } r = 1 \text{ THEN } f_{n-1}$$
$$\text{ELSE } \text{IF } r = 2 \text{ THEN } f_{n-2}$$
$$\text{ELSE IF} \ldots\ldots$$
$$\text{ELSE } f_1$$
$$\ldots\ldots$$
$$\text{FI}$$
$$\text{FI}$$
$$\text{FI};$$
$$k := k - 1; X$$

If the function which executes f_{n-i} when r has the value i is called $sf(r)$,

$$S == r := \mod(k, n); sf(r); k := k - 1; X$$

We can now write the iterative procedure Q equivalent to X. The resolution of the system is easy and is left as an exercise for the reader. We have introduced the action R to make a WHILE loop appear in $-X$:

$$Q == k := 1;$$
$$\text{DO}$$
$$\text{WHILE NOT } p \text{ DO}$$
$$f_0; k := n * k + n - 1$$
$$\text{OD};$$
$$a;$$
$$\text{WHILE } \mod(k, n) = 0 \text{ DO}$$
$$f_n; k := k : n$$
$$\text{OD};$$
$$\text{IF } k = 1 \text{ THEN EXIT FI};$$
$$sf(\mod(k, n));$$
$$k := k - 1$$
$$\text{OD};$$
$$Z$$

There are other possible simplifications, but they are of interest only when we have further information. In particular, the first WHILE loop accumulates the operations

$$k := n * k + n - 1$$

If we define a variable k' by $k' = k + 1$,

$$k' := n * k + n = n * (k + 1) = n * k'$$

If then the loop is done q times, k' is simply multiplied by n, q times,

$$k' := k' * n^q$$

so finally,

$$k := (k + 1) * n^q - 1$$

is the effect of the loop on k.

We shall make use of this from time to time.

We shall now compare our solution to that of Irlik. Irlik uses n supplementary variables $d, j_1, \ldots, j_{n-1}$.

The initial call defines these variables:

$$Q == j_1 := 0; \ldots; j_{n-1} := 0; d := 1; X; Z$$
$$X == \text{IF } p \text{ THEN } a; -X$$
$$\qquad \text{ELSE } j_1 := j_1 + d; \ldots; j_{n-1} := j_{n-1} + d; d := 2 * d; f_0;$$
$$\qquad\qquad X;$$
$$\qquad\qquad j_1 := j_1 - d:2; f_1; X;$$
$$\qquad\qquad \ldots\ldots$$
$$\qquad\qquad j_{n-1} := j_{n-1} - d:2; f_{n-1}; X;$$
$$\qquad\qquad d := d:2; f_n; -X$$
$$\qquad \text{FI}$$

The j_i and d are invariant over X. This can be demonstrated by recurrence; if it is true for each of the inner calls, it is true for the outer call. It is true if there is no recursion. This being so, we have the required predicates:

$$\text{in } Q, \quad \text{before } Z, \quad d = 1$$

In X, after the first X, $j_i \geq d:2$ for all i:

After $f_i: X$ we have $j_k < d:2$ for $k \leq i$, the others being greater than $d:2$.

By developing these computations, we obtain the procedure put forward by Irlik:

$$Q == j_1 := 0; \ldots; j_{n-1} := 0; d := 1;$$
$$\qquad \text{DO}$$
$$\qquad\qquad \text{WHILE NOT } p$$
$$\qquad\qquad\qquad \text{DO}$$
$$\qquad\qquad\qquad\qquad j_i := j_1 + d; \ldots; j_{n-1} := j_{n-1} + d; d := 2 * d; f_0$$
$$\qquad\qquad\qquad \text{OD};$$
$$\qquad\qquad a;$$
$$\qquad\qquad \text{DO}$$
$$\qquad\qquad\qquad \text{IF } d = 1 \text{ THEN EXIT(2) FI};$$
$$\qquad\qquad\qquad \text{IF } j_1 \geq d:2 \text{ THEN } j_1 := j_1 - d:2; f_1; \text{EXIT FI};$$
$$\qquad\qquad\qquad \ldots\ldots$$
$$\qquad\qquad\qquad \text{IF } j_{n-1} \geq d:2 \text{ THEN } j_{n-1} := j_{n-1}:2; f_{n-1}; \text{EXIT FI};$$
$$\qquad\qquad\qquad d := d:2$$
$$\qquad\qquad \text{OD}$$
$$\qquad \text{OD};$$
$$\qquad Z$$

Simplifications are possible here also. The relative merits of the two solutions cannot be discussed in absolute terms—they depend on what simplifications can be made. If none is possible, the first solution is better, as it requires only one variable k to control it; but it requires arithmetic in base n. Here the j are binary variables, each one attached to an occurrence of X.

What does appear interesting is that the method we have put forward allows due account to be taken of Irlik's transformation, if the supplementary variables are well chosen as recognising the several exits through $-$X. But it also allows others to be put forward. That is yet again the difference between a general method which can be adapted to particular cases and a catalogue of outline schemes which have very little chance to cope with the very wide variety of possible situations.

8.5 Formal Parameters and Global Variables

8.5.1 Local Variables

Let X be a procedure with local variables whose reach extends beyond a recursive call. The values of these variables must be globally invariant over a call of X. As they are local to X, this new call is in danger of redefining them. This leads us either to store them in a stack before the call of X and fetch them back at the exit:

$$U_i == \text{push(local variables)}; X;$$
$$\text{pop(local variables)}; Y_i;$$

or to make them global by binding their names to different activations of X, for example, by putting them into a table indexed on the level of activation of X.

Some examples of this will be given.

8.5.2 Formal Parameters

Formal result parameters may, in general, be taken directly as global variables. Their values are effectively fixed by the execution of the procedure. Their values at entry are destroyed. There are no difficulties arising out of these parameters.

On the other hand, parameters serving as data for the procedure (parameters called, or passed, by value) can pose very delicate semantic problems. To fix our ideas, we denote by t the n-tuple of formal parameters serving as data. We write $X(t)$ for the procedure with its parameters. The initial call is

$$U0 == X(t_0); Y0$$

The recursive calls are

$$Ui == X(f_i(t)); Yi$$

We make t global. The effect of the call by value is given by a preassignment to t:

$$U0 == t:=t_0; X; \dots$$
$$Ui == t:= f_i(t); X; \dots$$

The problem is due to the fact that, in general, the value of t at the entry to Ui is used in Yi; t must be restored before Yi.

Suppose first that

$-t$ is globally invariant over X:

$$[[t = t']] X [[t = t']]$$

$-$each f_i has an inverse.

We can then define Ui:

$$Ui == t:= f_i(t); X; t:= f_i^{-1}(t); Yi$$

meaning that t is effectively globally invariant over X provided only that it is not modified in the other branches of X.

If any f_i does not possess an inverse, recourse to the stack is necessary.

We shall see also that the invariance of t over X is a condition that can be too much of a constraint. We shall give cases where this condition can be relaxed.

Rather than treating these points formally, we shall present some examples illustrating the different ways of replacing the formal parameters and global variables by local variables.

8.6   A Known Recursive Scheme

We shall first restate the recursive function definition of Section 4.1.1:

$$f(x) \simeq \text{IF } c(x) \text{ THEN } a(x) \text{ ELSE } f(b(x)) \circ d(x) \text{ FI}$$

This scheme has already been studied at length, which should allow attention to be focussed on its manner of operation rather than on the perfectly understood result.

The first thing to do is to replace the function definition by a recursive sub-program assigning the value of the result to a formal parameter. Let us call this r:

$$F(x, r) \qquad \text{is the procedure which effects} \quad r := f(x)$$

We thus have a procedure body which, as a first approach, can be written

$$F(x, r) = = \text{IF } c(x) \text{ THEN } r := a(x)$$
$$\qquad\qquad\qquad \text{ELSE } \quad r := f(b(x)) \circ d(x)$$
$$\qquad \text{FI}$$

We must make F appear on the right, and for this f must be isolated in the right-hand side of the assignment:

$$F(x, r) = = \text{IF } c(x) \text{ THEN } r := a(x)$$
$$\qquad\qquad\qquad \text{ELSE } \quad r := f(b(x)); r := r \circ d(x)$$
$$\qquad \text{FI}$$

Now the second alternative is written with F:

$$F(x, r) = = \text{IF } c(x) \text{ THEN } r := a(x)$$
$$\qquad\qquad\qquad \text{ELSE } \quad F(b(x), r); r := r \circ d(x)$$
$$\qquad \text{FI}$$

A very free style of writing has been used here, giving formal parameters to something which looks like an action. We shall refine the presentation in order to have something which is properly an action, or rather a system of actions.

First, the exit action $-F$ has to be made to appear explicitly, and then $-F$ has to replace the terminal actions of value 0. There is one of these, in the form of an empty instruction, at the end of each alternative:

$$F(x, r) = = \text{IF } c(x) \text{ THEN } r := a(x); -F$$
$$\qquad\qquad\qquad \text{ELSE } \quad F(b(x), r) := r \circ d(x); -F$$
$$\qquad \text{FI}$$

The initial call of F has to be revealed. For this, we make a program which calls F, applied to a given d, and exits through Z:

$$P = = F(d, r); \text{result} := r; Z$$

Now the formal parameters must be replaced by global variables. As it is a result, r is taken as global. For the given parameter there must be a pre-assignment to the global variable x:

$$P = = x := d; F; \text{result} := r; Z$$

In F, the call $F(b(x), r)$ becomes

$$x := b(x); F$$

but x is used in the form $d(x)$ after the call of F. It must therefore be either saved or recomputed.

In the former case, we have again two possibilities:

$$F == \text{IF } c(x) \text{ THEN } r := a(x); \, -F$$
$$ \text{ELSE} \quad \text{save}(x); \, x := b(x); \, F;$$
$$\phantom{F == \text{ELSE} \quad } \text{restore}(x); \, r := r \circ d(x);$$
$$\phantom{F == \text{ELSE} \quad } -F$$
$$ \text{FI}$$

But we can also save the value $d(x)$:

$$F == \text{IF } c(x) \text{ THEN } r := a(x); \, -F$$
$$ \text{ELSE} \quad \text{save}(d(x)); \, x := b(x); \, F;$$
$$\phantom{F == \text{ELSE} \quad } \text{restore}(y); \, r := r \circ y;$$
$$\phantom{F == \text{ELSE} \quad } -F$$
$$ \text{FI}$$

The most general way of saving x is to use a global variable p (which could be an array, a character string, or any other structure considered adequate). We assume p to be globally invariant over F. For this, p has to be left unchanged by the non-recursive branch of F.

The saving of x is achieved by a combination of x and p, giving a new p and having an inverse:

$$F == \text{IF } c(x) \text{ THEN } r := a(x); \, -F$$
$$ \text{ELSE} \quad p := g(p, x); \, x := b(x); \, F;$$
$$\phantom{F == \text{ELSE} \quad } p, x := g^{-1}(p); \, r := r \circ d(x);$$
$$ \text{FI}$$

If p is invariant over the inner call F, it is also invariant over the outer call, and this assures us of the (global) invariance of p and thus of the safety of x.

The stack is only one way of achieving this.

We shall develop the iterative program associated with this recursive form. We must add to P an initialisation of p (which, by extension, we may call the stack):

$$P == p := p_0; \, x := d; \, F; \, \text{result} := r; \, Z$$
$$Z == \text{IF } c(x) \text{ THEN } r := a(x); \, -F$$
$$ \text{ELSE } p := g(p, x); \, x := b(x); \, U$$
$$ \text{FI}$$
$$U == F; \, Y$$
$$Y == p, x := g^{-1}(p); \, r := r \circ d(x); \, -F$$

We have a predicate for the first activation—$p = p_0$ is true in P, but not in U.

Thus we have the regularised system:

$$P == p := p_0; x := d; F$$
$$F == \text{IF } c(x) \text{ THEN } r := a(x); -F$$
$$\qquad\qquad \text{ELSE } p := g(p, x); x := b(x); F$$
$$\qquad \text{FI}$$
$$-F == \text{IF } p = p_0 \text{ THEN result} := r; Z$$
$$\qquad\qquad \text{ELSE Y}$$
$$\qquad \text{FI}$$
$$Y == p, x := g^{-1}(x); r := r \circ d(x); -F$$

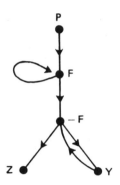

The resolution of this system is simple. We copy Y into $-F$. Then F and $-F$ are made iterative, which can be done with WHILE instructions. The details of the computations are without difficulty or interest:

$$p := p_0; x := d;$$
$$\text{WHILE NOT } c(x) \text{ DO}$$
$$\qquad\qquad\qquad p := g(p, x); X := b(x)$$
$$\qquad\qquad \text{OD};$$
$$r := a(x);$$
$$\text{WHILE } p \neq p_0 \text{ DO}$$
$$\qquad\qquad\qquad p, x := g^{-1}(x);$$
$$\qquad\qquad\qquad r := r \circ d(x)$$
$$\qquad\qquad \text{OD};$$
$$\text{result} := r$$

This is exactly the same program as that of Section 4.2. That is not surprising; the interesting point is that it has been obtained by a very different method.

We have seen one of the ways of saving x; $d(x)$ can be saved in the same way. Now let us consider the case where the recomputation of x is possible. We have

$$F(b(x), r)$$

We change this call to

$$x := b(x); F(x, r); x := b^{-1}(x)$$

assuming that b has an inverse. If we suppose x to be globally invariant over F, then it is globally invariant over this sequence also. We replace $F(x, r)$ by

F == IF c(x) THEN $r := a(x)$; $-$F
ELSE $x := b(x)$; F; $x := b^{-1}(x)$; $r := r \circ d(x)$; $-$F
   FI

This gives the system

P == $x := d$; F; result $:= r$; Z
F == IF c(x) THEN $r := a(x)$; $-$F
      ELSE $x := b(x)$; F; Y
   FI
Y == $x := b^{-1}(x)$; $r := r \circ d(x)$; $-$F

There is a predicate on x:

$$x = d$$

true in P after F (because x is globally invariant over F) and false after F in F (because if for some x in F we had $x = d$, then the sequence of the x would be periodic and F would not stop).

It is now easy to regularise the system:

P == $x := d$; F
F == IF c(x) THEN $r := a(x)$; $-$F
      ELSE $x := b(x)$; F
   FI
Y == $x := b^{-1}(x)$; $r := r \circ d(x)$; $-$F
$-$F == IF $x = d$ THEN result $:= r$; Z
        ELSE   Y
   FI

Here again, regularisation is simple:

$x := d$;
WHILE NOT c(x) DO $x := b(x)$ OD;
$r := a(x)$;
WHILE $x \neq d$ DO $x := b^{-1}(x)$; $r := r \circ d(x)$ OD;
result $:= r$

This is the program of Section 4.3.

It requires a little imagination to obtain a program with a single loop. The recursive procedure contains the operation

$$f(b(x)) \circ d(x)$$

Instead of F computing r, let us take F', combining the value of f operating on r:

$$\text{F}'(x, r) \qquad \text{effects} \quad r := f(x) \circ r$$

We proceed as above, giving first a form for F' with formal parameters:

$$\text{F}'(x, r) == \text{IF } c(x) \text{ THEN } r := a(x) \circ r$$
$$\text{ELSE } \quad r := f(b(x)) \circ d(x) \circ r$$
$$\text{FI}$$

If the operator $\circ$ is associative, we can compute the second operation first:

$$\text{F}'(x, r) == \text{IF } c(x) \text{ THEN } r := a(x) \circ r$$
$$\text{ELSE } \quad r := d(x) \circ r; r := f(b(x)) \circ r$$
$$\text{FI}$$

We can make F' appear on the right-hand side:

$$\text{F}'(x, r) == \text{IF } c(x) \text{ THEN } r := a(x) \circ r$$
$$\text{ELSE } \quad r := d(x) \circ r; \text{F}'(b(x), r)$$
$$\text{FI}$$

It is interesting that this time F' is in terminal position. If we can keep it in this position while the formal parameters are being replaced by global variables, we shall have a simpler, degenerate, case.

We form first the initial call. We wish to obtain

$$\text{result} := f(d)$$

by means of an operation $f(d) \circ r$. We take as r the right-hand neutral element

$$\text{P} == r := e; \text{F}'(d, r); \text{result} := r; Z$$

The parameter r is immediately made global. In F', x is not used after the call F'(b(x), r). There is no point in saving it.

$$\text{P} == r := e; x := d; \text{F}'; \text{result} := r; Z$$
$$\text{F}' == \text{IF } c(x) \text{ THEN } r := a(x) \circ r; -\text{F}'$$
$$\text{ELSE } \quad r := d(x) \circ r; x := b(x); \text{F}'$$
$$\text{FI}$$

As there is only one non-terminal call, we have directly

$$-\text{F}' == \text{result} := r; Z$$
$$\text{P} == r := e; x := d; \text{F}'$$
$$\text{F}' == \text{IF } c(x) \text{ THEN } r := a(x) \circ r; -\text{F}'$$
$$\text{ELSE } \quad r := d(x) \circ r; x := b(x); \text{F}'$$
$$\text{FI}$$

and after resolution,

$$r := e; x := d;$$
$$\text{WHILE NOT c}(x) \text{ DO}$$
$$\quad r := \text{d}(x) \circ r;$$
$$\quad x := \text{b}(x)$$
$$\text{OD};$$
$$\text{result} := \text{a}(x) \circ r$$

This is the program of Section 4.6.1.

We have, then, a considerable armoury of weapons for converting recursively defined functions into iterative procedures:

−by way of equivalent recurrent sequences, which are re-ordered and transformed into programs;

−by going directly to the iterative form and generalising the recursive form under the recurrence hypothesis;

−by writing a sub-program to compute the program, transforming this into regular actions, and resolving.

The preference of the programmer may fall on one or other of these according to the case in hand, but also according to his own aptitudes and tastes. We shall see, nevertheless, in Chapter 9 that the manipulation of actions tends to greater flexibility for the transformation of the program; as we saw in Chapter 7, actions provide an excellent means of transformation.

Exercises

E.8.1   Given a binary tree, that is, a tree each vertex of which may have only 0, 1 or 2 sub-trees (sons), the symmetric list of this tree is given by the procedure

$$\text{SYM}(r) == \text{IF } r = \text{null THEN}$$
$$\quad\quad\quad\quad\quad\quad\quad\quad \text{ELSE}\quad \text{SYM(leftson}(r));$$
$$\quad\quad\quad\quad\quad\quad\quad\quad\quad\quad\quad \text{write}(r);$$
$$\quad\quad\quad\quad\quad\quad\quad\quad\quad\quad\quad \text{SYM(rightson}(r))$$
$$\quad\quad\quad\quad \text{FI}$$

(null signifies an empty tree). Transform this into an iterative procedure.

E.8.2   The recursive procedure of the previous exercise can be modified so as not to look at a (sub-)tree unless it is not empty. Effect this modification, then transform the modified procedure into an iterative procedure, and compare the result with the solution of Exercise E.8.1.

E.8.3   The traversal in postfix order is given, with the same notation, by

POST(*r*) == IF *r* = null THEN

ELSE   POST(leftson(*r*));
            POST(rightson(*r*));
            write(*r*)

      FI

Transform this into iterative form.

E.8.4   A tree (not necessarily binary; a vertex can have any number of sons) is given such that there are for each vertex the functions

    son(*i*)   points to the leftmost son of vertex(*i*)
    brother(*i*)   points to the brother to the immediate right of *i*
    father(*i*)

When a vertex has no son or no brother, the corresponding function is null.

Write a recursive procedure for traversing this tree in postfix order (it contains a loop in which there is a recursive call), then transform it into an iterative procedure.

E.8.5   The eight queens problem is well known—place eight queens on a chess board in such a way that none attacks another. A queen attacks another if the two are on the same row, the same column, or the same diagonal.

A recursive solution of the problem can be given by creating a procedure HR(*k*), which finds all the solutions with the queens in rows 1 to *k* − 1 fixed;then this can be transformed into an iterative procedure.

Can the search for all the solutions be reduced by taking account of the symmetrical properties of the chessboard (a square array of eight rows and eight columns)?

E.8.6   Permutations in lexicographic order. Given: a sequence of *n* numbers, which can be taken equal to the integers from 0 to *n* − 1 and considered as the digits in base *n*. A permutation of this sequence can be read as an integer in base *n* (of *n* digits, all different). Generate all the permutations for which the corresponding integers are in ascending order.

Write first a recursive procedure, then transform this into an iterative procedure, and, finally, discuss the strategies involved.

E.8.7   To factorise an odd natural integer *n*, we might proceed as follows:

n is expressed in the form $n = x * y$ where x, y are both odd; *a* being a given even integer, *x* and *y* are divided by *a*:

$$x = a*u + c \qquad 0 < c < a \qquad c \text{ odd}$$
$$y = a*v + b \qquad 0 < b < a \qquad b \text{ odd}$$

whence it can be deduced, with a new variable p:

$$p = a * u * v + b * u + c * v$$
$$n = a * p + b * c$$

If p is even, u and v are of the same parity, whereas if p is odd, they are of opposite parity.

Expressing u in the form $2 * u$ or $2 * u + 1$, and similarly for v, we again find relations of the same form. If $p < a$, the product $u * v$ must be zero, and the only possible solutions are of the form

$$u = 0 \qquad v = p : c$$

or

$$v = 0 \qquad u = p : b$$

and they are acceptable if and only if the divisions have zero remainder.

Write a recursive procedure based on this idea.

Using the recursive procedure and beginning with the above relations, show that the only divisions carried out are of quantities p, b, c less than the square root of n.

Discuss the initial call of this procedure for an integer n. Put this procedure into iterative form. Discuss the efficiency of the iterative and recursive forms.

Chapter 9

Analytical Programming

9.1 Analytical Programming

We shall present by means of examples a new and still rather controversial method of programming. We have a problem to solve. We find a recursive solution. We transform the formal parameters and local variables into global variables. We thus obtain a system of generalised actions. We make this system regular.

From this point we can resolve the regular system and obtain a first iterative program.

But we might also examine the system for opportunities of simplification. By manipulation of the system, we simplify it, and we obtain a new iterative program whose merits are there to be considered.

Throughout this process, there are decisions to be taken and things to be done. It has to be borne in mind that the choice of one solution is the rejection of another. But at the moment of choice one is not necessarily in possession of all the information which might influence that choice. It is therefore recommended that the programmer should not hesitate to develop solutions corresponding to different choices, and to decide only afterwards which is the form best adapted to the purpose. This may appear to be a heavy-handed approach, above all to the reader who only sees the exercise of transformation practised by others. But when one has mastered a little of this computational technique it is only a matter of writing, requiring little thought, and for which after all the computer can be usefully employed.

So, instead of a program being created by necessarily inventive effort, it is obtained by computation. This has been compared to the case of Euclidean geometry. Suppose, for example, it is required to construct a square whose four sides, produced if necessary, pass through four given points of the plane. One could perhaps, with a lot of imagination, find the straight line to draw which solves the problem. That would depend only on very rudimentary knowledge of plane geometry. Alternatively, one might express the four lines by means of linear equations, taking account of those pairs which are parallel and those pairs which are perpendicular to each other. One would then express that the segments bounded on these lines by their points of intersection are equal. The resolution of the system gives the required answer. Invention has been replaced by computation. And it seems to me to be much easier to become good at computation (it only needs training, and the computer is there to help) than to acquire a sound creative imagination.

This comparison is due to Edsger Dijkstra. While I was presenting my ideas on program transformation at a meeting of the IFIP (International Federation for Information Processing) working group on programming methodology, he reproached me for committing "the error of my compatriot Descartes", which was, in my view, praise altogether too high. Dijkstra thinks that instead of spending time and energy processing a program, I would do better to reflect and obtain an elegant program by elegant means. But, again from his formulary, "there is no royal road to geometry", nor is there to programming. Faced with a problem, I can wait months for inspiration. At the very least, analytical programming does not leave me helpless.

It is true, however, that its domain of application is limited; it is designed to solve those problems where the chief difficulty is in the discovery of an algorithm. It would hardly help to write a payroll program. It would not be much better for parallel programming, at least in the present state of affairs. But in its own field it is effective, and it would be wrong to believe that this field is empty. I have proved in practice, by enquiries and surveys, that professional programmers in management find themselves sooner or later face to face with a problem in the organisation and manipulation of data for which they have no known algorithm. What they do in this situation is, to say the least, astonishing, and it is not done to enhance the brand image of programming...

We shall not construct a theory of "analytical programming" (so called by analogy with analytical geometry); we shall present applications of it. That makes sense only if the reader will work in the following way:

–read the statement of the problem;
–close the book, and try to solve the problem. If the solution comes directly, good for the reader—perhaps he has no need of analytical programming; the book can stay shut.

If he arrives at a solution by a transformational method, then perhaps he may like to open the book again to see whether I can compute as well as he...

If he does not find a solution, then perhaps he will search in this book for a possible starting point and try his luck again. But I ask him to do the computations himself. He will not otherwise begin to acquire that facility of technique without which analytical programming will be of no use to him.

9.2 An Old Friend

In Section 4.8.1, we considered the function defined recursively as follows:

$f(k, x) \simeq$ IF $k = 1$ THEN x
ELSE IF even(k) THEN $2 * f(k:2, x)$
ELSE $f(k:2, x) + f((k:2) + 1, x)$
FI
FI

We have associated with this scheme a simpler, monadic, scheme:

$g(k, x) \simeq$ IF $k = 0$ THEN $0, x$
ELSE IF even(k) THEN $2 * u, u + v$
ELSE $u + v, 2 * v$
FI
FI
WHERE $(u, v = g(k:2, x))$

the result $f(k, x)$ being the first component of the doublet $g(k, x)$—remember that

$$g(k, x) = f(k, x), f(k + 1, x)$$

9.2.1 Creation of the Recursive Sub-Program

The function g produces two results. We shall therefore take two result variables in F. The variable x is constant over g, and it can immediately be taken as global. Thus we can make use of a sub-program $F(k, u, v)$ computing

$$u, v := g(k, x)$$

Using this in g,

$F(k, u, v) == $ IF $k = 0$ THEN $u, v := 0, x$
ELSE $F(k:2, u, v)$;
IF even(k) THEN $u, v := 2 * u, u + v$
ELSE $u, v := u + v, 2 * v$
FI
FI

The program computing f(n, b) is

$$P == x := b; F(n, u, v); \text{result} := u; Z$$

It will be necessary to add an exit action at the end of the alternatives in F. This is not a problem. But k, u, v have to be made global. For u and v this can be done immediately as they are the result parameters. For k, the call $F(k:2, u, v)$ is changed to

$$k := k:2; F(k, u, v)$$

But k is destroyed and cannot be recovered, since the operation $k:2$ has no inverse; and we need k after this call in

$$\text{IF even}(k) \text{ THEN}$$

Therefore we have to save either k itself or $\text{mod}(k, 2)$ from which $\text{even}(k)$ can be computed, it being the same as $\text{mod}(k, 2) = 0$. So we replace

$$F(k:2, u, v); \text{IF even}(k) \text{ THEN} \dots$$

by

$$\text{push}(\text{mod}(k, 2)); k := k:2; f; \text{pop}(t);$$
$$\text{IF } t = 0 \text{ THEN} \dots$$

We now have the system of actions:

$$P == x := b; k := n; \text{stack} := \text{empty}; F; \text{result} := u; Z$$
$$F == \text{IF } k = 0 \text{ THEN } u := 0; v := x; -F$$
$$\qquad\qquad \text{ELSE} \quad \text{push}(\text{mod}(k, 2)); k := k:2; U$$
$$\quad \text{FI}$$
$$U == F;$$
$$Y == \text{pop}(t);$$
$$\qquad \text{IF } t = 0 \text{ THEN } v := u + v; u := 2*u$$
$$\qquad\qquad\qquad \text{ELSE} \quad u := u + v; v := 2*v$$
$$\quad \text{FI};$$
$$\quad -F$$

Up to now we have had no choices to make. The first decision was to replace a procedure with two calls of f in cascade by a monadic procedure. This is a classic transformation which imposes itself—see what has been said about this in connection with the Fibonacci sequence, in Section 2.7. The second has been to save not k but $\text{mod}(k, 2)$. There again there is no real choice, for the simple reason of quantity of information—$\text{mod}(k, 2)$ costs one bit against however many bits there are in k.

We shall for the moment leave the operations push and pop without detailed definition.

We regularise the system and then resolve it.

9.2.2   Regularisation

We have to define − F. This is easy, because we have an obvious predicate to characterise the first activation. In P, and only in P, the stack is empty after F.

By regularisation, U becomes

$$U == F$$

Thus we replace U by F in F. We obtain

$$P == x := b; k := n; \text{stack} := \text{empty}; F;$$
$$F == \text{IF } k = 0 \text{ THEN } u := 0; v := x; -F$$
$$\qquad\qquad\quad \text{ELSE push}(\text{mod}(k, 2)); k := k : 2; F$$
$$\quad \text{FI}$$
$$Y == \text{pop}(t);$$
$$\qquad \text{IF } t = 0 \text{ THEN } v := u + v; u := 2 * u$$
$$\qquad\qquad\quad \text{ELSE} \quad u := u + v; v := 2 * v$$
$$\qquad \text{FI};$$
$$\qquad -F$$
$$-F == \text{IF stack} = \text{empty THEN result} := u; Z$$
$$\qquad\qquad\qquad\qquad \text{ELSE} \quad Y$$
$$\qquad \text{FI}$$

The resolution of this system is simple. We make F iterative, which can be done with a WHILE instruction (one test only, at the beginning). We take Y into − F, so making − F recursive. We can then go on to iteration, here again with a WHILE instruction. We obtain, after detailed working:

$$x := b; k := n; \text{stack} := \text{empty};$$
$$\text{WHILE } k \neq 0 \text{ DO}$$
$$\qquad\qquad\qquad \text{push}(\text{mod}(k, 2)); k := k : 2$$
$$\qquad\qquad \text{OD};$$
$$u := 0; v := x;$$
$$\text{WHILE stack} \neq \text{empty DO}$$
$$\qquad\qquad\qquad \text{pop}(t);$$
$$\qquad\qquad\qquad \text{IF } t = 0 \text{ THEN } v := u + v; u := 2 * u$$
$$\qquad\qquad\qquad\qquad\qquad\quad \text{ELSE} \quad u := u + v; v := 2 * v$$
$$\qquad\qquad\qquad \text{FI}$$
$$\qquad\qquad \text{OD};$$
$$\text{result} := u$$

We now have to choose an implementation for the stack, taking account of the fact that it is a stack of bits.

9.2.3   First Realisation of the Stack

First we take the classic implementation of the stack as an integer variable in base 2. Let p be this integer:

$$\begin{array}{lll}
\text{stack} := \text{empty} & \text{becomes} & p := 1 \\
\text{push}(u) & & p := 2 * p + u \\
\text{pop}(u) & & p, u := \text{div}(p, 2) \\
\text{stack} = \text{empty} & & p = 1
\end{array}$$

(It was explained in Section B.2.5 why p has to be initialised to 1.) From this we have immediately a first form for the program:

$$x := b; k := n; p := 1;$$
WHILE $k \neq 0$ DO
$$\qquad\qquad k, r := \text{div}(k, 2); p := 2 * p + r$$
$$\qquad \text{OD};$$
$$u := 0; v := x;$$
WHILE $p \neq 1$ DO
$$\qquad\qquad p, t := \text{div}(p, 2);$$
$$\qquad\qquad \text{IF } t = 0 \text{ THEN } v := u + v; u := 2 * u$$
$$\qquad\qquad\qquad\qquad \text{ELSE } \ u := u + v; v := 2 * v$$
$$\qquad\quad \text{FI}$$
$$\qquad \text{OD};$$
$$\quad \text{result} := u$$

This is the program which was given, without detailed working, in Section 4.8.1. We may have forgotten what it does—p is closely bound to the integer whose binary representation is the mirror image of the binary representation of k. This is clear because the first loop removes the rightmost bit of k and concatenates it to the right of p.

9.2.4   Second Implementation of the Stack

The stack of bits is again considered as an integer represented in base 2 but is read in the opposite sense. Instead of stacking by concatenation to the right of the representation of p, we concatenate to the left. But in order to do this, we need access to a pointer which shows where to put the next binary digit. We use an integer h whose values are powers of 2:

$$\text{push}(t) \qquad t = 0 \quad \text{or} \quad 1 \qquad p := h * t + p; h := 2 * h$$

$$\text{pop}(t) \qquad\qquad\qquad\qquad h := h : 2;$$
$$\qquad\qquad\qquad\qquad\qquad\qquad \text{IF } p \geq h \text{ THEN } t := 1; p := p - h$$
$$\qquad\qquad\qquad\qquad\qquad\qquad\qquad \text{ELSE } t := 0$$
$$\qquad\qquad\qquad\qquad\qquad \text{FI}$$

This ensures that "pop" is indeed the inverse operation to "push". Initialisation remains to be done. The height of the stack being given by h, a stack is empty if h has reverted to its initial value. We do not have here the problem of distinguishing between a stack containing only elements of value 0 and an empty stack:

$$\text{stack} := \text{empty} \qquad p := 0; h := 1$$

The stack is empty when $h = 1$.

Putting this directly into the program,

$$x := b; k := n; p := 0; h := 1;$$
$$\text{WHILE } k \neq 0 \text{ DO}$$
$$\qquad\qquad k, r := \text{div}(k, 2);$$
$$\qquad\qquad \text{IF } r \neq 0 \text{ THEN } p := p + h \text{ FI};$$
$$\qquad\qquad h := 2 * h$$
$$\qquad \text{OD};$$
$$u := 0; v := x;$$
$$\text{WHILE } h \neq 1 \text{ DO}$$
$$\qquad\qquad h := h : 2;$$
$$\qquad\qquad \text{IF } p \geq h \text{ THEN } u := u + v; v := 2 * v; p := p - h$$
$$\qquad\qquad\qquad\qquad \text{ELSE } v := u + v; u := 2 * u$$
$$\qquad\qquad \text{FI}$$
$$\qquad \text{OD};$$
$$\text{result} := u$$

We have made one simplification—the operation "pop" defines t as 0 or 1 according to the relation between p and h, and then t is compared with 1 to select the operations on u and v. The two tests have been combined into one.

The first loop removes the rightmost bit of k and adds it to the left of p. Thus it must reconstitute k in p. More precisely, the bits which are no longer in k are in p and in such a way that the concatenations of the representations of k and p must give n:

$$n = p + h * k$$

Let us validate this assertion. It is true immediately after initialisation, when

$p = 0, h = 1, k = n$. Suppose it is also true after the first DO:

$$
\begin{aligned}
&\text{DO } [[p + h * k = n]] \\
&\qquad k, r := \text{div}(k, 2) \\
&\qquad [[p + h * (2 * k + r) = n \text{ AND } (r = 0 \text{ OR } r = 1)]] \\
&\qquad \text{IF } r \neq 0 \text{ THEN } [[p + 2 * h * k + h = n]] \\
&\qquad\qquad\qquad\qquad\quad p := p + h \\
&\qquad\qquad\qquad\qquad\quad [[p + 2 * h * k = n]] \\
&\qquad \text{FI}; \\
&\qquad [[p + 2 * h * k = n]] \\
&\qquad h := 2 * h \\
&\qquad [[p + h * k = n]]
\end{aligned}
$$

This establishes the property. At the exit from the loop

$$p + h * k = n \quad \text{AND} \quad k = 0 \qquad \text{giving} \quad p = n$$

This allows us to avoid the computation of p in the loop. But then we may ask ourselves what is the use of the variable k. If we can replace the test on k by a test on h, then the computation of k also is pointless. Now, by the assertion

$$p + h * k = n$$

h is less than n, while k is different from 0. We also have $p < h$. This is true after initialisation, and it remains true throughout the body of the loop. (Demonstration is left to the reader.) We can now affirm that

$$p + h * k = n < h * (k + 1)$$

$$
\begin{aligned}
&\text{for} \quad k > 1, \quad h < n \\
&\text{for} \quad k = 1, \quad h \leq n \\
&\text{for} \quad k = 0, \quad n < h
\end{aligned}
$$

From this we deduce a new program:

```
x := b; h := 1;
WHILE h ≤ n DO h := 2 * h OD;
u := 0; v := x; p := n;
WHILE h ≠ 1 DO
                h := h : 2;
                IF p ≥ h THEN u := u + v; v := 2 * v; p := p − h
                         ELSE v := u + v; u := 2 * u
                FI
        OD;
    result := u
```

There are no surprises in this version, and it could have been derived directly from the first. Here in effect the binary representation of n is turned around before the different digits are taken from the right. This means that the digits of n itself are used in order from left to right. This program first looks for the leftmost digit (first loop) and then extracts the successive digits from left to right. In other words, the problem here was to discover that it is necessary to operate by extracting the binary digits from left to right; this done, the rest is easy. A point of great importance should always be noted.

We formed first a program containing the operations "push", "pop", etc., without saying anything as to how these were to be implemented. This is consistent with the trend in current programming research on abstract types (a simplified description is to be found in [MEB]). Certain languages, and notably ADA, allow the use of a type, and its definition, to be isolated completely by a set of procedures sharing the use of variables to which the user may not have access. For example, in the case of a stack, the user does not know how the stack is implemented, and if it happens to be implemented by an array and a pointer, he has no access to either of these variables. With this method we should be obliged to remain with the first version of our program. Everything we have obtained beyond this has come from a study of the properties of the stack, whose particular implementation we have then decided is best adapted to our problem. Then we have interpreted this implementation by looking for a "physical" meaning for the variables used and the operations carried out.

This is not a condemnation of the work which has been done on types or the choices taken in ADA. It is a question asked of those who do the research in this subject. For me it is an extremely disquieting point, and I must admit that I am a long way from understanding all its implications. That is why I am very careful when I speak of data types, so much so that I can be accused of not giving this essential aspect of programming sufficient emphasis in my teaching. But to do more would require my mastery of the subject. How can I teach what I understand so inadequately?

9.2.5 Variations

We shall carry on with the foregoing implementation of the stack, except that the operation "pop(t)" will be realised in a different way. We know that t is the most significant bit of p and that its weight is $h:2$. As for the new stack, it is p deprived of this digit. Thus, "pop(t)" can now be realised by

$$h:= h:2; t, p:= \text{div}(p, h)$$

This affects only the second loop of the program. We have then without further computation:

$$x := b; h := 1;$$
$$\text{WHILE } h \leq n \text{ DO } h := 2*h \text{ OD};$$
$$u := 0; v := x; p := n;$$
$$\text{WHILE } h \neq 1 \text{ DO}$$
$$\qquad h := h:2; t, p := \text{div}(p, 2);$$
$$\qquad \text{IF } t = 0 \text{ THEN } v := u + v; u := 2*u$$
$$\qquad\qquad\qquad\qquad \text{ELSE } \; u := u + v; v := 2*v$$
$$\qquad \text{FI}$$
$$\text{OD};$$

result $:= u$

We know that this program, in the second loop, makes use of the successive binary digits of n and that t is the digit of weight h in n. Instead of breaking down p, initialised to n, we can consult n directly. The digit t of weight h is the units (least significant) digit of $n:h$. Its value is 0 if this number is even. Whence a new version

$$x := b; h := 1;$$
$$\text{WHILE } h \leq n \text{ DO } h := 2*h \text{ OD};$$
$$u := 0; v := x;$$
$$\text{WHILE } h \neq 1 \text{ DO}$$
$$\qquad h := h:2;$$
$$\qquad \text{IF even}(n:h) \text{ THEN } v := u + v; u := 2*u$$
$$\qquad\qquad\qquad\qquad\qquad \text{ELSE } \; u := u + v; v := 2*v$$
$$\qquad \text{FI}$$
$$\text{OD};$$

result $:= u$

The possible variations have not been exhausted. We leave it as an exercise for the reader to construct others. Perhaps he will have forgotten, after all this work, that the five programs which have been presented all compute

$$\text{result} := n*b$$

I must admit that I had myself lost sight of this point and so have taken the trouble to put one of these programs on a computer to "see" the result: "E pur si muove", to parody Galileo; yet it does work.

9.3 A Problem of Permutations

9.3.1 The Recursive Procedure

Here is an example with a local variable. We are given a vector $a[0 \ldots n - 1]$ of n elements. Warning: the first choice, as usual, was $a[1 \ldots n]$, but in the course of the work some properties appeared which allowed some simplification with 0 rather than 1 as origin of indices. In the first study, 1 was taken as origin; this possibility of simplification was revealed, the origin was changed, and the computations were repeated. One iteration of them is omitted here so as not to weary the reader. But make no mistake. There was no brilliant flash of genius to show that this problem needed 0 as origin of indices. No, 1 was taken as usual, it was seen that it was not the best choice, and the work was begun again (see the last proverb of Ledgard [LE1]).

We require a program which will write out all the permutations of the vector a (whose elements are supposed all different, to avoid the problem of dealing with repetitions). We work recursively. Suppose that we have a procedure which writes out all the permutations of a which leave unchanged the part from $i + 1$ to $n - 1$, and, moreover, that at the exit from this procedure, a has the same value as at entry.

The vector a being given

$$a_0 \quad a_1 \quad a_2 \quad \ldots \quad a_{n-1}$$

we execute $P(n - 2)$. This gives all the permutations ending with a_{n-1}. It leaves at the end

$$a_0 \quad a_1 \quad a_2 \quad \ldots \quad a_{n-1}$$

We can now, by the simple interchange of two elements, move into the last position, one after the other, all the elements of the sequence, and so obtain all the permutations. Denoting by sw(i,j) the interchange operation of the two elements $a[i]$, $a[j]$, what has to be done is

$$P(n - 1) \quad \text{sw}(n - 1, n - 2) \quad P(n - 1)$$

But it does not end up with the initial vector; it leaves a_{n-2} in the last position. We put a_{n-1} in its place:

$$P(n - 1) \quad \text{sw}(n - 1, n - 2) \quad P(n - 1) \quad \text{sw}(n - 1, n - 2)$$

We can continue:

$$\text{sw}(n - 1, n - 3) \quad P(n - 1) \quad \text{sw}(n - 1, n - 3)$$
$$\ldots\ldots$$
$$\text{sw}(n - 1, 0) \quad P(n - 1) \quad \text{sw}(n - 1, 0)$$

All the permutations have been written, and the vector a has resumed its initial value. The first call does not have the general form. Observing that

$$\text{sw}(n - 1, n - 1)$$

is an empty operation, we write the first call as

$$\text{sw}(n - 1, n - 1) \quad P(n - 1) \quad \text{sw}(n - 1, n - 1)$$

We now have the essential part of the recursive procedure for effecting $P(i)$:

```
j := i;
WHILE j ≥ 0 DO
                sw(i,j); P(i − 1); sw(i,j);
                j := j − 1
        OD
```

It remains to find a non-recursive case. One will be produced if i is decreased sufficiently. For $i = 0$, all the permutations leaving the part from 1 to $n - 1$ unchanged must be found and written out. But there is only one term in the lower part, and so no permutation to do. Finally,

$$P(i) == \text{ IF } i = 0 \text{ THEN write}(a)$$
$$\text{ELSE } \quad j := i;$$
$$\text{WHILE } j \geq 0 \text{ DO}$$
$$\text{sw}(i,j); P(i - 1); \text{sw}(i,j);$$
$$j := j - 1$$
$$\text{OD}$$
$$\text{FI}$$
$$\text{PERM} == P(n - 1); Z$$

9.3.2 First Iterative Form

Note that at the beginning the vector a was taken as global. It is easy to make i global. Suppose i to be globally invariant over $P(i)$. We change

$$P(i - 1) \quad \text{into} \quad i := i - 1; P(i); i := i + 1$$

and

$$P(n - 1) \quad \text{into} \quad i := n - 1; P(i)$$

The variable j, local to $P(i)$, must either be stacked and restored or be made global. There is one j for each i. Thus, we form a vector $c[i]$ conserving the j attached to each i.

In this way we obtain the system

$$P == \text{ IF } i = 0 \text{ THEN write}(a); -P$$
$$\text{ELSE } \quad c[i] := i;$$
$$\text{WHILE } c[i] \geq 0 \text{ DO}$$
$$\text{sw}(i, c[i]);$$
$$i := i - 1; P; i := i + 1;$$
$$\text{sw}(i, c[i]);$$
$$c[i] := c[i] - 1$$
$$\text{OD}; -P$$
$$\text{FI}$$
$$\text{PERM} == i := n - 1; P; Z$$

This system contains one loop, which has to be replaced by a terminal recursion. We name the loop Q:

$$P == \text{ IF } i = 0 \text{ THEN write}(a); -P$$
$$\text{ELSE } c[i] := i; Q$$
$$\text{FI}$$

$$Q == DO$$
$$\quad\quad IF\ c[i] < 0\ THEN\ EXIT\ FI;$$
$$\quad\quad sw(i, c[i]);$$
$$\quad\quad i := i - 1;\ P;\ i := i + 1;$$
$$\quad\quad sw(i, c[i]);$$
$$\quad\quad c[i] := c[i] - 1$$
$$\quad OD;$$
$$\quad -P$$

The loop is replaced by a terminal recursion. We obtain the system

$$P == IF\ i = 0\ THEN\ write(a);\ -P$$
$$\quad\quad\quad\quad ELSE\ c[i] := i;\ Q$$
$$\quad\quad FI$$
$$Q == IF\ c[i] < 0\ THEN\ -P$$
$$\quad\quad\quad\quad ELSE\ sw(i, c[i]);\ i := i - 1;\ U$$
$$\quad\quad FI$$
$$U == P;\ Y$$
$$Y == i := i + 1;\ sw(i, c[i]);\ c[i] := c[i] - 1;\ Q$$
$$PERM == i := n - 1;\ P;\ Z$$

Now i is globally invariant over P. We thus have a predicate for the first activation; $i = n - 1$ only between P and Z in PERM, for i is decremented before every call of P by U in Q. Regularisation is then simple.

$$P == IF\ i = 0\ THEN\ write(a);\ -P$$
$$\quad\quad\quad\quad ELSE\ c[i] := i;\ Q$$
$$\quad\quad FI$$
$$Q == IF\ c[i] < 0\ THEN\ -P$$
$$\quad\quad\quad\quad ELSE\ sw(i, c[i]);\ i := i - 1;\ P$$
$$\quad\quad FI$$
$$Y == i := i + 1;\ sw(i, c[i]);\ c[i] := c[i] - 1;\ Q$$
$$-P == IF\ i = n - 1\ THEN\ Z\ ELSE\ Y\ FI$$
$$PERM == i := n - 1;$$

To resolve this system, we first take Q into P to make the loop over P appear:

$$P == IF\ i = 0\ THEN\ write(a);\ -P$$
$$\quad\quad ELSE\ c[i] := i;$$
$$\quad\quad\quad\quad IF\ c[i] < 0\ THEN\ -P$$
$$\quad\quad\quad\quad\quad\quad ELSE\ sw(i, c[i]);\ i := i - 1;\ P$$
$$\quad\quad\quad\quad FI$$
$$\quad FI$$

Simplification is possible. In the ELSE branch of the first test, i is non-zero; thus, so is $c[i]$; as P is called with i non-negative, $c[i]$ is strictly positive, and the subsequent test is not needed. There remains only the sequence

$$\text{sw}(i, c[i]); i := i - 1; P$$

But since $i = c[i]$, $\text{sw}(i, c[i])$ is an empty instruction (interchange of elements with the same index), and can be suppressed. This is quite a remarkable phenomenon. For convenience, two instructions $\text{sw}(i, j)$ with no effect were introduced before and after the first call of P, and now one has been eliminated. What should we make of this? There remains for P:

$$P == \text{IF } i = 0 \text{ THEN write}(a); -P$$
$$\quad\quad\quad\quad \text{ELSE } c[i] := i; i := i - 1; P$$
$$\quad\text{FI}$$

which is quickly transformed into

$$P == \text{WHILE } i \neq 0 \text{ DO}$$
$$\quad\quad\quad\quad\quad\quad c[i] := i; i := i - 1$$
$$\quad\quad\quad\quad \text{OD};$$
$$\quad\text{write}(a); -P$$

The resolution is now simple. We take Y into $-P$, then Q into $-P$. We make $-P$ iterative; it has two exits, Z and P. We take it into P, which in turn we make iterative:

$$P == \text{DO}$$
$$\quad\quad \text{WHILE } i \neq 0 \text{ DO}$$
$$\quad\quad\quad\quad\quad\quad\quad c[i] := i; i := i - 1$$
$$\quad\quad\quad\quad\quad \text{OD};$$
$$\quad\quad \text{write}(a);$$
$$\quad\quad \text{DO}$$
$$\quad\quad\quad\quad \text{IF } i = n - 1 \text{ THEN } Z + 2$$
$$\quad\quad\quad\quad\quad\quad\quad\quad \text{ELSE } i := i + 1; \text{sw}(i, c[i]);$$
$$\quad\quad\quad\quad\quad\quad\quad\quad\quad\quad c[i] := c[i] - 1;$$
$$\quad\quad\quad\quad\quad\quad\quad\quad\quad\quad \text{IF } c[i] < 0 \text{ THEN}$$
$$\quad\quad\quad\quad\quad\quad\quad\quad\quad\quad\quad\quad \text{ELSE sw}(i, c[i]);$$
$$\quad\quad\quad\quad\quad\quad\quad\quad\quad\quad\quad\quad\quad i := i - 1; \text{EXIT}$$
$$\quad\quad\quad\quad\quad\quad\quad \text{FI}$$
$$\quad\quad\quad\quad \text{FI}$$
$$\quad\quad \text{OD}$$
$$\quad \text{OD}$$

To improve the structure of the loop, we reverse the test $c[i] < 0$. The sequence of instructions

$$\text{sw}(i, c[i]); i := i - 1; \text{EXIT}$$

is pushed by the expansion out of the loop. We thus obtain the first "good" version of our program:

$$i := n - 1;$$
DO
    WHILE $i \neq 0$ DO
$$c[i] := i; i := i - 1$$
      OD;
    write(a);
    DO
      IF $i = n - 1$ THEN EXIT(2) FI;
      $i := i + 1$; sw($i, c[i]$);
      $c[i] := c[i] - 1$;
      IF $c[i] \geq 0$ THEN EXIT FI
    OD;
    sw($i, c[i]$); $i := i - 1$
OD

This program is right because the recursive procedure which we have left behind was correct and because we have carried out only correct transformations. It none the less poses a serious problem. We should be able to show directly why it writes all the permutations of a. I have not been able to do this. I presented this example during the course of a panel discussion in the World Congress of Information Processing held at Melbourne in 1980. I have received a letter from Australia informing me that research carried out in an Australian university has met with no more success.

9.3.3   Second Iterative Form

Starting with the recursive form, we have tried to find a form without parameters or local variables. We took the decision to attach j to i by means of the array c. The other solution is to save j in a stack. The instruction $P(i - 1)$ is changed to

$$\text{push}(j); i := i - 1; P; i := i + 1; \text{pop}(j)$$

We thus obtain the generalised system:

PERM $== i := n - 1$; stack $:=$ empty; P; Z
   P $==$ IF $i = 0$ THEN write(a); $-$ P
            ELSE $j := i$; Q
     FI
   Q $==$ IF $j < 0$ THEN $-$ P
            ELSE sw(i, j); push(j); $i := i - 1$; P; Y
     FI
   Y $== i := i + 1$; pop(j); sw(i, j); $j := j - 1$; Q

The definition of $-P$ has not been modified:

$$-P == \text{IF } i = n - 1 \text{ THEN Z ELSE Y FI}$$

Thus, we need only concern ourselves with the stack. From the form of the recursive procedure, the variable j associated with i takes its values from the sequence of natural integers from 0 to i. We represent the stack by an integer k:

$$\begin{array}{ll} \text{push}(j) & k := k * (i + 1) + j \\ \text{pop}(j) & k, j := \text{div}(k, i + 1) \end{array}$$

As we do not make any test as to the emptiness of the stack, this property need not be characterised. The initialisation

$$\text{stack} := \text{empty}$$

can be realised by

$$k := 0$$

We thus have the regularised version:

$$\begin{array}{ll} \text{PERM} == & i := n - 1; k := 0; P \\ P == & \text{IF } i = 0 \text{ THEN write}(a); -P \\ & \qquad\qquad \text{ELSE } j := i; Q \\ & \text{FI} \\ Q == & \text{IF } j < 0 \quad \text{THEN } -P \\ & \qquad\qquad \text{ELSE } \text{sw}(i, j); k := k * (i + 1) + j; \\ & \qquad\qquad\qquad\quad i := i - 1; P \\ & \text{FI} \\ Y == & i := i + 1; k, j := \text{div}(k, i + 1); \text{sw}(i, j); \\ & \qquad j := j - 1; Q \\ -P == & \text{IF } i = n - 1 \text{ THEN Z ELSE Y FI} \end{array}$$

In this form, the program shows hardly any advantages over its predecessor. We have replaced the stack, represented by the vector c, by a stack represented by the integer k. This is of interest only if the arithmetic properties of k come into play. We have said that the first loop of an iterative program associated with a recursive program can often be simplified. Let us then form the loop P. We take Q into P:

$$\begin{array}{ll} P == & \text{IF } i = 0 \text{ THEN write}(a); -P \\ & \qquad \text{ELSE } j := i; \\ & \qquad\qquad \text{IF } j < 0 \text{ THEN } -P \\ & \qquad\qquad\qquad \text{ELSE sw}(i, j); k := k * (i + 1) + j; \\ & \qquad\qquad\qquad\qquad\quad i := i - 1; P \\ & \qquad\qquad \text{FI} \\ & \text{FI} \end{array}$$

As in the previous case, j cannot be negative, and sw(i, j) is an empty instruction because we have just effected the assignment

$$j := i$$

Whence the new form,

> P == IF $i = 0$ THEN write(a); $-$P
>   ELSE $j := i$; $k := k * (i + 1) + i$; $i := i - 1$; P
>   FI

Writing $k' = k + 1$ (see Section 8.4), the assignment to k becomes

$$k' := k * (i + 1) + i + 1 = (k + 1) * (i + 1) = k' * (i + 1)$$

Now the loop is based on decreasing values of i, the last-used value of i being $i = 1$. Thus k' becomes multiplied by $(i + 1)!$ which we denote by fac$(i + 1)$. At the exit from the loop, i is zero. The value of j is of no consequence, for P is followed by $-$P, which does not use j, and $-$P exits either through Z where j is of no concern or through Y where j is redefined before being used. We can thus express P in the following form (where k has been reinstated using $k = k' - 1$):

$$\text{P} == \ k := (k + 1) * \text{fac}(i + 1) - 1; i := 0; \text{write}(a); -\text{P}$$

So the first loop has disappeared to be replaced by a sequence of assignments. But this is an illusory advantage unless further possibilities for simplification appear, because it now requires a loop to compute fac$(i + 1)$.

    Now let us look at $-$P. We take Q into Y, and then Y into $-$P to construct the loop around $-$P:

> $-$P == IF $i = n - 1$ THEN Z
>   ELSE $i := i + 1$; $k, j := \text{div}(k, i + 1)$; sw$(i, j)$;
> $j := j - 1$;
>   IF $j < 0$ THEN $-$P
>   ELSE sw(i, j); $k := k * (i + 1) + j$;
> $i := i - 1$; P
>   FI
>   FI

Here k is divided by the increasing $i + 1$ each time the previous division has had zero remainder. The first time, $-$P is entered from P, and thus with $i = 0$. Then k is divided by a factorial. More precisely, suppose that at the entry

$$k = (q * (m + 2) + r) * \text{fac}(m + 1)$$

We know $i = 0$.

In the first step of the loop, in $-P$, i becomes 1, and k is divided by 2 giving $j = 0$, sw(1, 0). Then $-P$ is re-entered with

$$k = (q * (m + 2) + r) * \text{fac}(m + 1)/2 \text{ AND } i = 1$$

We take then as invariant for the loop

$$[[k = (q * (m + 2) + r) * \text{fac}(m + 1)/\text{fac}(i + 1) \text{ AND } i < m < n]]$$
$-P == \text{IF } i = n - 1 \text{ THEN } Z$
$\qquad\qquad\quad \text{ELSE } i := i + 1;$
$\qquad\qquad\qquad\qquad [[k = (q * (m + 2) + r) * \text{fac}(m + 1)/\text{fac}(i)$
$\qquad\qquad\qquad\qquad\qquad\qquad\qquad\qquad \text{AND } i \le m < n]]$
$\qquad\qquad\qquad\qquad k, j := \text{div}(k, i + 1);$
$\qquad\qquad\qquad\qquad [[k = (q * (m + 2) + r) * \text{fac}(m + 1)/\text{fac}(i + 1)$
$\qquad\qquad\qquad\qquad\qquad\qquad\qquad \text{AND } i \le m < n \text{ AND } j = 0]]$
$\qquad\qquad\qquad\qquad \text{sw}(i, j); j := j - 1;$
$\qquad\qquad\qquad\qquad \dots\dots\dots$

Here sw(i, 0) is executed and j becomes -1, causing the loop over $-P$.

The loop will not be left until either $i = n - 1$ or a division has produced a non-zero remainder. Consider first the case where $i = m$ in $-P$:

$$[[k = q * (m + 2) + r \text{ AND } i = m < n - 1]]$$
$-P == \text{IF } i = n - 1$
$\qquad\qquad \text{THEN } Z$
$\qquad\qquad \text{ELSE } i := i + 1;$
$\qquad\qquad\qquad\qquad [[k = q * (m + 2) + r \text{ AND } i = m + 1]]$
$\qquad\qquad\qquad\qquad k, j := \text{div}(k, i + 1);$
$\qquad\qquad\qquad\qquad [[k = q \text{ AND } j = r]]$
$\qquad\qquad\qquad\qquad \text{sw}(i, j); j := j - 1;$
$\qquad\qquad\qquad\qquad [[j = r - 1 \ge 0]]$
$\qquad\qquad\qquad\qquad \text{IF } j < 0 \text{ THEN } -P$
$\qquad\qquad\qquad\qquad\qquad\qquad \text{ELSE } \text{sw}(i, j);$
$\qquad\qquad\qquad\qquad\qquad\qquad\qquad\quad k := k * (i + 1) + j;$
$\qquad\qquad\qquad\qquad\qquad\qquad\qquad\quad [[k = q * (m + 2) + r - 1]]$
$\qquad\qquad\qquad\qquad\qquad\qquad\qquad\quad i := i - 1;$
$\qquad\qquad\qquad\qquad\qquad\qquad\qquad\quad [[k = q * (m + 2) + r - 1 \text{ AND } i = m]]$
$\qquad\qquad\qquad\qquad\qquad\qquad\qquad\quad k := (k + 1) * \text{fac}(i + 1) - 1;$
$\qquad\qquad\qquad\qquad\qquad\qquad\qquad\quad [[k = (q * (m + 2) + r) * \text{fac}(m + 1) - 1$
$\qquad\qquad\qquad\qquad\qquad\qquad\qquad\quad \text{AND } i = m]]$
$\qquad\qquad\qquad\qquad\qquad\qquad\qquad\quad i := 0; \text{write}(a); -P$
$\qquad\qquad\qquad\qquad \text{FI}$
$\qquad\qquad \text{FI}$

We re-enter $-P$, having written a, with a value of k, which is the preceding value decremented by 1. We can thus shorten the computations on k in the following way:

After writing a and before calling $-P$, save k in kp.

When $-P$ is left with non-negative j, give k the saved value kp decreased by 1:

$$-P == \text{IF } i = n - 1 \text{ THEN } Z$$
$$\text{ELSE } i := i + 1;$$
$$k, j := \text{div}(k, i + 1);$$
$$\text{sw}(i, j); j := j - 1;$$
$$\text{IF } j < 0 \text{ THEN } -P$$
$$\text{ELSE } \text{sw}(i, j);$$
$$k := kp - 1;$$
$$i := 0;$$
$$kp := k;$$
$$\text{write}(a); -P$$
$$\text{FI}$$
$$\text{FI}$$

Now we can take P into PERM:

$$\text{PERM} == i := n - 1; k := 0;$$
$$k := (k + 1) * \text{fac}(i + 1) - 1; i := 0; kp := k; \text{write}(a); -P$$

The two assignments to k can be merged:

$$\text{PERM} == i := n - 1;$$
$$k := \text{fac}(i + 1) - 1; i := 0; kp := k; \text{write}(a); -P$$

The first assignment to i can be absorbed in the two assignments which follow it:

$$\text{PERM} == k := \text{fac}(n) - 1; i := 0; kp := k; \text{write}(a); -P$$

As the last part of this sequence occurs twice, we give it a name:

$$\text{PERM} == k := \text{fac}(n) - 1; R$$
$$R == i := 0; kp := k; \text{write}(a); -P$$
$$-P == \text{IF } i = n - 1 \text{ THEN } Z$$
$$\text{ELSE } i := i + 1;$$
$$k, j := \text{div}(k, i + 1);$$
$$\text{sw}(i, j); j := j - 1;$$
$$\text{IF } j < 0 \text{ THEN } -P$$
$$\text{ELSE } \text{sw}(i, j);$$
$$k := kp - 1; R$$
$$\text{FI}$$
$$\text{FI}$$

Now we try to find a condition such that k, taken in the interval of natural integers less than fac(n) (this comes from the initialisation and from the decrementation by steps of 1), will make $-P$ terminate with Z. Any integer k can be written uniquely in the form

$$k = (q*(m + 2) + r)*\text{fac}(m + 1) \qquad r \neq 0$$

With $i = m$, the assertion at entry to $-P$ is

$$k = q*(m + 2) + r \qquad r \neq 0 \quad i = m$$

If $i = n - 1$, then since r is non-zero, k is at least equal to 1. Now $q = 0$ and $r = 1$ are the lowest possible values. They give, for k, $k = \text{fac}(m + 1)$ and $m = n - 1$; that is, $k = \text{fac}(n)$, a value outside the interval. The only other value which will give zero j for all i is the value $k = 0$.

We should remark that there is no surprise in this; when $k = 0$, the stack which k represents is empty. But we do not have the reciprocal property— $k = 0$ is equivalent to stack $=$ empty.

To make the test $k = 0$ appear in the program, we enclose $-P$ in a tautology on $k = 0$. To reduce the amout of writing, we apply the hypotheses $k = 0$ and $k \neq 0$ to the simplification of each alternative, that is, in each case to the body of $-P$.

When $k = 0$, any division of k gives $k = 0$, $j = 0$. When decremented by 1, j becomes negative. Thus we have

$$\text{P1} == \text{IF } i = n - 1 \text{ THEN Z}$$
$$\text{ELSE } \quad i:= i + 1; \text{sw}(i, 0); -P$$

In the case where $k \neq 0$, $i = n - 1$ is always false. Call this alternative P2:

$$\text{P2} == i:= i + 1; k, j:= \text{div}(k, i + 1);$$
$$\text{sw}(i, j); j:= j - 1;$$
$$\text{IF } j < 0 \text{ THEN } -P$$
$$\text{ELSE } \quad \text{sw}(i, j); k:= kp - 1; R$$
$$\text{FI}$$

Finally,

$$-P == \text{IF } k = 0 \text{ THEN P1 ELSE P2 FI}$$

We now take $-P$ into P1:

$$\text{P1} == \text{IF } i = n - 1 \text{ THEN Z}$$
$$\text{ELSE } \quad i:= i + 1; \text{sw}(i, 0);$$
$$\text{IF } k = 0 \text{ THEN P1 ELSE P2 FI}$$
$$\text{FI}$$

As P1 does not alter k, $k = 0$ remains true, and so this reduces to

$$P1 == \text{IF } i = n - 1 \text{ THEN Z}$$
$$\text{ELSE } i := i + 1; sw(i, 0); P1$$
$$\text{FI}$$

or, finally,

$$P1 == \text{WHILE } i \neq n - 1 \text{ DO } i := i + 1; sw(i, 0) \text{ OD}; Z$$

Similarly, in P2 we look for possible simplifications. We have obtained as preassertion for $-P$:

$$k = (q * (m + 2) + r) * \text{fac}(m + 1)/\text{fac}(i + 1) \qquad r \neq 0$$

which cannot give $k = 0$, even with $i = m$. But, for $i = m$, the division gives $k = q$ and $j = r$, and causes the loop on $-P$ to be left through R. Thus in P2, k remains non-zero, and $-P$ can be replaced by P2, whence a new system:

$$\text{PERM} == k := \text{fac}(n) - 1; R$$
$$R == i := 0; kp := k; \text{write}(a); -P$$
$$-P == \text{IF } k = 0 \text{ THEN P1 ELSE P2 FI}$$
$$P1 == \text{WHILE } i \neq n - 1 \text{ DO } i := i + 1; sw(i, 0) \text{ OD}; Z$$
$$P2 == i := i + 1; k, j := \text{div}(k, i + 1);$$
$$sw(i, j); j := j - 1;$$
$$\text{IF } j < 0 \text{ THEN P2}$$
$$\text{ELSE } sw(i, j); k := kp - 1; R$$
$$\text{FI}$$

Resolution of the system gives the following form directly:

```
k := fac(n) − 1;
DO
        i := 0; kp := k; write(a);
        IF k = 0 THEN EXIT FI;
        DO
                i := i + 1; k, j := div(k, i + 1);
                sw(i, j); j := j − 1;
                IF j ≥ 0 THEN sw(i, j); k := kp − 1; EXIT FI
        OD
OD;
WHILE i ≠ n − 1 DO i := i + 1; sw(i, 0) OD
```

This program can still be improved slightly. The little loop which ends it does not write any permutations; it only restores the vector to its initial state. If that was not part of the statement of the problem, the final loop can be omitted. Consequently, the assignment $i := 0$ in the main loop, written to initialise both this outer loop and the second inner loop, can be postponed until after the test IF $k = 0...$, and similarly, for the initialisation of kp. We use a simple expansion:

$$k := \text{fac}(n) - 1;$$
$$\text{DO}$$
$$\quad \text{write}(a);$$
$$\quad \text{IF } k = 0 \text{ THEN EXIT FI};$$
$$\quad i := 0; kp := k;$$
$$\quad \text{DO}$$
$$\quad\quad i := i + 1; k, j := \text{div}(k, i + 1);$$
$$\quad\quad \text{sw}(i, j); j := j - 1;$$
$$\quad\quad \text{IF } j \geq 0 \text{ THEN EXIT FI}$$
$$\quad \text{OD};$$
$$\quad \text{sw}(i, j); k := kp - 1;$$
$$\text{OD}$$

In this form, the method is very clear; k is initialised to $\text{fac}(n) - 1$, then decreased in steps of 1 to 0, and so the number of permutations produced is $\text{fac}(n)$. For each value of k, a permutation is constructed based on the arithmetic properties of k, which have not been spelt out and which have not been made use of in the writing of the program. Here again, we have made small transformations, chiefly on the variable k. We have demostrated some assertions concerning k, but these are directly bound to the form of the program rather than to the properties of the permutations. It is very remarkable that with such crude implements we have been able to produce a program whose direct construction would require no little mathematics.

9.4   The Towers of Hanoi

9.4.1   Recursive Procedure

The puzzle of the Towers of Hanoi is well known. Three vertical rods (numbered here $0, 1, 2$) are mounted vertically on a baseboard. Circular discs, pierced at their centres, can be threaded on the rods. Initially, all the discs form a "tower" on rod 0. Their diameters are all different, decreasing towards the top; the largest disc is at the base and the smallest at the top. We take the diameter of the smallest disc as unity. We shall call this smallest disc "disc 1", and number the discs with successive integers; we can say that the diameter of disc p is p. The object of the puzzle is to rebuild the tower on rod 1; but only one disc may be moved at a time, and at no stage may any disc be placed on a smaller disc.

The solution is very simple. We write $H(p, d, a)$ for the procedure which transports discs p to 1 from the "departure" rod d (where they are assumed to be, in proper order) to the "arrival" rod a. We note that, because we are concerned with the p smallest discs, this procedure can be carried out whatever the disposition of the remaining larger discs.

$H(p, d, a)$ involves rods d and a, but we can also make use of the third rod, x say, as an intermediary. Suppose we move the $p - 1$ smallest discs from d to x. This is $H(p - 1, d, x)$.

The disc p is now at the top of the tower on rod d, and a is either empty or has only discs larger than p. We may thus take disc p from d and place it on a. To finish, we have to move the $p - 1$ smallest discs from x to a.

It is easy to compute x as a function of d and a, for the sum of the numbers of the three rods is $0 + 1 + 2 = 3$, and so $x = 3 - a - d$. Finally, when $p = 1$, $H(p, d, a)$ reduces simply to moving disc 1 from d to a; that is always possible, since disc 1 is the smallest:

$$H(p, d, a) == \text{IF } p = 1 \text{ THEN } m(1, d, a)$$
$$\qquad\qquad\qquad \text{ELSE } \quad H(p - 1, d, 3 - a - d);$$
$$\qquad\qquad\qquad\qquad\qquad m(p, d, a);$$
$$\qquad\qquad\qquad\qquad\qquad H(p - 1, 3 - a - d, d)$$
$$\qquad \text{FI}$$

where $m(p, d, a)$ might reduce to PRINT p, "is moved from", d, "to", a. The program calling H is

$$H(n, 0, 1)$$

9.4.2   The First Form

The formal parameters have to be made global. We can assume that the global variables p, d, a are globally invariant over H. A call such as

$$H(p - 1, d, 3 - a - d)$$

will thus be changed into

$$p := p - 1; a := 3 - a - d; H; a := 3 - a - d; p := p + 1$$

We obtain

$$H == \text{IF } p = 1 \text{ THEN } m(1, d, a); -H$$
$$\qquad\qquad \text{ELSE } \quad p := p - 1; a := 3 - a - d; H;$$
$$\qquad\qquad\qquad\qquad a := 3 - a - d; p := p + 1;$$
$$\qquad\qquad\qquad\qquad m(p, d, a);$$
$$\qquad\qquad\qquad\qquad p := p - 1; d := 3 - a - d; H;$$
$$\qquad\qquad\qquad\qquad d := 3 - a - d; p := p + 1;$$
$$\qquad\qquad\qquad\qquad -H$$
$$\qquad \text{FI}$$

The most inconvenient feature of this is that the second call of H, which was terminal, no longer is because of the assignments restoring the values of the two variables p, d. We put the system into canonical form by the creation of new actions and by the definition of the program:

$$\text{HANOI} == p := n; d := 0; a := 1; \text{H}; \text{Z}$$
$$\text{H} == \text{IF } p = 1 \text{ THEN } m(1, d, a); -\text{H}$$
$$\text{ELSE } p := p - 1; a := 3 - a - d; \text{U1}$$
$$\text{FI}$$
$$\text{Y1} == a := 3 - a - d; p := p + 1;$$
$$m(p, d, a);$$
$$p := p - 1; d := 3 - a - \text{d}; \text{U2}$$
$$\text{U1} == \text{H}; \text{Y1}$$
$$\text{U2} == \text{H}; \text{Y2}$$
$$\text{Y2} == d := 3 - a - d; p := p + 1; -\text{H}$$

We have three non-terminal calls. The initial call in HANOI can easily be recognised, as it is the only one which leaves $p = n$ (before each of the two other calls there is $p := p - 1$).

There is no obvious property which can be used to distinguish between the two other calls. A binary counter k must be introduced in order to mark them and so enable each to be recognised.

We have described this technique in Section 8.2.5. But the counter can also be for the recognition of the initial call. We have two possible tests for this. The previous example suggests that it may be worthwhile to use the same variable for all the tests; we had a test for exit, $i = n - 1$, which we replaced by a test on k. So here we take the same variable k to test for the initial call and to distinguish between the recursive calls. We take k as globally invariant over H, and we modify HANOI, U1, and U2:

$$\text{HANOI} == p := n; d := 0; a := 1; k := 1; \text{H}; \text{Z}$$
$$\text{U1} == k := 2 * k + 1; \text{H}; k := k - 1; \text{Y1}$$
$$\text{U2} == \text{H}; k := k : 2; \text{Y2}$$

Now k is not modified in the non-recursive branch of H; it is incremented in U1 and then decremented by 1 between H and Y1; it is finally restored to its initial value between H and Y2; thus, it is globally invariant over H. We can define $-\text{H}$:

$$-\text{H} == \text{IF } k = 1 \text{ THEN } \text{Z}$$
$$\text{ELSE } \text{IF even}(k) \text{ THEN } k := k : 2; \text{Y2}$$
$$\text{ELSE } k := k - 1; \text{Y1}$$
$$\text{FI}$$
$$\text{FI}$$

$H == \text{IF } p = 1 \text{ THEN } m(1, d, a); \quad H$
$\qquad\qquad \text{ELSE} \quad p := p - 1; a := 3 - a - d; k := 2 * k + 1; H$
$\qquad \text{FI}$
$Y1 == a := 3 - a - d; p := p + 1; m(p, d, a);$
$\qquad\quad p := p - 1; d := 3 - a - d; H$
$Y2 == d := 3 - a - d; p := p + 1; -H$

We have here a form which is easy to resolve, and thence an iterative program. It must be simplified. We first examine the loop on H, in which we can expect simplification.

The iterative form of H is

$H == \text{WHILE } p \neq 1 \text{ DO}$
$\qquad\qquad\qquad\qquad\qquad p := p - 1; a := 3 - a - d; k := 2 * k + 1$
$\qquad\quad \text{OD};$
$\quad m(1, d, a); -H$

The body of the loop is executed $p - 1$ times. The final value of p is 1. Let a_0 be the initial value of a. At the end of the execution of the first step of the loop, a is $3 - a_0 - d$, and after the second, it is $3 - (3 - a_0 - d) - d = a_0$.

The final value of a is thus a_0 if $p - 1$ is even; otherwise, $3 - a_0 - d$. There remains k. We observe, as in the previous section, that $k + 1$ is changed to $2 * k + 1 + 1 = 2 * (k + 1)$, that is, multiplied by 2, in each step of the loop. We can thus replace H by the resolved form:

$H == \text{IF odd}(p - 1) \text{ THEN } a := 3 - a - d \text{ FI};$
$\qquad k := (k + 1) * 2^{p-1} - 1; p := 1; m(1, d, a); -H$

which in turn simplifies to

$H == \text{IF even } (p) \text{ THEN } a := 3 - a - d \text{ FI};$
$\qquad k := (k + 1) * 2^{p-1} - 1; p := 1; m(1, d, a); -H$

Note that if $p = 1$, k, p, a remain unchanged. This is consistent with the fact that the body of the loop is not executed.

Now we consider $-H$. The action $Y2$ ends with $-H$, $Y1$ with H. There is thus only one branch of $-H$ to cause an iteration, and it would be interesting to isolate it in the first alternatives of the selections. The iteration occurs for even k, and in this case k cannot have the value 1.

The simplest way is to enclose $-H$ in a tautology on even(k) and then to simplify the result by removing all the redundant tests. That is left as an exercise for the reader:

$-H == \text{IF even}(k) \text{ THEN } k := k:2; d := 3 - a - d; p := p + 1; -H$
$\qquad\qquad\qquad \text{ELSE} \quad R$
$\qquad\quad \text{FI}$
$R == \text{IF } k = 1 \text{ THEN } Z$
$\qquad\qquad\qquad \text{ELSE} \quad k := k - 1; Y1$
$\qquad \text{FI}$

We put $-H$ into iterative form:

$-H ==$ WHILE even(k) DO
$$k:=k:2; d:=3-a-d; p:=p+1$$
OD;

    R

This works in a manner similar to that of H. Let q be the number of steps of the loop. At each step of the loop k is divided by 2, which has the effect of removing a zero from the right-hand end of its binary representation. The loop stops when k is odd, that is, when every zero at the right of k has been removed. We denote by nzr(k) the number of zero bits at the right of the binary representation of k:

$$q = \text{nzr}(k)$$

The effect of $-H$ is thus

$-H == q:= \text{nzr}(k); \text{IF odd}(q) \text{ THEN } d:=3-a-d \text{ FI};$
$\quad\quad\text{p}:=p+q; k:=k:2^q; R$

Before continuing, we note that $-H$ is called by H, with $p = 1$. We can therefore simplify

$$p:=p+q$$

into

$$p:=q+1$$

This being so, q can be replaced by $p-1$:

$-H == p:= \text{nzr}(k)+1; \text{IF even}(p) \text{ THEN } d:=3-a-d \text{ FI};$
$\quad\quad k:=k:2^{p-1}; R$

We now take R into $-H$, after the necessary substitutions. We simplify in Y1:

$p:=p+1; m(p,d,a); p:=p-1$ becoming $m(p+1,d,a)$
$-H == p:= \text{nzr}(k)+1; \text{IF even}(p) \text{ THEN } d:=3-a-\text{d FI};$
$\quad\quad k:=k:2^{p-1};$
$\quad\quad\text{IF } k=1 \text{ THEN Z}$
$\quad\quad\quad\quad\quad\text{ELSE } k:=k-1;$
$\quad\quad\quad\quad\quad\quad\quad\quad a:=3-a-d; m(p+1,d,a); d:=3-a-d;$
$\quad\quad\quad\quad\quad\quad\quad\quad\text{IF even}(p) \text{ THEN } a:=3-a-d \text{ FI};$
$\quad\quad\quad\quad\quad\quad\quad\quad k:=(k+1)*2^{p-1}-1; p:=1; m(1,d,a); -H$
$\quad\quad\text{FI}$

We move the assignment $k := k - 1$ down to merge it with

$$k := (k + 1) * 2^{p-1} - 1$$

Then we move the assignment $k := k : 2^{p-1}$ to merge with the previously merged assignment; the result is $k := k - 1$. This modifies the test

$$k = 1 \quad \text{into} \quad k = 2^{p-1}$$

$-\text{H} == p := \text{nzr}(k) + 1; \text{IF even}(p) \text{ THEN } d := 3 - a - d \text{ FI};$
$\quad \text{IF } k = 2^{p-1} \text{ THEN Z}$
$\qquad \text{ELSE } a := 3 - a - d; \text{m}(p + 1, d, a); d := 3 - a - d;$
$\qquad\qquad \text{IF even}(p) \text{ THEN } a := 3 - a - d \text{ FI};$
$\qquad\qquad k := k - 1; p := 1; \text{m}(1, d, a); -\text{H}$
$\quad \text{FI}$

We have a new form of the program in which H no longer appears. To eliminate this action, we take it into HANOI:

$\text{HANOI} == p := n; d := 0; a := 1; k := 1;$
$\qquad \text{IF even}(p) \text{ THEN } a := 3 - a - d \text{ FI};$
$\qquad k := (k + 1) * 2^{p-1} - 1; p := 1; \text{m}(1, d, a); -\text{H}$

All the evident simplifications are made:

$\text{HANOI} == d := 0; \text{IF even}(n) \text{ THEN } a := 2 \text{ ELSE } a := 1 \text{ FI};$
$\qquad k := 2^n - 1; p := 1; \text{m}(1, d, a); -\text{H}$

The sequence

$$p := 1; \text{m}(1, d, a); -\text{H}$$

occurs twice; let us call it G. As p is redefined in $-\text{H}$, there is no point in making the assignment to p. There remains

$\text{HANOI} == d := 0; \text{IF even}(n) \text{ THEN } a := 2 \text{ ELSE } a := 1 \text{ FI};$
$\qquad k := 2^n - 1; \text{G}$
$\text{G} == \text{m}(1, d, a); -\text{H}$
$-\text{H} == p := \text{nzr}(k) + 1; \text{IF even}(p) \text{ THEN } d := 3 - a - d \text{ FI};$
$\qquad \text{IF } k = 2^{p-1} \text{ THEN Z}$
$\qquad\qquad \text{ELSE } a := 3 - a - d; \text{m}(p + 1, d, a);$
$\qquad\qquad\qquad d := 3 - a - d;$
$\qquad\qquad\qquad \text{IF even}(p) \text{ THEN } a := 3 - a - d \text{ FI};$
$\qquad\qquad\qquad k := k - 1; \text{G}$
$\quad \text{FI}$

Note first the change of status of the variable k. It was introduced as a binary counter to distinguish the calls of H. Now it is decremented by 1 at each step of the loop, and its value serves to determine which disc is to be moved.

In fact, k begins at $2^n - 1$ and is decreased in steps of 1 until the next lower power of 2 is encountered, which is 2^{n-1}. Let us try to change this interval of variation to $2^{n-1} \ldots 0$. We put k into the form $k = 2^{n-1} + k'$.

For all non-zero k', $\text{nzr}(k) = \text{nzr}(k')$, and so k can be replaced by k'. When k' is zero, $\text{nzr}(k)$ cannot be computed. It will therefore be necessary in $-\text{H}$ to anticipate the test $k' = 0$, which ensures that the modification to d does not take place. This is once again what we have seen already in the permutation program. The program in its present form re-establishes the variables p, d, a with their initial values. If we anticipate the test on k, this will not happen, but it does not matter. We have then a new form:

$$\text{HANOI} == d := 0; a := \text{IF even}(n) \text{ THEN } 2 \text{ ELSE } 1 \text{ FI};$$
$$k := 2^n - 1; G$$
$$G == m(1, d, a);$$
$$\text{IF } k = 0 \text{ THEN Z}$$
$$\text{ELSE} \quad p := \text{nzr}(k) + 1;$$
$$\text{IF even}(p) \text{ THEN } d := 3 - a - d \text{ FI};$$
$$a := 3 - a - d; m(p + 1, d, a);$$
$$d := 3 - a - d;$$
$$\text{IF even}(p) \text{ THEN } a := 3 - a - d \text{ FI};$$
$$k := k - 1; G$$
$$\text{FI}$$

We shall now try to follow the values of d and a. Let d_0, a_0, and x_0 be the values of d, a, and x at the entry to G:

$$G == m(1, d, a);$$
$$\text{IF } k = 0 \text{ THEN Z}$$
$$\text{ELSE} \quad p := \text{nzr}(k) + 1;$$
$$[[a = a_0 \quad d = d_0 \quad x = x_0]]$$
$$\text{IF even}(p) \text{ THEN } d := 3 - a - d \text{ FI};$$
$$[[\text{even}(p) \to a = a_0 \quad d = x_0 \quad x = d_0$$
$$\text{odd}(p) \to a = a_0 \quad d = d_0 \quad x = x_0]]$$
$$a := 3 - a - d;$$
$$[[\text{even}(p) \to a = d_0 \quad d = x_0 \quad x = a_0$$
$$\text{odd}(p) \to a = x_0 \quad d = d_0 \quad x = a_0]]$$
$$m(p + 1, d, a);$$
$$d := 3 - a - d;$$
$$[[\text{even}(p) \to a = d_0 \quad d = a_0 \quad x = x_0$$
$$\text{odd}(p) \to a = x_0 \quad d = a_0 \quad x = d_0]]$$
$$\text{IF even}(p) \text{ THEN } a := 3 - a - d \text{ FI};$$
$$[[\text{even}(p) \to a = x_0 \quad d = a_0 \quad x = d_0$$
$$\text{odd}(p) \to a = x_0 \quad d = a_0 \quad x = d_0]]$$
$$k := k - 1; G$$
$$\text{FI}$$

The effect of G is now clear. The move m($p + 1, d, a$) takes disc $p + 1$ from x_0 to d_0 if p is even and from d_0 to x_0 if p is odd. We note that this takes place after m($1, d, a$), which has put disc 1 on a_0. As no other disc can be placed on top of disc 1, and because this move is not a move of disc 1, it must necessarily be a move between the two other towers d_0 and x_0 and affects the smaller of the discs on top of these two towers. The parity of p provides the necessary information.

Taking account of the assertions above, we simplify G to

> G == m($1, d, a$);
>   IF $k = 0$ THEN Z
>   ELSE $x := 3 - a - d$; $p := $ nzr(k) $+ 1$;
>   IF even(p) THEN m($p + 1, x, d$)
>   ELSE m($p + 1, d, x$)
>   FI;
> $d := a$; $a := x$;
> $k := k - 1$; G
>   FI

The work is finished, and we can now give the final program:

> $d := 0$; $a := $ IF even(n) THEN 2 ELSE 1 FI;
> $k := 2^{n-1} - 1$;
> DO
>   m($1, d, a$);
>   IF $k = 0$ THEN EXIT FI;
> $x := 3 - a - d$; $p := $ nzr(k) $+ 1$;
>   IF even(p) THEN m($p + 1, x, d$) ELSE m($p + 1, d, x$) FI;
> $d := a$; $a := x$;
> $k := k - 1$
> OD

At the risk of repetitiveness, we must insist that we have not been looking for this particular program. We started with an undoubted, well-known, recursive procedure. We made one choice; for H to save its arguments, which implied that the second call did not stay terminal, and thus that there were three non-terminal calls. We applied a general technique to distinguish the calls by means of a binary counter. Then, in the resultant program, we identified certain actions on the counter, in terms not of a strategy for the Towers of Hanoi, but of local properties. We considered in detail the assignments to the variables a and d and made consequent simplifications. All that done, we found the following strategy:

move the smallest disc from d to a,
move the next smallest disc,
make a cyclic permutation of the three towers.

In other words, the smallest disc takes part in every alternate move and always in the same (cyclic) direction. The next move is completely determined each time.

We have thus found a remarkably simple strategy for the Towers of Hanoi without, we repeat, having sought it directly. This strategy is the simplest possible.

Had we been asked directly to write an iterative program for the Towers of Hanoi based on the serial numbering of the moves (the variable k), would we have been able to find this strategy? I regard it as unimportant among the results of the program that

the number of moves is $2^n - 1$

This result can, in fact, easily be obtained from the recursive procedure, but that would require a deliberate effort. Here it has appeared without being asked for.

The development of this program is a good illustration of what we call "analytical programming". We begin with a "raw", axiomatic form and with no apparent strategy. We operate on the program, following general methods, always trying to make good use of whatever may come to light.

This, then, is "analytical programming". The operations are carried out on the basis of the possible simplifications, not directed towards an unknown goal. The result is often a program which one had not dared to hope for...

9.5 A General Result

We made a choice, and we underlined this choice: the second call of H was not kept terminal, because with the formal parameters becoming global, it was an easy matter to arrange for the exit. To keep H terminal, it would have been necessary to know how H modified the global variables which replaced the formal parameters.

Consider a recursive procedure

$$F(x) == \text{IF } t \text{ THEN a ELSE } \beta; F(h(x)) \text{ FI}$$

where x represents the n-tuple of formal parameters, a is a sequence of instructions not containing any call of F, and β a sequence which does contain one or more calls of F. We suppose moreover that a does not modify x.

We have considered the solution obtained by supposing that F globally preserves x, a global variable:

$$F == \text{IF } t \text{ THEN } a; -F$$
$$\text{ELSE } \beta[F(g(x)) \rightarrow x := g(x); F; x := g^{-1}(x)];$$
$$x := h(x); F; x := h^{-1}(x); -F$$
$$FI$$

If the inverse functions do not exist, this is impossible. It is the same if we wish to keep the second call terminal. Two solutions are then usable.

9.5.1   The Stack

We can save x in a stack:

$$F == \text{IF } t \text{ THEN } a; -F$$
$$\text{ELSE } \beta[F(g(x)) \rightarrow \text{push}(x); x := g(x); F; \text{pop}(x)];$$
$$x := h(x); F$$
$$FI$$

The last call of F remains terminal and does not have to be regularised. This is an advantage paid for by the price of stack manipulation. If, for example, this were to be used without other precautions in the case of the Towers of Hanoi, it would be necessary to stack p, d, a at every call—something we would wish to avoid.

9.5.2   Recomputing the Arguments

If the procedure F does not save its arguments, it modifies them in a way that we can try to determine. Let δ be the transformation which F imposes on the global variables representing the formal parameters:

$$[[x = x_0]] \, F \, [[x = \delta(x_0)]]$$

Note that the effect of δ depends on the value of t: when t is true, a, which is supposed not to modify x, is executed. For this case, δ is thus the identity function. If on the other hand t is false, β is executed, and β is supposed to preserve x (otherwise the call $F(h(x))$ would pose problems...):

$$[[x = x_0]] \, F == \text{IF } t \text{ THEN } a[[x = x_0 = \delta(x_0)]]$$
$$\text{ELSE } \beta;$$
$$[[x = x_0]]$$
$$x := h(x); \qquad [[x = h(x_0)]]$$
$$F \, [[x = \delta(h(x_0))]]$$
$$FI \, [[x = \delta(x_0)]]$$

We deduce from this a recursive definition of the function δ:

$$\delta(x) \simeq \text{IF } t \text{ THEN } x$$
$$\text{ELSE } \delta(h(x))$$
$$\text{FI}$$

With δ, and provided that all the inverse functions exist, we have a new form for F:

$$F == \text{IF } t \text{ THEN } a ; -F$$
$$\text{ELSE } \beta[F(g(x)) \rightarrow x := g(x); F; x := g^{-1}(\delta^{-1}(x))] ;$$
$$x := h(x); F$$
$$\text{FI}$$

This form is interesting because it keeps F terminal and avoids the need for a stack.

In certain cases, it may be necessary to have recourse to a compromise between the two techniques. This is what we are about to see with the Towers of Hanoi.

9.6   The Towers of Hanoi—Second Form

We return to the recursive form of Section 9.4.1. This gives directly the recursive definition of δ:

$$\delta(p, d, a) \simeq \text{IF } p = 1 \text{ THEN } p, d, a$$
$$\text{ELSE } \delta(p - 1, 3 - a - d, a)$$
$$\text{FI}$$

We have to find the explicit form of this recursive (or implicit) definition. In every case, the third argument is unchanged; that is, preserved by δ. At exit from δ, p is necessarily equal to 1:

$$\delta(p, d, a) = 1, \ldots, a$$

After every two calls, d takes its original value. We may then conjecture that

$$\delta(p, d, a) = 1, \text{ IF even}(p) \text{ THEN } 3 - a - d \text{ ELSE } d \text{ FI}, a$$

Show by means of recurrence that this is so. It is true for $p = 1$. If it is assumed true for the inner call, it is also true for the outer call (left as an exercise for the reader).

Because it is invariant through F, a can easily be recomputed. If the value of p after F is known, d can be recomputed. But p cannot be recomputed since all initial values give the same final value 1.

Thus, we have to stack p. After F, the stack gives p; a has kept its value; and d is unchanged if p is odd, otherwise $3 - a - d$. As it is $p - 1$ rather than p which is needed, we shall stack $p - 1$. We return to the form of generalised actions defining H, and add to it some assertions about p, d, a, using the notation $x = 3 - a - d$:

$$[[\, p = p_0 \qquad d = d_0 \qquad a = a_0 \qquad x = x_0 \,]]$$

$$\begin{aligned}
\text{H} = = \ &\text{IF } p = 1 \text{ THEN } m(1, d, a); \ -\text{H} \\
&\text{ELSE } \ p := p - 1; a := 3 - a - d; \text{push}(p); \\
&\qquad\quad [[\, p = \text{top} = p_0 - 1 \qquad d = d_0 \qquad a = x_0 \\
&\qquad\qquad\quad x = a_0 \,]] \\
&\qquad\quad \text{H}; \\
&\qquad\quad [[\, p = 1 \qquad \text{top} = p_0 - 1 \qquad a = x_0 \\
&\qquad\qquad\quad d = \text{IF even(top) THEN } a_0 \text{ ELSE } d_0 \text{ FI} \,]] \\
&\qquad\quad \textbf{c} \text{ the variables } p, d, a \text{ can be recovered } \textbf{c} \\
&\qquad\quad \text{pop}(p); \\
&\qquad\quad [[\, p = p_0 - 1 \\
&\qquad\qquad\quad \text{even}(p) \rightarrow a = x_0 \qquad d = a_0 \qquad x = d_0 \\
&\qquad\qquad\quad \text{odd}(p) \ \rightarrow a = x_0 \qquad d = d_0 \qquad x = a_0 \,]] \\
&\qquad\quad x := a; \\
&\qquad\quad \text{IF even}(p) \text{ THEN } a := d; d := 3 - a - x \\
&\qquad\qquad\qquad\qquad \text{ELSE } \ a := 3 - d - x \\
&\qquad\quad \text{FI} \\
&\text{FI}
\end{aligned}$$

We obtain a new generalised system, without formal parameters:

$$\begin{aligned}
\text{H} = = \ &\text{IF } p = 1 \text{ THEN } m(1, d, a); \ -\text{H} \\
&\qquad\qquad \text{ELSE } \ p := p - 1; a := 3 - a - d; \text{push}(p); \text{H}; \text{K} \\
&\text{FI} \\[4pt]
\text{K} = = \ &\text{pop}(p); x := a; \\
&\text{IF even}(p) \text{ THEN } a := d; d := 3 - a - x \\
&\qquad\qquad\quad \text{ELSE } \ a := 3 - d - x \\
&\text{FI}; \\
&m(p + 1, d, a); \\
&d := 3 - a - d; \\
&\text{H} \\[4pt]
\text{HANOI} = = \ &p := n; d := 0; a := 1; \text{stack} := \text{empty}; \text{H}; \text{Z}
\end{aligned}$$

There are only two non-terminal calls, and the initial call in Z is characterised by stack = empty. Regularisation is immediate:

$$H == \text{IF } p = 1 \text{ THEN } m(1,d,a); -H$$
$$\text{ELSE } p := p - 1; a := 3 - a - d; \text{push}(p); H$$
$$\text{FI}$$
$$K == \text{pop}(p); x := a;$$
$$\text{IF even}(p) \text{ THEN } a := d; d := 3 - a - x$$
$$\text{ELSE } a := 3 - d - x$$
$$\text{FI};$$
$$m(p + 1, d, a); d := 3 - a - d; H$$
$$\text{HANOI} == p := n; d := 0; a := 1; \text{stack} := \text{empty}; H$$
$$-H == \text{IF stack} = \text{empty THEN Z ELSE K FI}$$

Operations procede as before. The loop in H cannot be suppressed, because of its successive stackings, but its effect on a can be synthesized.

$$H == \text{IF even}(p) \text{ THEN } a := 3 - a - d \text{ FI};$$
$$\text{WHILE } p \neq 1 \text{ DO } p := p - 1; \text{push}(p) \text{ OD};$$
$$m(1, d, a); -H$$

Let us now follow the effect of K on the variables a, d, x. Let a', d', x' be the respective values of these three variables at the point of entry into K:

$$[[a', d', x']]$$
$$K == \text{pop}(p); x := a; [[a', d', a']]$$
$$\text{IF even}(p) \text{ THEN } a := d; [[d', d', a']]$$
$$d := 3 - a - x [[d', x', a']]$$
$$\text{ELSE } a := 3 - d - x [[x', d', a']]$$
$$\text{FI};$$
$$m(p + 1, d, a);$$
$$d := 3 - a - d; [[\text{even}(p) \rightarrow d', a', a'$$
$$\text{odd}(p) \ x', a', a']]$$
$$H$$

But H begins by modifying a if p is even:

$$H == \text{IF even}(p) \text{ THEN } a := 3 - a - d [[x', a', a']] \text{ FI};$$
$$\text{WHILE} \ldots$$

We isolate this loop:

$$H == \text{IF even}(p) \text{ THEN } a := 3 - a - d \text{ FI}; S$$
$$S == \text{WHILE} \ldots \text{OD}; m(1, d, a); -H$$

We take H into $-H$ and into HANOI, and simplify where possible. The details are omitted here:

$$\text{HANOI} == p := n;\, d := 0;\, \text{stack} := \text{empty};$$
$$a := \text{IF even}(n)\ \text{THEN 2 ELSE 1 FI};$$
$$\text{S}$$
$$\text{S} == \text{WHILE } p \neq 1\ \text{DO } p := p - 1;\, \text{push}(p)\ \text{OD};$$
$$m(1, d, a);\, -\text{H}$$
$$-\text{H} == \text{IF stack} = \text{empty THEN Z ELSE K FI}$$

We write K in terms of a', d', x':

$$\text{K} == \text{pop}(p);$$
$$\text{IF even}(p)\ \text{THEN } m(p + 1, x', d')\ \text{ELSE } m(p + 1, d', x')\ \text{FI};$$
$$d := a';\, a := x';\, \text{S}$$

It is sufficient to compute x to obtain the required form:

$$\text{K} == \text{pop}(p);\, x := 3 - a - d;$$
$$\text{IF even}(p)\ \text{THEN } m(p + 1, x, d)\ \text{ELSE } m(p + 1, d, x)\ \text{FI};$$
$$d := a;\, a := x;\, \text{S}$$

Here is the program:

$$p := n;\, d := 0;\, \text{stack} := \text{empty};\, a := \text{IF even}(n)\ \text{THEN 2 ELSE 1 FI};$$
$$\text{DO}$$
$$\quad \text{WHILE } p \neq 1\ \text{DO } p := p - 1;\, \text{push}(p)\ \text{OD};$$
$$\quad m(1, d, a);$$
$$\quad \text{IF stack} = \text{empty THEN EXIT FI};$$
$$\quad \text{pop}(p);\, x := 3 - a - d;$$
$$\quad \text{IF even}(p)\ \text{THEN } m(p + 1, x, d)\ \text{ELSE } m(p + 1, d, x)\ \text{FI};$$
$$\quad d := a;\, a := x;$$
$$\text{OD}$$

This program strongly resembles the previous one, in particular in its treatment of a, d, x. The choice of the move

$$m(p + 1, d, x) \qquad \text{or} \qquad m(p + 1, x, d)$$

is decided by the stack and not by k.

9.7 Remarks on the Two Solutions of the Towers of Hanoi

The two solutions which we have achieved resemble each other, and that should not surprise us. They have one essential point in common; they do not make use of any representation of the puzzle. That is a surprising fact.

A "conventional" approach to this program, with the aim of finding an iterative solution, would have been to define the types of the data of the problem and to consider ways of representing these data in a program. Two solutions come to mind:

  −represent each of the towers by a vector or a list;
  −attach to each disc the number of the tower in which it is.

It is also necessary to unearth an iterative strategy. At a given point in the solution of the puzzle, there are only two movable discs:

  −the smallest one at the top of a tower, which can go to either of the two others;
  −the smaller of the two discs at the tops of the other towers, which can go to the tower which does not have the smallest disc.

It is easy to see that the smallest disc takes part in every second move. Suppose it has just been moved. At the next move, if the smallest disc is moved again, that move will be annulled. We have to take the only move possible— there is no choice. The smaller of the two other top discs has to go onto the larger. After that, there are again only two discs which can be moved—that which is not the smallest, being the one which has just been moved. Suppose it is disc p which has just been moved. There is now at the top of the tower it has left a disc larger than p, and p is still the smaller of the discs other than disc 1.

The puzzle of the Towers of Hanoi is thus strongly determinate. We must move alternately the smallest disc and the only other movable disc. The only choice to make thus concerns the movement of the smallest disc; it has two possible moves at each stage.

What the foregoing programs have shown us is that the smallest disc must always move in the same (cyclic) direction. (We can imagine a cyclic permutation of the three towers.)

Another way to obtain this result is by experimentation. We can write out the recursive procedure and run it on a computer. We would then find out

  that the smallest disc takes part in alternate moves, and that the smallest disc moves always in the same (cyclic) direction.

This demonstration is insufficient for a valid construction, but it provides a starting point. We might show, by recurrence, that these properties are true. After that, the construction of an iterative program becomes simple:

find the direction of movement of the smallest disc;
          DO
                  move the smallest disc in this direction;
                  IF all the pieces are in tower 1 THEN EXIT FI;
                  move the only possible disc other than the smallest
          OD

But we should need to know where the smallest disc is—a variable y would suffice. It would then be necessary to have a representation of the puzzle in mind so as to be able to tell which disc is at the top of each tower, and hence what moves are possible.

We could represent the puzzle by a vector $t[1 \ldots n]$.
$t[i]$ is the number of the tower containing disc i.

To move disc 1 in the direction s, add s to $t[i]$ modulo 3. The only other movable disc is the smallest of those which are not under disc 1. We run through the array t looking for the first element different from $t[i]$. We give without further development the following program:

$t[1 \ldots n] := 0; t[n + 1] := 3;$
$s := $ IF even(n) THEN 2 ELSE 1 FI;
DO
    $q := t[1] + s;$ IF $q > 2$ THEN $q := q - 3$ FI;
    m$(1, t[1], q); t[1] := q;$
    $p := 1;$
    WHILE $t[p] = q$ DO $p := p + 1$ OD;
    IF $p > n$ THEN EXIT FI;
    $x := 3 - q - t[p];$ m$(p, t[p], x); t[p] := x$
OD

We leave it to the reader to decide carefully which program of those put forward appears to him to be the best. Remember that the last one given would not have been found if we had not first "computed" the others.

A final point remains to be cleared up. We have obtained simple programs by computation. There must be a simple way of deriving them. Now, if we can indeed find the means to clear up some points, others will remain obscure. Thus, why go by the number of zeros on the right of the serial number of the move, and by the parity of this number?

Even granted that this point can be resolved [AR2], what can be done to make those properties which have first to be established—theorems to be proved, say—appear naturally? If it is true that I can, after the event, justify the program which I have computed, which is a way of verifying that I have not made any computing errors, I have no simple way of bringing the solution to the reader.

We are still in the state of analytical geometry.

Two types of transformations have been presented:

–semantic transformations based on assertions;
–syntactic or strongly local semantic transformations. These latter can be realised by a computer with an adequate program. I have written two

experimental systems of this type, one in SNOBOL for an IBM370/68, the other in LSE, first for a MITRA15CII, then for a THEMIS EFCIS-THOMSON (a microcomputer with 64K store and discs, based on the MOTOROLA 6800 microprocessor).

These systems are an interesting aid, because they produce the rewritten programs while avoiding errors in copying and transliteration. But make no mistake—they do not "think"; they can neither take the initiative nor make suggestions. It is for the user to say what transformation he wants to be done and where. For that he has to be able to anticipate the effect of each transformation; and the result of the transformation as it appears on the screen has to be in such a form as to be not entirely unfamiliar to him. In other words, he must have had much practice doing the work by hand for the machine to be of any real use.

This is a serious handicap. Many people reel before the prospect of "analytical programming" because it requires a thorough apprenticeship, which, I am ready to admit, can be tedious. And there is not any interactive system which can ease this apprenticeship, at least not in the form in which we have written such systems—perhaps a system more inspired by the methods of computer-assisted learning?

The purpose of this book has been to show the reader that there are important tools for the creation of programs. Perhaps he is still unconvinced that programming with these tools is worth all the trouble, all the "gymnastic exercises", and all the tiresome computation. But he should know that some others have succeeded with this method and that in my view there is only one other possibility—to develop one's imagination, one's creativity, and the rigour of one's thought... I do not know which of these two ways will appear the more attractive to him. This book states clearly what has been my own choice.

Exercises

E.9.1 One way of sorting a vector consists of sorting its upper and lower halves and then merging these two sorted segments. Normally, the two halves are merged into another vector; this allows a form of merging whose execution time is linear in n. But the two sorted vectors could be merged in their own space. We shall confine ourselves, for simplicity, to the case of the merging of two parts of a vector whose length is a power of 2.

Let a be a vector. Let i and j be two indices in the domain of a, and l a power of 2 such that $j \geq i + l$. The merging operation $F(i, j, l)$ produces in the two parts of a, of equal length l, and beginning at i and j, the sorted sequence resulting from the merging of the sorted sequences of length l which were initially in a in the segments beginning at i and j:

$$F(i,j,l) == \text{IF } l = 1 \text{ THEN } \text{csw}(i,j)$$
$$\text{ELSE } F(i,j,l:2);$$
$$F(i + l:2, j + l:2, l:2);$$
$$F(i + l:2, j, l:2)$$
$$\text{FI}$$

The operation $\text{csw}(i, j)$ is a conditional interchange of the elements of ranks i and j; it is defined here, but, to avoid tedious computations, it should not be written explicitly in F:

$$\text{csw}(i,j) == \text{IF } a[i] > a[j] \text{ THEN } x := a[i]; a[i] := a[j]; a[j] := x \text{ FI}$$

There are several ways of transforming F into an iterative procedure.

E.9.1.1 Suppose that F conserves the global variables i, j, l. Use an arithmetic variable in base 3 to distinguish the calls.

E.9.1.2 Same hypothesis. Use two counters in base 2.

E.9.1.3 Same hypothesis. Do not use counters, but make use of the properties of i and j to distinguish the calls. Supposing that the initial call is

$$F(0, 2^n, 2^n)$$

discuss the peculiarities of the binary representations of i, j.

E.9.1.4 Keep the third call terminal.

E.9.2 "Le Baguenaudier"*: This is a patience game represented by a rectangular board divided into squares, which can be regarded as a vector $a[1 \ldots n]$. There are n pieces which can be placed in or removed from the squares. The rules of the game are these: at each move, one may play only

–on the first square, or
–on the square following the first occupied square,

"playing on a square" meaning that one may place a piece on the square if it is empty or remove the piece from the square if it is occupied.
There are two possible games:

ON(n)   The board is completely empty; put the n pieces on it.
OFF(n)   The board is fully occupied by the n pieces. Take them all off.

---

* This game may be more familiar to the reader in the form of "The Chinese Rings" [*Translator*].

E.9.3   Ackerman's function is defined by

$$A(m, n) \simeq \text{IF } m = 0 \text{ THEN } n + 1$$
$$\text{ELSE   IF } n < 0 \text{ THEN } 1$$
$$\text{ELSE   } A(m - 1, A(m, n - 1))$$
$$\text{FI}$$
$$\text{FI}$$

Transform this into a recursive sub-program. (The only recursive call occurs in a loop.)

Further transform it into an iterative procedure using a stack to save one of the arguments (say why the other argument does not have to be saved).

Consider the structure of the stack, and show that it can be replaced by a vector giving the number of times that each integer in a certain interval occurs in stack.

E.9.4   Consider again the recursive sub-program for merging, of Exercise E.9.1. The first two calls could be made in parallel, or their sequence could be reversed. Write a new recursive procedure $PF(i, j, l, k)$ which implements the k calls:

$$F(i + x * k, j + x * k, l) \qquad \text{for} \quad x = 0, 1, \ldots, k - 1$$

Beginning with F, define it and then make it iterative. Take this investigation as far as you can. There will appear some altogether unexpected properties of the binary representations of i and j.

E.9.5   To sort a vector a of n elements, we may proceed thus:

$$T(p) = = \text{IF } p > n : 2 \text{ THEN}$$
$$\text{ELSE } T(2 * p); T(3 * p); \text{run}(p)$$
$$\text{FI}$$

The sort is given by $T(1)$.

The idea is this: $T(p)$ is the sorting process at step p, meaning that for all i such that the indices concerned are in the interval of validity $1 \ldots n$:

$$a[i] \leq a[i - p]$$

The operation run(p) is given by

$$\text{run}(p) = = i := 1;$$
$$\text{WHILE } i + p \leq n \text{ DO csw}(i, i + p) \text{ OD}$$

csw being the conditional interchange defined in Exercise E.9.1.

Write an iterative procedure beginning with this recursive procedure.

Work systematically through your first version.

The detailed behaviour of this procedure should be carefully studied; it will show that certain steps in the sorting process are repeated unnecessarily [BER].

Bibliography

[AR1]   J. ARSAC, *Premières leçons de programmation*, Nathan (Paris, 1980).

[AR2]   J. ARSAC, *La construction de programmes structurés*, Dunod (Paris, 1977).

[AR3]   J. ARSAC, *La science informatique*, Dunod (Paris, 1970).

[ARK]   J. ARSAC and Y. KODRATOFF, Some techniques for recursion removal from recursive functions, *ACM Transactions on Programming Languages*, Vol. 4, No. 2 (April 1982).

[ASH]   E. A. ASHCROFT and W. W. WADGE, Lucid, a non procedural language with iteration, *Comm. ACM* 20, 7 (July 1977), pp. 519–526.

[BAR]   D. W. BARRON, *Recursive Techniques in Programming*, Macdonald (London, 1969).

[BD1]   R. M. BURSTALL and J. DARLINGTON, A system which automatically improves programs, *Acta Informatica* 6 (1976), *pp.* 41–60.

[BD2]   R. M. BURSTALL and J. DARLINGTON, A transformation system for developing recursive programs, *JACM* 24, 1 (January 1977), pp. 44–61.

[BER]   P. BERLIOUX, Application des propriétés de composition séquentielle et parallèle des instructions à la transformation de programmes récursifs. Dans B. ROBINET, Transformation de programmes, *Actes du 3ᵉ Coll. international sur la programmation*, Dunod (Paris, 1978), pp. 187–202.

[BOE]   B. W. BOEHM, *The High Cost of Software*, Proc. of a symposium SRI, Menlo Park (Monterey, 1973).

[BOI]   N. BOILEAU, *L'Art poétique*, 1674 (Paris, 1894).

[BUR]   A. W. BURGE, *Recursive Programming Techniques*, Addison Wesley (Reading, Massachusetts., 1976).

[CAI]   D. CAILLE, Le langage LSE, *L'ordinateur individuel* (January–February 1979), pp. 50–52.

[CHA]   D. D. CHAMBERLAIN, The single assignment approach to parallel processing, *AFIPS Conf. FJCC*, Vol. 79 (1971), pp. 263–269.

[CO1]   G. COUSINEAU, Thèse d'Etat, Institut de programmation (Paris, 1978): *Un système formel complet pour l'équivalence de schémas itératifs*.

[CO2]   G. COUSINEAU, Transformation de programmes itératifs dans programmation, *Actes du 2ᵉ Coll. international*, Dunod (Paris, 1976), pp. 53–74.

[DI1]   O. J. DAHL, E. W. DIJKSTRA, and C. A. R. HOARE, *Structural Programming*, Academic Press (London, 1972).

[DI2]   E. W. DIJKSTRA, Go To statements considered as harmful, *Comm. ACM*, Vol. 11, No. 3 (March 1968).

[DI3]   E. W. DIJKSTRA, *A Discipline of Programming*, Prentice Hall (1976).

[DUM]   J. DUMONTET, *Etude de la preuve de programmes numériques: contrôle, précision et minimisation des erreurs de calcul*, Thèse d'Etat, Institut de programmation (Paris, 1979).

[FLK]   R. W. FLOYD and D. E. KNUTH, Notes on avoiding Go To statements, *Information Processing Letters*, Vol. 1 (1979), pp. 23–31.

[FLO]   R. W. FLOYD, *Assigning Meaning to Programs*, Proc. of a symp. in applied math., Vol. 19, Math. aspects of computer science (Providence, Rhode Island, 1967).

[GER]   S. GERHARDT, Proof theory of partial correctness verification systems, *SIAM Journal of Computing*, Vol. 5, No. 3 (1976), pp. 355–377.

[GRI]   D. GRIES, *The Science of Programming*, Springer-Verlag (1981).

[HEN]   C. HENRY, *Structures de contrôle et puissance d'expression*, 4ᵉ Coll. international, Springer-Verlag, Lecture notes in comp. sci. No. 83, pp. 147–162.

[HOA]   C. A. R. HOARE, An axiomatic basis for computer programming, *Comm. ACM*, Vol. 12 (1969), pp. 576–583.

[HOO]   P. HOOGVORST, Thèse d'Etat, Ecole normale supérieure (Paris, 1982).

[HOP]   J. E. HOPCROFT, *Complexity of Computer Computations*, Proc. of the IFIP conference Stockholm, North-Holland (Amsterdam, August 1974), p. 620.

[IRL]   J. IRLIK, Translating some recursive procedures into iterative schemas, *Programmation*, 2ᵉ Coll., Dunod (Paris, 1978), pp. 39–52.

[KNU]   D. E. KNUTH, *The Art of Computer Programming*, Vol. 1, Addison Wesley (Reading, 1968).

[KOS]   R. KOSARAJU, Analysis of structured programs, *Journal of Computer and Systems Science*, Vol. 9 (December 1974), pp. 232–255.

[LE1]   H. F. LEDGARD, *Proverbs de programmation*, French translation by J. ARSAC, Dunod (Paris, 1978).

[LE2]   H. F. LEDGARD and M. MARCOTTY, A genealogy of control structures, *Comm. ACM*, Vol. 18 (November 1975).

[LUS]   B. LUSSATO, Chronique Journal Le Monde, 8 July 1981.

[MAN]   Z. MANNA, *Mathematical Theory of Computation*, McGraw-Hill (New York, 1974).

[MEB]   B. MEYER and C. BAUDOIN, *Méthodes de programmation*, Eyrolles (Paris, 1978).

[MOR]   R. MOREAU, *Ainsi naquit l'informatique*, Dunod (Paris, 1981).

[MYC]   A. MYCROFT, *The Theory and Practice of Transforming Call by Need into Call by Value*, 4ᵉ Coll. intern., Springer-Verlag, Lecture notes in comp. sci., Vol. 83 (1980), pp. 269–281.

[ROH]   J. S. ROHL, Recursion via Pascal. In *Sophisters and Calculators* (Australia, 1984).

[ROU]   G. ROUCAIROL, *Transformation de programmes séquentiels en programmes parallèles*, 1ᵉʳ Coll. intern., Springer-Verlag, Lecture notes in comp. sci., Vol. 19 (1974), pp. 327–349.

[TES]   L. G. TESLER and M. J. ENEA, A language design for concurrent programming, *Proc. SJCC* (1968).

[VUI]   J. VUILLEMIN, *Proof Techniques for Recursive Programs*, Comp. Sci. Dept., Standard University (October 1973).

[WEG]   B. WEGBREIT, Goal directed program transformations, *IEEE Trans. on Software Engineering*, SE 2, 2 (1976), pp. 69–80.

[WIL]   J. W. WILLIAMS, Heap sort, *Comm. ACM*, Vol. 7, No. 6 (June 1964), p. 232.

[WIR]   N. WIRTH, *Algorithms + Data Structure = Programs*, Prentice Hall (Englewood Cliffs, New Jersey, 1976).

Index

Note. Certain words appear many times in the text. There is no point in listing all their occurrences. Only the most significant are given here.

A

Absorption, 161, 163, 165, 174
Action, 129, 135, 212, 224
  generalised, 195, 221
  regular, 131, 133, 135, 143, 150, 217, 221
Addition (recursive definitions), 98, 99
Algorithm, 51
  recurrent, 60
Artificial intelligence, 103
Assertion, 2, 12, 152, 171, 173, 175, 184, 189,
  227, 238, 240, 248, 253
Assignment, 2, 4, 34, 52, 56, 57, 60, 75, 137,
  170, 249
Associativity, 93, 101, 105, 106, 107, 216
Automaton, 136, 150
Axiom, 35, 113, 193, 250

B

Branch instruction, 6, 133, 135, 140, 145, 199

C

Calendar, perpetual, 53
Call by need, 46, 65, 66, 67
  value, 46, 67
Catalogue, 103, 210
Choice, 13, 39, 221, 224, 226, 231, 249, 250,
  256
Complexity, 38, 40, 41, 42, 118
Construction, 11, 28, 70, 136, 156, 193, 222,
  223, 256
  of algorithms, 53

Copy, 54, 59, 138, 144, 198, 214, 258
Correctness, partial, 13
Counter, 201, 204, 244, 249
Creation, *see* Construction

D

Depth, of an instruction, 159
Depth, of recursion, 43, 201
"De-structuring", 136
Division, 88
Dyadic, 33, 40, 41, 100

E

Efficiency, 43, 46, 186, 205, 222
Eratosthenes, 118
Execution, 65, 84, 150
Exit, 8, 14, 132, 142, 144, 145
Expansion, 133, 145, 161, 162, 165, 235, 242
Exponential, 1, 27, 29, 36

F

Factorial, 92, 237
Fibonacci, 31, 41, 64, 100, 224
File, sequential, 168
Formal parameter, 136, 138, 210, 212, 216,
  221, 243, 253
Functional programming, 34, 46

G

Generalisation, 103, 107, 117, 120
Graph, precedence, 55, 59, 137, 146, 198, 199

H

Hamming sequence, 43, 125
Hanoi, Towers of, 242, 252
Happy numbers, 118
Hypothesis, recurrence, 11, 13, 14, 16, 120, 193, 217

I

Identification, 150, 180
Indexed variable, 172, 230
Instruction, terminal, 159, 162, 163, 196
Intelligence, artificial, 103
Interpretation, 9, 76, 93, 133, 136, 142, 143, 197, 229
Invariance, invariant, 8, 11, 105, 107, 169, 200, 202, 210, 211, 213, 215, 232, 243, 244
Invention, 156, 186, 222, 229
Inverse, 211, 213, 224, 227, 251
Inversion
   proper, 167
   of selections, 174
Iteration, 11, 76, 141, 143, 145, 175, 213, 217, 221, 225, 256

L

Label, 6, 133, 135
"Lazy" evaluation, 58
Loop, *see* Iteration

M

Merging, of two assignments, 172, 247
Method, 103, 125, 127, 210, 217, 221, 222, 229, 250, 257
Monadic, 32, 40, 42, 80, 100, 223, 224

N

Need, call by, 46, 59
Neutral element, 94, 95, 161, 216
Numbers
   happy, 118
   prime, 118

O

Objective, 186, 192, 250

P

Parallel, 57, 222
Parameter, formal, 136, 138, 210, 212, 216, 221, 243, 253

Parenthesis, 48, 85, 195, 204
Permutability, 95
Permutation, 11, 95, 128, 171, 230
Position, terminal, 131, 133, 135, 136, 139, 143, 196, 216
Preassertion, 3, 8, 131, 137, 151, 187, 188, 200, 240
Precedence, 55, 137, 197
Precision, 36
Predicate, 3, 131, 200, 202, 209, 213, 215, 225, 233
Prefix, 113
Prime numbers, 118
Procedure, 59, 136, 197, 199
Product, 32, 60, 100
Program synthesis, 113, 254
Programming
   analytical, 221
   applicative, 34
   functional, 34, 46
   imperative, 34
Proper inversion, 167
Proper sequence, 160, 167, 198
Property, 35, 230, 240, 244, 249, 257

R

Recurrence, 11, 27, 31, 35, 37, 60, 64, 76, 119, 132, 209, 217, 252, 256
Recurrence hypothesis, 11, 13, 14, 16, 120, 217
Recursion, 27, 32, 34, 35, 43, 125, 140, 221, 223, 230, 249
Reducibility, 159, 162, 163, 166
Redundant selection, 173, 176, 180, 245
Regular action, 131, 133, 135, 143, 150, 217, 221
Regularisation, 200, 214, 215, 221, 225, 233
Repetition, 170
Resolution, 144, 181, 192, 214, 217, 221, 225, 234, 241
Reverse of a string, 30, 108, 113
Root, square, 70

S

Scheme, 205, 210, 211, 223
Selection, 6, 131, 145, 173
   redundant, 173, 176, 180, 245
Semantics, 3, 138, 200, 210
Sequence, 61, 62, 63, 82, 217
   proper, 160, 167, 198
   reducible, 159

Side-effect, 6, 47, 136, 171, 173
Situation, *see also* State, 5, 7, 11, 129, 136
Sorting, 11
  topological, 56
Specification, 113, 115
Square root, 70
Stack, 43, 85, 89, 202, 205, 210, 211, 213, 224, 225, 226, 229, 235, 251
State, 2, 57, 60, 129
Strategy, 33, 35, 113, 117, 120, 150, 184, 190, 192, 249, 256
String, 30, 88, 113, 114, 129, 145, 165, 195
Structure, 145
Substitution, 52, 59, 108, 138, 143, 198
Synthesis, of a program, 113, 254

T

Tautology, 174, 176, 177, 187, 240, 245
Terminal instruction, 159, 161, 196
Terminal position, 131, 133, 135, 136, 139, 143, 196, 216
Terminal recursion, 140, 176, 232, 244, 249, 252
Terminal value, 159, 212
Termination, 14, 28, 39, 107, 136, 182, 215
Tests, of programs, 2
Transformation
  semantic, 138, 148, 151, 170, 190, 257
  syntactic, 159, 175, 257

Transformation of definitions
  recurrent, 70
  recursive, 41
Transformation of predicate, 3
Transformation of program, 13, 67, 85, 106, 113, 135, 140, 170, 186, 217, 221, 242, 257
Transformation of situation, 5, 11, 34
Transmitter, 139
Tricks in programming, 169
Type, of data, 229, 255

U

Unification, 108

V

Value
  call by, 46
  final, 245
  terminal, 159, 212
Variable
  global, 200, 210, 212, 216, 221, 223, 232, 243, 250
  indexed, 171, 230
  local, 136, 210, 221, 230

W

WHILE, 7, 169, 175, 177, 214, 225

A.P.I.C. Studies in Data Processing
General Editors: Fraser Duncan and M. J. R. Shave

1. Some Commercial Autocodes. A Comparative Study*
    E. L. Willey, A. d'Agapeyeff, Marion Tribe, B. J. Gibbens and
    Michelle Clarke

2. A Primer of ALGOL 60 Programming
    E. W. Dijkstra

3. Input Language for Automatic Programming*
    A. P. Yershov, G. I. Kozhukhin and U. Voloshin

4. Introduction to System Programming*
    Edited by Peter Wegner

5. ALGOL 60 Implementation. The Translation and Use of ALGOL 60
    Programs on a Computer
    B. Randell and L. J. Russell

6. Dictionary for Computer Languages*
    Hans Breuer

7. The Alpha Automatic Programming System*
    Edited by A. P. Yershov

8. Structured Programming
    O.-J. Dahl, E. W. Dijkstra and C. A. R. Hoare

9. Operating Systems Techniques
    Edited by C. A. R. Hoare and R. H. Perrott

10. ALGOL 60. Compilation and Assessment
    B. A. Wichmann

11. Definition of Programming Languages by Interpreting Automata
    Alexander Ollongren

12. Principles of Program Design
    M. A. Jackson

13. Studies in Operating Systems
    R. M. McKeag and R. Wilson

14. Software Engineering
    R. J. Perrott

15. Computer Architecture: A Structured Approach
    R. W. Doran

* Out of print.

16. Logic Programming
    Edited by K. L. Clark and S.-A. Tärnlund

17. Fortran Optimization
    Michael Metcalf

18. Multi-microprocessor Systems
    Y. Paker

19. Introduction to the Graphical Kernel System—GKS
    F. R. A. Hopgood, D. A. Duce, J. R. Gallop and
    D. C. Sutcliffe

20. Distributed Computing
    Edited by Fred B. Chambers, David A. Duce
    and Gillian P. Jones

21. Introduction to Logic Programming
    Christopher John Hogger

22. Lucid, the Dataflow Programming Language
    William W. Wadge and Edward A. Ashcroft

23. Foundations of Programming
    Jacques Arsac

24. Prolog for Programmers
    Feliks Kluźniak and Stanisław Szpakowicz